BECOMING SOCIALIZED IN
STUDENT AFFAIRS ADMINISTRATION

D1516749

BECOMING SOCIALIZED IN STUDENT AFFAIRS ADMINISTRATION

A Guide for New Professionals
and Their Supervisors

Edited by
Ashley Tull, Joan B. Hirt,
and Sue A. Saunders

STERLING, VIRGINIA

Published by Stylus Publishing, LLC
22883 Quicksilver Drive
Sterling, Virginia 20166-2102

Library of Congress Cataloging-in-Publication-Data

Becoming socialized in student affairs administration : a guide for new professionals and their supervisors / edited by Ashley Tull, Joan B. Hirt, and Sue Saunders.
    p. cm.
    Includes bibliographical references and index.
    ISBN 978-1-57922-275-8 (hardcover : alk. paper)—
ISBN 978-1-57922-276-5 (pbk. : alk. paper) 1. Student affairs administrators—In-service training—United States. 2. Student affairs administrators—Supervision of—United States. 3. Student affairs administrators—Professional relationships—United States. 4. Professional socialization—United States. I. Tull, Ashley, 1972– II. Hirt, Joan B. III. Saunders, Sue, 1950–
LB2342.92.B4 2009
378.1'970715—dc22

                             2008054641

13-digit ISBN: 978-1-57922-275-8 (cloth)
13-digit ISBN: 978-1-57922-276-5(paper)

Printed in the United States of America

All first editions printed on acid free paper that meets the American National Standards Institute Z39-48 Standard.

Bulk Purchases

Quantity discounts are available for use in workshops and for staff development.
Call 1-800-232-0223

First Edition, 2009

10 9 8 7 6 5 4 3

CONTENTS

ACKNOWLEDGMENTS   *vii*

PREFACE   *ix*

PART ONE: EFFECTIVE SOCIALIZATION OF NEW PROFESSIONALS: PROCESSES AND IMPORTANCE

1. THE SOCIALIZATION PROCESS FOR NEW
   PROFESSIONALS   *3*
   Denise Collins

2. QUALITY OF WORK LIFE   *28*
   Why Socialization Matters
   Vicki J. Rosser and Jan Minoru Javinar

PART TWO: CONTEXTS THAT INFLUENCE SOCIALIZATION OF NEW PROFESSIONALS

3. THE INFLUENCE OF INSTITUTIONAL TYPE ON
   SOCIALIZATION   *45*
   Joan B. Hirt

4. CHANGING STUDENT CHARACTERISTICS AND
   SOCIALIZATION   *67*
   Jerrid P. Freeman and Colette Taylor

PART THREE: STRATEGIES TO ENHANCE SOCIALIZATION OF NEW PROFESSIONALS

5. GRADUATE PREPARATION PROGRAMS   *89*
   The First Step in Socialization
   Linda Kuk and Michael J. Cuyjet

v

6. ORIENTATION IN THE SOCIALIZATION PROCESS 109
   Sue A. Saunders and Diane L. Cooper

7. SUPERVISION AND MENTORSHIP IN THE
   SOCIALIZATION PROCESS 129
   Ashley Tull

8. STAFF-PEER RELATIONSHIPS IN THE SOCIALIZATION
   PROCESS 152
   Terrell L. Strayhorn

9. INSTITUTIONAL SOCIALIZATION INITIATIVES 174
   Stan Carpenter and Linda Carpenter

10. PROFESSIONAL ASSOCIATIONS AND SOCIALIZATION 194
   Steven M. Janosik

PART 4: IMPLICATIONS AND FUTURE DIRECTIONS
FOR EFFECTIVE SOCIALIZATION

11. CONCLUSIONS AND RECOMMENDATIONS 217
   Ashley Tull, Joan B. Hirt, and Sue A. Saunders

CONTRIBUTORS 233

INDEX 243

ACKNOWLEDGMENTS

We would like to thank Rosa Edwards, administrative assistant in the Campus Life Center at the University of Arkansas, for her editorial assistance throughout the preparation of this book.

E very year student affairs divisions at the over 4,300 colleges and universities across the United States welcome new staff members to their ranks. Hundreds of aspiring administrators bring a wealth of talents, interests, and abilities to their positions. A sense of revitalization is typical when recent hires arrive on campus, and seasoned professionals benefit from the enthusiasm their new colleagues bring with them. In turn, senior administrators offer wisdom and astuteness to novices who are just beginning to chart their professional journeys.

The roads these new staff members have traveled to gain entry to the profession are varied. Certainly many have followed the traditional route— active involvement as undergraduates led them to master's programs in higher education and student affairs administration. There are other career paths, however. For instance, newly minted alumni who served as senior resident assistants or campus ambassadors as undergraduates often are hired as hall directors or admission counselors. Likewise, some new hires completed graduate degrees in other fields (e.g., psychology, sociology, communication) but were employed in assistantships in student affairs offices. They became enamored of the profession and elected to pursue postgraduate employment in the postsecondary sector.

Regardless of the path they have taken, these new employees join a robust profession. The American College Personnel Association (ACPA) and the National Association of Student Personnel Administrators (NASPA), the two major general associations for the profession, boast 20,000 members. Thousands of others join functionally specific organizations, such as the Association of College and University Housing Officers–International (ACUHO–I), the National Orientation Directors Association (NODA), the National Association for Campus Activities (NACA), or the Association of College Unions International (ACUI), to name but a few. Indeed, the hundreds of new staff members who join the echelons of student affairs administrators indicate the vocation is healthy and vigorous.

This is not to suggest that the profession does not have challenges to face. As we welcome hundreds of new colleagues to our ranks each year, hundreds of others leave the profession. Certainly some aspiring administrators are hired for newly created positions that reflect the expansion higher education continues to undergo each year. Most new appointees, however, are filling jobs that have been vacated by others—at times because of promotions but frequently because a predecessor has abandoned the field.

Estimates of departures from the student affairs profession range from 20% to 40%, most of which takes place within the first six years of the career. This attrition rate obviously carries some serious costs. Faculty members in graduate preparation programs invest countless hours educating future professionals. Those who supervise graduate assistants or interns spend valuable time training people who aspire to administrative careers. Managers devote hours to supervising newly hired staff members and providing guidance to novices in the field. Human resource personnel process appointment papers and benefit portfolios—the resources institutions call upon to recruit, hire, train, supervise, and develop staff talent are considerable. When relatively new professionals leave the field, we lose not only the resources we have invested in them, but the ideas and innovations they might have contributed to the campus had they persisted.

What can be done to turn the tide on professional attrition? We believe one solution lies in the efforts we make to socialize new professionals. Socialization is the process by which new members of an organization come to understand, appreciate, and adopt the customs, traditions, values, and goals of their profession and their new organization. It is the mechanism that offers agency to recent hires and a sense of belonging to those who have been around longer. People in organizations need to feel they matter, and the socialization process can lead to that outcome. But socialization is multifaceted and not always easily accomplished. Many seasoned professionals are unaware of (or have forgotten) the bevy of interrelated activities and relationships that led them to feel comfortable in the profession when they first started out.

The importance of the socialization process was the genesis of this book. We wanted to educate student affairs administrators of all ranks on the importance of socialization and the role they can play in socializing their new employees. So we sought the best thinking of scholars who have studied this process and the best practices of professionals who have worked with novice staff members. The result of their endeavors is *Becoming Socialized in Student Affairs Administration: A Guide for New Professionals and Their Supervisors*

The book is organized in four sections. Part one is designed to define the concept, offer a model of socialization, and explain why socializing new professionals is so important to the vitality of our work. Denise Collins opens the volume with an illuminating explanation of the stages in and elements of socialization. She combines these into a model of socialization that is comprehensive and comprehensible. Vicki J. Rosser and Jan Minoru Javinar follow with a chapter on quality of work life for student affairs administrators. They demonstrate how job satisfaction and morale are important predictors of departure, explaining why we should care about the appropriate socialization of our new colleagues.

Part two examines the context in which the socialization of new professionals occurs. In chapter 3, Joan B. Hirt discusses the different types of colleges and universities that employ nascent administrators and how institutional type influences the socialization process. This is followed by a chapter on the changing characteristics of college students. Jerrid Freeman and Colette Taylor describe the characteristics of students that professionals can expect on their campuses in the coming years and offer insights into how those characteristics may change the way we conduct our work.

The book then moves to part three, strategies to promote positive socialization of new professionals. We start in chapter 5 with a discussion of the role that graduate education plays in preparing new professionals for work in student affairs. Michael Cuyjet and Linda Kuk explicate the elements of graduate education and the function that each element plays in the socialization process. They offer guidance to faculty and practitioners who are involved in graduate education about what they can do to introduce graduate students to professional life.

The next four chapters address aspects of on-the-job socialization. In chapter 6, Sue Saunders and Diane Cooper talk about the importance of orienting new professionals to the unit, the division of student affairs, the campus, and the profession. Their cogent discussion of the cognitive apprenticeship is particularly compelling. Next, Ashley Tull addresses the role of supervision and mentorship in the socialization process. While closely related, these are, in fact, distinct functions, and Tull's explanation of how they differ and where they intersect is useful to those who serve in one or both these roles. But new professionals interact with others as well, and in chapter 8 Terrell L. Strayhorn points out how peers in the work setting play a major role in the socialization process. He offers concrete evidence of the power that peers play in decisions to stay in the field or leave it. Such decisions have an impact on institutions, and Stan Carpenter and Linda Carpenter describe some of those impacts in their chapter on socialization and institutional initiatives. They suggest opportunities for and obstacles to successful socialization at the personal, unit/divisional, and institutional levels. Last, no book on socialization in student affairs would be complete without a discussion of professional associations. Steve Janosik describes in chapter 10 the obligations that associations have to their members and the profession to ensure continuing professional development opportunities.

We conclude the book in part four with a chapter that summarizes the key points the authors have made. We describe the implications of socialization for a variety of campus constituencies, including faculty in graduate preparation programs, supervisors of new professionals, divisional leaders, and, not least of all, new professionals themselves. Since we view this volume as an initial dialogue on the subject of socialization, we offer recommendations for future research and practice in an effort to propel that discussion to the next level.

We hope to appeal to several audiences with this volume. First, while many faculty members understand that they are among the first agents of socialization, this book elucidates a model of socialization that clearly situates graduate education in the socialization process. It also identifies areas where more data are needed, laying out a research agenda for those interested in expanding the knowledge base about this important topic. Second, senior student affairs officers (SSAOs) should benefit from the recommendations the experts in this book offer. Recruiting, hiring, training, supervising, evaluating, and developing staff is a resource-intense endeavor and one that is essential to the success of the division. Surely they have a vested interest in retaining the new staff members they hire. This volume offers SSAOs information on a broad array of socialization elements and provides a model of socialization they might adopt when developing policies and programs related to human resource management. Likewise, administrators who supervise or collaborate with new staff members daily can gain a better understanding of the critical role they play in inculcating novices to the profession they have grown up in and care about so deeply.

Finally, this book opens doors for new professionals. We offer them perspectives on socialization that we hope will make their transition to student affairs administration a bit easier. At a minimum, we hope they will understand the professional journey they are embarking on, the checkpoints they may encounter on that journey, and the destination we hope they achieve—a commitment to professional excellence. That is what impelled us to publish this work in the first place. So, to our new and future colleagues, we wish you a speedy and successful trip!

PART ONE

EFFECTIVE SOCIALIZATION OF NEW PROFESSIONALS: PROCESSES AND IMPORTANCE

THE SOCIALIZATION PROCESS FOR NEW PROFESSIONALS

Denise Collins

S ocialization is the process by which new professionals enter the student affairs profession. During this process, the new professional "acquires the social knowledge and skills necessary to assume an organizational role" (Van Maanen & Schein, 1979, p. 211). Although the notion of "acquiring" skills, values, and organizational cultures has been criticized for its unidirectionality (Tierney, 1997), socialization is an interactive act that involves interpretation by the new professional and agents of the organization. The new professional entering a position in student affairs brings along individual traits, personal beliefs and values, and cultural contexts (Tierney; Van Maanen & Schein) that shape and color the experience of entering a new campus or position. Likewise, organizations have distinctive cultures that reflect rituals, routines, values, and norms of the group. Being "socialized" involves interaction between individual and organizational cultures (Chipman & Kuh, 1988; Thornton & Nardi, 1975; Tierney). Through a process of mutually influencing adaptation, the new professional secures an identity within the organization, and the culture of the organization alters to include the new professional among its members (Thornton & Nardi; Tierney).

The stages of socialization help illuminate the process. Additionally, negotiating the socialization process in student affairs occurs on several levels: identity and self-definition, institutional knowledge and contexts, external influences, and the student affairs profession as a whole (Hirt & Creamer, 1998). In this chapter, I first describe the socialization stages as conceptualized by Thornton and Nardi (1975) and then describe Hirt and Creamer's realms of professional practice. The four socialization stages and the four realms of professional practice are then merged to illustrate how new professionals in student affairs experience and negotiate transitions.

Stages of Socialization

Socialization has been conceptualized by Thornton and Nardi (1975) as occurring in four stages: anticipatory, formal, informal, and personal. The stages are developmental, "whereby individuals move from passively accepting roles to actively engaging in and shaping them" (p. 872). In the anticipatory stage, new professionals develop expectations of what the role will be like, basing their assumptions on observations of those already in the role, depictions in media, or other people's notions of what the role entails (Weidman, Twale, & Stein, 2001). Because of their distance from the actual intricacies of the job, they have "very generalized and stereotyped conceptions" (Thornton & Nardi, p. 874) of the work role. A sense of anticipation is apparent at this stage, as new professionals are eager to enter the new position.

During the formal stage, the perspective shifts from outsider to insider, as the new professional is no longer anticipating but is now entering the work role (Thornton & Nardi, 1975). Formal orientation and training programs transmit the expectations of behaviors, attitudes, and values enacted by members of the organization. Communication is informative, regulative, and integrative as the more seasoned administrators help newcomers "learn about normative role expectations and how they are carried out" (Weidman et al., 2001, p. 13). These expectations apply to the role itself rather than to the person in the role (Thornton & Nardi). The central task during this stage is mastering the role and negotiating the new environment, as new professionals learn their way in the institution (Weidman et al.).

Informal socialization occurs when new professionals observe the variations in implementing formal rules and expectations and develop their own individual styles for inhabiting the role. More experienced colleagues will provide insight into the ways that rules and expectations are typically interpreted and enacted, giving the new professional the freedom to insert personal forms of expression. Although informal socialization may occur in explicit and implicit communication, it is more likely to be implicit and relate to attitudinal characteristics rather than behavior or knowledge requirements (Thornton & Nardi, 1975).

Finally, the personal stage involves the integration of the self and the professional role. New professionals at this stage combine personal and work identities to form an integrated whole and "form a professional identity" (Weidman et al., 2001, p. 14). By bringing together others' expectations and self-expectations for the role, a personal style emerges, linking the role and the person (Thornton & Nardi, 1975).

Building on these four stages, Weidman et al. (2001) proposed developmental tasks for the socialization process, particularly as it related to students entering graduate work. They reconceptualized the process not as stages, but as "states of identity and commitment" (Weidman et al., p. 11), providing an understanding of the fluid and overlapping nature of the socialization experience. A similar analysis of Thornton and Nardi's socialization stages reveals how each is manifested in the four realms of professional practice proposed by Hirt and Creamer (1998).

Realms of Professional Practice

Professional practice occurs in four contexts that influence the actions of student affairs professionals: the personal, the institutional, the extra-institutional, and the professional (Hirt & Creamer, 1998). The personal realm includes concerns of the student affairs professional as an individual. Hirt and Creamer indicated that pressing issues in the personal realm are "career mobility and prospects, familial opportunities and obligations, and quality of life" (p. 48). Additional influences in the personal realm might include individual skill sets, work-life balance, and cultural and social identities.

Issues in the institutional realm relate to demands placed on the professional by campus agents and contexts. These issues include changing demographics, trends in enrollment management, assessment and accountability, technology, and diminishing resources (Hirt & Creamer, 1998). Other institutional contexts are the mission of the institution and student affairs division, institutional type, relationships with colleagues and supervisors, and institution-specific cultures. The extra-institutional realm is mediated by influences outside the institution: "governing boards, state and federal agencies, and public sentiment" (Hirt & Creamer, p. 54). These are manifested by regulations, policies, and expectations imposed by outside forces. In addition to those external agents identified by Hirt and Creamer, student affairs professionals will also face scrutiny from a myriad of constituent groups, including parents and families, alumni, corporate donors, members of the local community, national offices of Greek-letter organizations, and even the public at large, particularly following a campus-based scandal or tragedy.

The fourth context is the student affairs profession as a whole. The professional realm is embodied in functional and national associations, standards promulgated by the Council for the Advancement of Standards in Higher Education (CAS, 2006), and the initiatives toward credentialing or registering student affairs professionals or accrediting graduate preparation programs (Hirt & Creamer, 1998). What it means to be a member of the profession is communicated through ethical standards, a philosophical and theoretical knowledge base, and standards of practice. Ethical statements from the national associations are readily available on their Web sites (National Association of Student Personnel Administrators [NASPA], www.naspa.org; American College Personnel Association [ACPA], www.myacpa.org). Functional organizations, such as National Orientation Directors Association (NODA), Association of College and University Housing Officers–International (ACUHO–I), or National Career Development Association (NCDA), also have ethical standards that relate to work in those areas. Foundational philosophy statements and standards of practice have been collected by the Student Affairs History Project, coordinated at Bowling Green State University and available at http://www.bgsu.edu/colleges/library/cac/sahp/. Conferences, workshops, Webinars and seminars, and a wide range of information available on the Internet (see, for example, http://www.studentaffairs.com) provide important professional development, particularly for those new professionals who have not attended graduate school, and complement formal instruction for those who pursue graduate education.

Understanding the Stages of Socialization in the Realms of Professional Practice

Combining the Thornton and Nardi (1975) socialization model with the four realms of professional practice as proposed by Hirt and Creamer (1998) offers a model for understanding the experiences of new professionals in student affairs. The socialization stages will be illustrated as they relate to each realm of professional practice, with some examples of what might occur for new professionals at each level.

Anticipatory Stage

For those who have made the decision to pursue a career in student affairs, the period between realizing that student affairs is a legitimate option and landing the first professional job is one of great anticipation. As an undergraduate student, involvement in a student organization, employment as a resident assistant or admissions tour guide, or the desire to emulate a trusted advisor can spur an interest in student affairs work. Those who move directly into a professional position from undergraduate work or who come to student affairs from an allied graduate program such as counseling or human resources draw their expectations about the student affairs professional role from their exposure, typically as a student staff member or graduate assistant, to others in the field. Their expectations of what the professional role will be come from an external view and are largely based on generalizations (Thornton & Nardi, 1975). These preprofessionals may tell their mentors, "I want your job" or they may say, "I know I can do it better than *my* hall director." To gain a more realistic view of the nature of professional work in student affairs, undergraduate students who aspire to a career in student affairs would benefit from mentoring and job shadowing programs.

Those who enroll in a master's degree program in student affairs, however, take on an apprentice role during which they formulate more specific expectations and understandings about the professional role they aspire to, which can also come from an idealized stance. A practicum or internship experience can serve to give the student a more realistic view of professional practice. For example, a current graduate student reflected on the value of her practicum that "it was through that experiential learning that I was able to find out first hand which areas of student affairs fit me and my strengths as a professional." Graduate assistantships, as preprofessional employment, serve a similar training function, where students learn skills that will enhance their success as professionals. One student affairs professional shared the importance of her graduate assistantship in learning to negotiate the political landscape:

> Many grads do not see all the politics related to higher education and are faced with many challenges when starting a first full time position. I was

lucky enough to work at a small school, where the political landscape affected everyone in the student affairs department—from the VP down to the graduate assistants. I learned to watch what I said and learned how to manage the balance between being professional while still being a student.

Having good role models who are competent, ethical, and committed to mentoring undergraduate or graduate students toward a career in student affairs is important to a successful outcome in the anticipatory stage. Because a key factor during this stage is developing an expectation for the way professional practice *should* be, guiding the preprofessional student toward appropriate behavior is essential. In the absence of intentional mentoring, new professionals will base their practice on whatever examples they can glean from others and will reproduce those things that make intuitive sense. The worst-case scenario here is that bad practice will beget bad practice. Good mentorship, however, that emphasizes critical inquiry and continual professional development provides the positive foundation for a successful transition into good practice. As an experienced student affairs professional explained,

> Mentoring during the graduate program by professionals in the field is key in how new professionals transition into their first positions. It's evident when interviewing who has had mentoring throughout their graduate program and who has not. One of the most prevalent issues I see is making the transition from being a student to being a professional. Many new professionals have difficulty creating boundaries with students—what type of social behavior is appropriate, being a friend versus a supervisor or advisor, etc.

Regardless of the path, whether directly from an undergraduate degree or through a graduate program, experiences in the preemployment phase in each of the four realms of practice set the groundwork for a successful progression through the anticipatory stage of the socialization process. It is during this stage that the individual develops a view of the profession or a particular aspect of the profession through interactions with and observations of others in those roles.

Personal Realm

In preparation for entering student affairs, preprofessionals acquire knowledge, develop skills, and form an appropriate disposition for working with students. This happens most explicitly through graduate preparation in student affairs. The graduate school experience accentuates the personal aspect of anticipation—students are encouraged to critically examine their strengths and weaknesses and must have "the capacity to be open to self-assessment and growth" (Miller, 2003, p. 293). Classes in student development theory offer the opportunity for self-assessment along developmental models with a focus on identity development and learning/work styles. By paying attention to "who I am" in multiple areas of identity, students connect to "who I will be" in a professional role. Looking at "how I learn/work best" leads to anticipation of the kinds of professional positions or functional areas that the student will seek. Mentors working with undergraduate students who intend to move directly into a professional position can encourage them to do some of this reflection as well.

The anticipatory stage is most enacted in the job search process. In the personal realm, looking for a job is first an exercise in self-exploration as individual goals and priorities are negotiated. Decisions about the type of position (e.g., admissions counselor, residence hall director [RHD], Greek advisor) are based in part on some understanding of personal interests, values, and goals. In addition, factors such as institutional type and mission are tied to individual preferences and values. Mentors and peers exert influence in considerations for the job search as well. Their experiences in previous positions most certainly affect the advice they give to information-hungry job searchers. The new professionals must balance the sometimes conflicting advice they receive with their own self-analyses.

Particular aspects of one's personal situation have important implications for some preprofessionals. For example, relationships and familial obligations are important factors for some who are deciding whether to relocate for a new job. The dual career search holds particular challenges since both partners' goals come into play (Gardner & Woodsmall, 2004). Having discussions about shared and individual priorities is an important first step. Researching institutions' hiring policies, finding a location with multiple job opportunities for both partners, and having the patience to wait for the right opportunity are key elements for success in the dual career search.

Social and cultural identities provide further personal context considerations in the anticipatory stage. People of color may be concerned about aspects of the job search that white applicants do not worry about. One African American new professional expressed her fear of being "pigeonholed" into working only in multicultural affairs. "I wanted no limitation placed on my career before it even began" (Johnson, 2004, p. 28). A former graduate student told me how being a woman of color affected her job search: "I was happy that my white classmates could have a completely open search. However, that was not a reality for me. An important aspect for me was finding a diverse community where I would be safe."

People with disabilities use other considerations to determine where to seek employment. A woman with a physical disability wrote, "what truly guided my decision was the knowledge that if I were going to be an independent person, I had to live in a location where my physical disability was not going to be an issue" (McCarthy, 2004, p. 138). Being a gay, lesbian, bisexual, or transgendered person can pose a dilemma that heterosexual people do not encounter of whether to reveal one's sexual or gender identity during the job search (Simpkins, 2004). Assessing the climate for diversity on the campus and in the community is an important part of the interview process.

The common aspect of the personal realm of anticipation is negotiating personal experiences, identities, and expectations with the perceived expectations of others. Having a strong sense of self in the multiple aspects of identity can be a key element to successful progress in the anticipatory stage. Strengthening personal identity development is best facilitated through reflection activities, which can occur in undergraduate or graduate classes, through personal journaling, or through guided reflection with a mentor. By having the opportunity to consider elements of identity and the impacts of identity on values and goals, the emerging professional can be more equipped to consider the interactions of identities with external expectations in the job search process.

Institutional Realm

The institutional realm involves learning about professional practice in the positions and institutions that one might enter. For many preprofessionals, this learning occurs formally in graduate preparation programs. Courses or units on campus environments, for example, provide insight into the institutional milieus new professionals can expect to enter. Practicum requirements allow graduate students to practice their developing skills in a specific institutional context. From this experience, they develop expectations of what the institutional factors may be in their first professional position (see chapter 3 for further information about institutional type). For all preprofessionals, including those who do not attend graduate school, this learning also occurs informally through talking with others and searching the Internet.

The interview process is another venue to anticipate the institutional realm of practice. Researching institutions, interviewing, and making campus visits contribute to building notions of what the institutional expectations will be. Applicants measure their comfort levels with the staff they meet, the institutional mission, and the campus environment and try to find the position that best represents their own values and needs (Jones & Segawa, 2004). These expectations are still formed from an outsider's perspective, however, and give only a broad view of the institution based on generalities. During recruitment and job placement, institutional officials are likely to "put their best foot forward" and therefore the institutional view is not necessarily complete. The goal is to find the best "fit" for the employee and the institution. Fit happens when what employers are looking for in a candidate matches what applicants are looking for in a job (Kretovics, 2002).

Extra-institutional Realm

The anticipatory stage relates to experiences prior to beginning the first professional position; extra-institutional issues—most often realized as regulations placed by external agencies—are less relevant or familiar to the preprofessional. During the undergraduate experience in student leadership roles, regulations like those imposed by the Family Educational Rights and Privacy Act (FERPA), Health Insurance Portability and Accountability Act (HIPAA), or Americans with Disabilities Act (ADA) are most often addressed by professional staff members. Although undergraduate students may be aware generally of external concerns, they are not consciously affected by those concerns. Similarly, graduate students in student affairs preparation programs are somewhat protected from extra-institutional issues. Indeed, when surveyed about areas of emphasis in their graduate preparation programs, new professionals indicated that higher education legal issues were addressed only moderately (Cuyjet, Arminio, & Woods, 2005), indicating that students may not have an extensive understanding of how external factors will influence their future work as student affairs professionals.

Other extra-institutional forces may have more impact on preprofessionals, depending on their areas of experience. For example, those who are members of or graduate advisors to Greek-letter organizations will have greater knowledge of regulations imposed by national offices and therefore may be more ready to deal with other types of external influences. Mentoring preprofessionals to learn about extra-institutional factors will prepare them for the transition.

Professional Realm

Graduate school is the primary way preprofessionals are socialized into the professional realm. Graduate preparation programs teach professional ethics and inculcate students with what it means to be a student affairs professional. Professional associations have mentoring programs and graduate student conferences that introduce students to the profession as a whole. Resources like ACPA's Standing Committee for Graduate Students and New Professionals and NASPA's New Professionals and Graduate Students Knowledge Community provide an entrée to the professional associations and help build personal networks. These groups also produce newsletters, sponsor educational and social programming at the national conventions, and offer structured opportunities for emerging professionals to connect with senior-level administrators to build mentoring relationships. The informal professional networks that graduate students and new professionals develop are important in supporting them through the first years of their professional careers.

Opportunities for those not in graduate programs are fewer but still available. The NASPA Undergraduate Fellows Program, for example, is a pipeline program that targets undergraduates from those populations underrepresented in student affairs to provide mentoring (NASPA, 2007). Several national and regional associations have special program tracks at their annual conferences for undergraduate networking and mentoring, for example ACPA's Next Generation Conference that occurs in conjunction with the national convention or NASPA Region IV-East's Bring a Student Challenge at its annual meeting. These are examples of many programs that provide an initial view of the student affairs profession.

In all realms of professional practice, the anticipatory stage emphasizes the preprofessionals' expectations of and assumptions about the nature of professional work. A successful transition into the professional world is more likely if these expectations and assumptions are closely matched to reality. Mentoring, experiential learning, and thorough research are all important to easing the shift from the anticipatory to the formal stage of socialization.

Formal Stage

Formal socialization in student affairs typically begins when the offer of employment is made and accepted. Moving from outsider to insider status, the new professional begins the relationship with the hiring institution in formal ways: signing contracts, completing payroll forms, and negotiating terms of employment. Formal orientation and training programs, when provided, address issues in all realms of professional practice. This stage generally occupies the first one to two months in the new position (Renn & Hodges, 2007), as the new professional is learning the ropes (see chapter 6 for further information).

Personal Realm

In the personal realm, orientation programs often cover such information as payment procedures, benefits, institutional ethical standards, and contract terms. (For a more complete treatment of these institutional issues, see chapter 9.) Formal orientation is not generally designed to address the more individualized issues faced by new professionals entering a new position in a different location. Obtaining housing (if it is not provided by the institution), moving, arranging child care or enrolling children in school, establishing bank accounts, and changing drivers' licenses and car registrations all require procedures that are specific to or regulated by the communities in which the new professionals live. Through these processes, new professionals are learning about the expectations of behaviors, attitudes, and values (Thornton & Nardi, 1975) in their new communities in formalized, structured ways.

Institutional Realm

The institutional realm is the primary locus for formal socialization. Although formal orientation programs are not always provided, new professionals need these opportunities to learn about institutional expectations (Rosen, Taube, & Wadsworth, 1980). As indicated in chapter 6, effective orientation programs increase the likelihood of success and retention in the first professional position (Saunders & Cooper, 2003). Formal training also communicates aspects of institutional culture including those related to institutional type, size, and mission. "Knowledge about matters such as institutional cultures, including the faculty and student cultures, is vital to new staff members" (Winston & Creamer, 1997, p. 163). Learning about faculty culture involves such things as tenure processes, governance systems, and student affairs/academic affairs collaborations. Student culture, in the formal stage, refers to learning about demographic information, predominant majors, array of student organizations, judicial statistics, and other information.

Supervisory relationships begin in the formal stage of socialization. "By establishing synergistic relationships with new professionals, supervisors are able to communicate the organization's goals, norms, and values" (Tull, 2006, p. 476). Although most of the relationship building for the supervisory relationship occurs in the informal stage, expectations about frequency of supervision meetings, reporting procedures, and methods of communication are most often transmitted in more formal terms.

Hirt addresses factors related to institutional type more thoroughly in chapter 3. Institutional size affects the relationships that student affairs professionals have with colleagues in other functional units (Hirt & Collins, 2004). Those who work in smaller campus environments are more likely to have overlapping responsibilities across functional units. Effective orientation and training make the patterns of collaboration within and between departments apparent.

Extra-institutional Realm

Instruction about the new professional's responsibilities with regard to external relationships and regulations is an element of formal socialization. These responsibilities might include preparing materials that will contribute to reports to the institution's board of trustees, obligations related to FERPA and ADA compliance, or procedures for responding to inquiries from members of the media. The increasing involvement of parents in college students' lives has prompted further clarification of FERPA regulations and concomitant revision of campus policies. New professionals should stay informed of the evolving clarification of FERPA and other similar regulations. Institutions also have an obligation to provide current information about these extra-institutional regulations as part of regular professional development for all staff.

Professional Realm

The relationship of the new professional with professional organizations is sometimes defined by formal policies and practices. New professionals learn whether membership fees are paid by the institution, whether membership in professional associations is required or encouraged, to what extent conference attendance is supported, and the degree of professional development provided by the institution. New professionals who join professional associations receive information from those associations, usually through publications or Web sites, about ethical and professional standards.

Formal socialization, across the realms of professional practice, is primarily transmitted through structured means, such as orientation programs, handbooks, and manuals. New professionals' sense of the organization and how to behave will also come from more informal means. Conversations with more experienced staff members, observing others' behaviors and interactions, and even making a few gaffes will enrich the new professionals' transition.

Informal Stage

Although Thornton and Nardi (1975) indicate that the informal stage of socialization follows the completion of the formal stage, many aspects of informal socialization occur from the beginning of the new professional's relationship with the institution. During the job search, the preprofessional has many opportunities to start developing insight into the informal aspects of working within the office, department, or institution. Still tempered by the tendency to emphasize the positive aspects of the position during the recruitment and hiring phase, interactions through telephone conversations and social functions can provide a glimpse into the realities of working life in the position. However, it is not until the new professional has been in the position for a while—after what Renn and Hodges (2007) call the "transition phase"—that she or he begins to personalize the role and develop an individual style based on the informal information acquired.

Personal Realm

The issues of transition experienced by new professionals relate to personal and social integration in the new environment. These include feelings of competency; relationships with family, partner, and/or friends; developing a social network; and striving for work-life balance. During the anticipatory stage, fears of competence are common as new professionals wonder whether they will actually be able to do the jobs they are hired to do (Renn & Hodges, 2007; Saunders & Cooper, 2003). After being in the job for a while, new professionals are able to assess areas in which they have competence and those in which they still need further training and professional development (Renn & Hodges).

Relationships with families, partners, and friends become more settled as the new professional transitions into the job. As the routines of the work environment are better established, routine can also return to personal relationships. Partners or children who have relocated for the new professional's job experience their own transitions, and new patterns of living emerge for all. An RHD explained his struggle to balance competing demands:

My wife and I celebrated our first anniversary shortly before I began my first professional position. Once I started the hours grew longer, and I felt overwhelmed by my work. Most nights I would come home for an hour and then leave to work again, other nights I wouldn't come home until 8 or 9 p.m. Although I lived where I worked, I definitely felt torn between my job and my wife. I spent most of my first year, and part of my second, learning how to balance work and family.

Because many new professionals are in their middle to late 20s, other major life changes are likely to accompany a new job, including marriage or committed partner relationships, having children, moving farther distances from their parents or families, home ownership, or even living off campus for the first time. Managing all the multiple transitions is a daunting task and can exacerbate job stress at this phase.

Friendships are also renegotiated, and friends find new ways of relating, particularly when they find themselves in different cities or states. Reliance on technology-mediated conversation, through telephones, e-mail, text messaging, or blogging, requires redefinition of relationships. Whether strengthened or weakened by the changes, it is during the informal transition that friendships are revised, again compounding job-related stress.

Developing social networks is another task of the informal stage of socialization. Participants in Renn and Hodges' (2007) study of the first professional year indicated that forming relationships with others outside the job was important to their transition. Although new professionals do not always seek networking opportunities (Jones & Segawa, 2004), these support systems can provide invaluable bolstering during the uneasy times in a new position. Particularly for those new professionals who belong to identity groups that are underrepresented at the institution (for example, a person of color at a predominantly white institution, a person with a disability on a campus with few other such people, or a person at a religiously affiliated institution who holds a different faith), it is important to develop a support network that includes "people from their identity groups to serve as much-needed sounding boards and support systems" (Ortiz & Shintaku, 2004, p. 174). These support networks provide one means for helping new professionals develop work-life balance.

Balancing personal and professional lives was identified as a major concern by ACPA's *New Professional Needs Study* (Cilente, Henning, Skinner Jackson, Kennedy, & Sloane, 2007). Although rarely addressed in formal orientation programs, the informal culture regarding how long one spends in the office after hours, at what programs and events attendance is expected, and when it is acceptable to take vacation days is part of the new professional's informal socialization. Making decisions on these factors involves interplay between the personal realm and the institutional realm of professional practice.

Institutional Realm

The new professional is learning the "unwritten rules" (Amey, 2002, p. 13) of the job during the informal socialization stage. These rules relate to role clarification, organizational culture, and working relationships. During formal orientation and training programs, new professionals learn the "duties and tasks" version of their work roles; through informal interactions they make the leap from the job description to the realities of the job (Amey). Because of the disparity between what is presented in orientation programs and what they subsequently learn in on-the-job training, new professionals can find their formal training inadequate (Renn & Hodges, 2007; Rosen et al., 1980). They look to coworkers to determine acceptable behaviors (Cilente et al., 2007) and "learn how to be" (Helm, 2004, p. 201) by observing how others behave and how they are rewarded.

Another aspect of role clarification in this stage is the transition from student to professional. For those who enter professional positions directly from undergraduate degrees, this transition can be particularly fraught, especially when remaining at the same institution. Boundary issues arise when going from being one of the gang to being the supervisor (Amey, 2002). New professionals learn to define their roles with students, sometimes by making mistakes. Although those who take the intermediary step of graduate school may have already established professional boundaries with students, they are also negotiating the change from an apprentice role to a professional role. Some new professionals may be frustrated that more senior staff members do not give them the credibility they believe they have earned in graduate school or that they are mistaken for students because of their youthful appearance (Reas, 2004). One new professional told me that he countered these concerns by adopting more professional attire:

> My first hall director position began less than a year after I graduated from the same institution. I quickly realized that I needed to find a way to stand out from the student population. I decided that I would wear a tie Monday through Thursday for the entire year (relatively unheard of for a hall director). I did it, and it made a terrific difference!

Reconciling boundary issues is an important task for the new professionals to become socialized in their positions and organizations. The burden for this does not rest solely on the new professional, however, as socialization is an interactive process whereby the individual and the organization adjust to each other (Thornton & Nardi, 1975; Tierney, 1997). Helping new professionals negotiate these role changes can be facilitated by mentors or supervisors with reflection.

Although formal orientation programs should include descriptions of organizational culture, the cultural aspects are often left to be learned informally (Saunders & Cooper, 2003; Winston & Creamer, 1997). Understanding the institutional culture is essential for success, but new professionals are not always sure how to get the information necessary to do this (Cilente et al., 2007). The supervisor or others in the department or institution can help the new professional understand and interpret the organizational culture (Winston & Hirt, 2003).

Institutional fit can become salient again during the informal stage as new professionals learn the realities of the job (Renn & Hodges, 2007). Determining whether the institution is a good fit is a primary task in the anticipatory stage during the job search. During the informal stage, new professionals learn whether their assessments of fit were accurate through interactions in more candid fashion with others at the institution. Some will reinforce their initial perceptions, but others will realize that there are inaccuracies in their initial perceptions that become apparent from their day-to-day experiences (Jaramillo, 2004; Renn & Hodges). A skilled supervisor can help the new professional determine if the institutional mismatch is irrecoverable and can assist the new professional in finding a better position.

Another aspect of organizational culture encountered in the informal stage of socialization is the disconnection between graduate preparation and organizational realities (Cilente et al., 2007; Helm, 2004). New professionals who have spent time in graduate school studying theories and best practices in student affairs are anxious to put their learning into practice, sometimes having unrealistic expectations of their ability to enter a new environment and make broad changes (Cilente et al.). Those new professionals without formal training can experience a disconnection as well, particularly those who assume different roles at their current institutions. The view of the culture varies depending on the role one has and it can be particularly surprising to change roles from student to administrator when new professionals are now privy to what happens behind the scenes.

Some new professionals meet resistance to change from long-term employees who have been through several generations of entry-level staff (Helm, 2004). Reconciling these differences requires interpretation that can be facilitated by consulting with institutional guides, such as more experienced colleagues who can help translate the cultural dynamics at play. For example, a new professional who meets resistance to an idea for a new program from a longtime associate director who says, "We tried that before and it didn't work," might seek advice from a more supportive colleague who can offer ways to approach the associate director or provide a historical context in which to understand the resistance. Learning to read the social, cultural, and political dynamics of the organization can be assisted by leaning on the experience of more practiced professionals.

Learning more about institution-specific student and faculty cultures occurs during the informal stage as well. In addition to the demographic profile of the student body, it is important to understand the ways students interact with each other, with faculty and professional staff, and with their environments. One indicator of student culture is the multicultural composition of the students. It is important for a new professional to learn what cultures are represented among the students, including racial and ethnic groups, sexual orientation identities, religious affiliations, age ranges, and first-generation student status. Beyond knowing the numbers of students in different identity groups, however, the new professional needs to learn how these identities affect the students' experiences on the campus. For example, do students from different racial or ethnic groups have support services on campus? Are gay and lesbian students able to be open and out on campus? Do nontraditionally aged students participate in campus activities?

Social interactions of students are another indicator of student culture. For example, do students tend to stay on campus during the weekends or is it a "suitcase campus?" If there are fraternities and sororities, how influential are they on campuswide programming and activities? Where do students hang out on campus? To what degree do student parties occupy students' free time? Learning about the social culture will help new professionals connect with students in meaningful ways and can indicate developmental needs of students as well. A first-year professional at an elite, private college described the student culture there as being very driven. "They do everything at one hundred percent: study *and* party." As an RHD, she has been surprised at what she perceives as a "sense of entitlement" among the students. Discovering and adapting to this student population has enabled her to implement some developmental interventions in helping students learn communication skills that are more effective than the demanding e-mails and text messages they have been sending.

The use of technology on campus has increasing implications for student culture and the interactions between students and student affairs professionals. The use of text messaging and Internet-based social networking sites (e.g. Facebook, MySpace) is supplanting e-mail and telephone communication. As technologies change, student affairs professionals must adapt and find new ways to reach students. Learning how students prefer to receive information will help new professionals make better connections with their students.

The primary method to learning about student cultures is to interact with students. Spending time in the student union can provide valuable insight into how students interact with each other. Reading the student newspaper or listening to the campus radio station will indicate what current issues are important to students. Attending student activities and programs allows the informal interactions that promote connection with students. New professionals can therefore increase their effectiveness with students through a better understanding of the student cultures.

Faculty cultures are also important to assess as a new professional. Although student affairs professionals sometimes bemoan the lack of involvement that faculty members seem to have in the out-of-classroom lives of students, understanding the work life of the faculty may increase the probability of successful collaborations (McCluskey-Titus, 2005). Factors to consider in determining the faculty culture include the tenure and promotion process and expectations for teaching, research, and service activities; the service-learning and community engagement missions at the institution; whether the faculty are unionized or otherwise heavily involved in university governance; and the presence of faculty affiliates in learning communities or other student affairs programs. New professionals might look to more experienced colleagues for insight into faculty culture. Other avenues to explore include attending colloquium or research presentations, serving on a university-wide committee that includes faculty representatives, and inviting faculty members to lunch for informal relationship building.

The final aspect to be considered in this analysis of the institutional realm of informal socialization is the new professionals' relationships with supervisors. Having an identified mentor is an important value for new professionals (Cilente et al., 2007), and many expect that their supervisors will fill that role (Renn & Hodges, 2007). This is a logical expectation, considering that supervisors of paraprofessional and graduate assistant staff frequently served as mentors "as part of a seamless learning environment" (Renn & Hodges, p. 377). However, there are problems inherent in combining the roles of supervisor and mentor, including the appearance of favoritism and difficulty in employee evaluation (Winston & Hirt, 2003). New professionals may realize that they need to look elsewhere for mentoring (Cilente et al.). Developing relationships with colleagues from other departments (Renn & Hodges) provides a source for finding an appropriate mentor relationship, also referred to as interorganizational mentors. Chapter 7 provides a more complete discussion of these roles.

Extra-institutional Realm

New professionals' informal roles with external stakeholders tend to be minimized. An entry-level professional seldom has direct contact with legislators or the institution's trustees. Any interaction is generally formalized and mediated through the supervisor. Even interactions with parents and members of the media are typically bound by policy; there is little room for personal interpretation in this realm. For some new professionals, this may be a source of comfort, knowing that they can "pass the buck" on potentially sensitive interactions. For others, it may be a source of frustration that they are not regarded as competent to handle such matters. It is important for supervisors to clarify new professionals' roles in the extra-institutional realm to avoid missteps or misunderstandings (Winston & Creamer, 1997).

Professional Realm

In the formal stage of socialization, new professionals learn about relationships with professional organizations from a policy perspective. The informal stage involves making decisions about affiliations with professional organizations and the degree of involvement in those organizations. Reesor (2002) describes four levels of involvement in professional associations: being a passive member or consumer, becoming a contributor, serving as a coordinator, and holding an officer position. New professionals are more likely to participate in the first or second level, attending conferences, volunteering, presenting sessions, or serving on committees. The decision about level of involvement is best made in consultation with the supervisor who can clarify the departmental policies and practices for supporting such activities (Reesor). See chapter 10 for a fuller exploration of the issues related to professional associations and their role in professional development.

The first three stages of socialization—anticipatory, informal, and formal—lead cumulatively to the personal stage, where they come together. Because of the integrated nature of the personal stage, the four realms of professional practice converge at this point.

Personal Stage

Thornton and Nardi (1975) assert that the personal stage of socialization involves "individuals imposing their own expectations and conceptions on roles and modifying role expectations according to their own unique personalities" (p. 880). Having learned the ropes in the formal stage and decoded the unwritten rules in the informal stage, the new professional truly inhabits the professional role and develops a personal style consistent with the role. This stage crosses the realms of professional practice as the individual creates a professional identity across boundaries. The line between "who I am" and "what I do" becomes more blurred as the new professional puts a personal stamp on her or his work. This becomes apparent with a staff that includes several new professionals, such as a group of new RHDs.

During the early weeks and months of employment, the new RHDs look to the more experienced staff for how to do the job: developing training, supervising staff, managing their offices, and other common functions of the RHD position. The formal stage of socialization promotes conformity, with orientation and training sessions that offer best practices on how to proceed. The informal stage also promotes some level of uniform response, with an emphasis on the informal norms and practices. It is during the personal stage of socialization, however, that the new RHDs make the job their own, putting their personalities more fully into their jobs, altering processes to fit their personal work styles, and customizing standard practices in ways that mesh with their own preferences.

The personal stage is related to what Renn and Hodges (2007) term the "Settling In" phase of the new professional experience. The new professional merges personal and professional identities, while still maintaining an awareness of the difference between identity and competency (Renn & Hodges). Having developed a richer, more nuanced understanding of the organizational cultures, relationships, and roles, new professionals are ready to take responsibility for their own professional development and continued learning (Hirt & Winston, 2003; Magolda & Carnaghi, 2004; Renn & Hodges). During this stage, the realms of professional practice converge as the new professional moves seamlessly among the different constituency groups with a well-developed sense of purpose. Although challenges may still arise in the new professional's position, a firm foundation has been established for success.

Implications

Understanding the socialization process can promote a successful transition through the first professional year. The socialization model has implications for new professionals, mentors and graduate preparation faculty, and supervisors of new professionals.

For new professionals, awareness of the process will offer perspective and a framework for knowing what to expect as you anticipate and negotiate your first year in a new position. It may help ease the transition if you give yourself permission to experience the full range of concerns, emotions, and tasks that are included in the socialization process. In addition, attending to all of the realms of professional practice will permit a more complete, conscious transition. Preparing for a new job involves not only academic and experiential learning, but also personal and social factors. Key to the socialization process is taking time to reflect on personal goals, values, and beliefs and determining how these fit with those of the institution. Another suggestion for success is to seek multiple mentors at each stage of the socialization process. Having diverse perspectives will expand the range of perspectives on the realities of work life, helping you to choose your own way rather than reproducing the experience of your mentor.

For preemployment mentors, helping preprofessionals develop a realistic appraisal of professional life will make the transition to working behind the scenes less jarring. Job shadowing is a valuable technique that allows students to see actual work life rather than an idealized view of student affairs administration. Taking time to talk with the students about what they have observed will permit you to clarify and correct misperceptions.

Preparation program faculty can also provide opportunities for reflection on professional practice during course work and experiential learning in practica and internships. Taking a developmental path from high structure to ambiguity will promote self-sufficiency among new professionals as they experience more autonomy in their first professional jobs than they have had in classes. In addition, maintaining contact with recent graduates will allow a feedback loop for curricular improvement for optimal relevancy of the graduate experience.

Finally, supervisors of new professionals can use the socialization model to plan orientation and training sessions for new staff that address all realms of professional practice. In addition, attending to the stages of socialization throughout the first year will provide developmental support to the new professional. Understanding that new professionals will see you as key to their success (Renn & Hodges, 2007), you can help them find multiple means of support and mentoring.

Conclusion

According to Thornton and Nardi (1975), "a role is not fully acquired until an individual has anticipated it, learned anticipatory, formal, and informal expectations comprised in it, formulated his [or her] own expectations, reacted to and reconciled these various expectations, and accepted the final outcome" (p. 873). It is important to help new professionals succeed in their first professional positions. In addition to avoiding the high cost of job turnover (Lorden, 1998), facilitating a successful transition enhances job satisfaction, commitment to the organization (Boehman, 2007), and, ultimately, effectiveness in the position. The socialization model presented here presents a way of conceptualizing the process of developing a professional identity across the four realms of professional practice. New professionals are the vitality of the student affairs profession; promoting their success is key to advancing the work of student affairs.

References

Amey, M. J. (2002). Unwritten rules: Organizational and political realities of the job. In M. J. Amey & L. M. Reesor (Eds.), *Beginning your journey: A guide for new professionals in student affairs* (pp. 13–30). Washington, DC: National Association of Student Personnel Administrators.

Boehman, J. (2007). Affective commitment among student affairs professionals. *NASPA Journal, 44,* 307–325.

Chipman, J. T., & Kuh, G. D. (1988). Organizational entry into student affairs: A metaphorical analysis. *NASPA Journal, 25,* 274–280.

Cilente, K., Henning, G., Skinner Jackson, J., Kennedy, D., & Sloane, T. (2007). *Report on the new professional needs study.* Washington, DC: American College Personnel Association.

Council for the Advancement of Standards in Higher Education. (2006). *CAS professional standards for higher education* (6th ed.). Washington, DC: Author.

Cuyjet, M., Arminio, J., & Woods, E. (2005, April). *Interactive research: Surveying new professionals about their preparation program competencies.* Paper presented at the annual meeting of the American College Personnel Association, Nashville, TN.

Gardner, K., & Woodsmall, C. (2004). The art of compromise and other secrets of the dual-career job search. In P. M. Magolda & J. E. Carnaghi (Eds.), *Job one: Experiences of new professionals in student affairs* (pp. 41–58). Washington, DC: American College Personnel Association.

Helm, M. P. (2004). Professional identity, sense-making, and the market effect: Perspectives from new student affairs professionals. *Dissertation Abstracts International, 65*(04), 1274.

Hirt, J. B., & Collins, D. (2004). Work, relationships, and rewards in student affairs: Differences by institutional type. *College Student Affairs Journal, 24*(1), 4–19.

Hirt, J. B., & Creamer, D. G. (1998). Issues facing student affairs professionals: The four realms of professional life. In N. J. Evans & C. E. Phelps Tobin (Eds.), *State of the art of preparation and practice in student affairs: Another look* (pp. 47–60). Lanham, MD: University Press of America, American College Personnel Association.

Hirt, J. B., & Winston, R. B., Jr. (2003). Professional development: Its integration with supervision processes. In S. M. Janosik, D. G. Creamer, J. B. Hirt, R. B.

Winston, S. A. Saunders, & D. L. Cooper (Eds.), *Supervising new professionals in student affairs* (pp. 85–121). New York: Brunner-Routledge.

Jaramillo, D. (2004). The perfect job. In P. M. Magolda & J. E. Carnaghi (Eds.), *Job one: Experiences of new professionals in student affairs* (pp. 103–114). Washington, DC: American College Personnel Association.

Johnson, C. (2004). Are they hiring me because of the color of my skin? The job search and ethnic fit. In P. M. Magolda & J. E. Carnaghi (Eds.), *Job one: Experiences of new professionals in student affairs* (pp. 27–40). Washington, DC: American College Personnel Association.

Jones S. R., & Segawa, J. M. (2004). Crossing the bridge from graduate school to job one. In P. M. Magolda & J. E. Carnaghi (Eds.), *Job one: Experiences of new professionals in student affairs* (pp. 59–76). Washington, DC: American College Personnel Association.

Kretovics, M. (2002). Entry-level competencies: What student affairs administrators consider when screening candidates. *Journal of College Student Development, 43,* 912–920.

Lorden, L. P. (1998). Attrition in the student affairs profession. *NASPA Journal, 35,* 207–216.

Magolda, P. M., & Carnaghi, J. E. (2004). Preparing the next generation of student affairs professionals. In P. M. Magolda & J. E. Carnaghi (Eds.), *Job one: Experiences of new professionals in student affairs* (pp. 201–227). Washington, DC: American College Personnel Association.

McCarthy, D. (2004). Playing it safe or being real: Integrating a disability and a profession. In P. M. Magolda & J. E. Carnaghi (Eds.), *Job one: Experiences of new professionals in student affairs* (pp. 137–148). Washington, DC: American College Personnel Association.

McCluskey-Titus, P. (2005). The housing professionals' challenge: To involve faculty members meaningfully in our residence hall programs. *Journal of College and University Student Housing, 33*(2), 10–13.

Miller, T. K. (Ed.). (2003). *Book of professional standards for higher education* (3rd ed.). Washington, DC: Council for the Advancement of Standards in Higher Education.

National Association of Student Personnel Administrators. (2007). NASPA undergraduate fellows program. Retrieved December 17, 2007, from http://www.naspa .org/programs/nufp

Ortiz, A. M., & Shintaku, R. H. (2004). Professional and personal identities at the crossroads. In P. M. Magolda & J. E. Carnaghi (Eds.), *Job one: Experiences of new professionals in student affairs* (pp. 163–178). Washington, DC: American College Personnel Association.

Reas, M. (2004). The early days in the real world: Establishing a professional identity. In P. M. Magolda & J. E. Carnaghi (Eds.), *Job one: Experiences of new professionals in student affairs* (pp. 77–90). Washington, DC: American College
Personnel Association.

Reesor, L. M. (2002). Making professional connections. In M. J. Amey & L. M.
Reesor (Eds.), *Beginning your journey: A guide for new professionals in student
affairs* (pp. 81–96). Washington, DC: National Association of Student Personnel
Administrators.

Renn, K. A., & Hodges, J. P. (2007). The first year on the job: Experiences of new
professionals in student affairs. *NASPA Journal, 44,* 367–391.

Rosen, J. A., Taube, S. R., & Wadsworth, E. L. (1980). The first professional year:
Interviews with the new professionals at SUNY-Stony Brook. *NASPA Journal,
17*(3), 52–59.

Saunders, S. A., & Cooper, D. L. (2003). Orientation: Building the foundations for
success. In S. M. Janosik, D. G. Creamer, J. B. Hirt, R. B. Winston, S. A. Saunders, & D. L. Cooper (Eds.), *Supervising new professionals in student affairs* (pp.
17–41). New York: Brunner-Routledge.

Simpkins, W. D. (2004). Part of the crowd: One man's journey through identity. In
P. M. Magolda & J. E. Carnaghi (Eds.), *Job one: Experiences of new professionals
in student affairs* (pp. 149–162). Washington, DC: American College Personnel
Association.

Thornton, R., & Nardi, P. M. (1975). The dynamics of role acquisition. *American
Journal of Sociology, 80,* 870–885.

Tierney, W. G. (1997). Organizational socialization in higher education. *Journal of
Higher Education, 68,* 1–16.

Tull, A. (2006). Synergistic supervision, job satisfaction, and intention to turnover
of new professionals in student affairs. *Journal of College Student Development, 47,*
465–480.

Van Maanen, J., & Schein, E. H. (1979). Toward a theory of organizational socialization. *Research in Organizational Behavior, 1,* 209–264.

Weidman, J. C., Twale, D. J., & Stein, E. L. (2001). *Socialization of graduate and
professional students in higher education: A perilous passage?* ASHE-ERIC Higher
Education Research Report, Vol. 28, No. 3. San Francisco: Jossey-Bass.

Winston, R. B., Jr., & Creamer, D. G. (1997). *Improving staffing practices in student
affairs.* San Francisco: Jossey-Bass.

Winston, R. B., Jr., & Hirt, J. B. (2003). Activating synergistic supervision
approaches: Practical suggestions. In S. M. Janosik, D. G. Creamer, J. B. Hirt,
R. B. Winston, S. A. Saunders, & D. L. Cooper (Eds.). *Supervising new professionals in student affairs* (pp. 43–83). New York: Brunner-Routledge.

2

QUALITY OF WORK LIFE
Why Socialization Matters

Vicki J. Rosser and Jan Minoru Javinar

S tudent affairs professionals are a critically important group of institutional leaders within postsecondary education. As a result, they are among the cadre of midlevel administrators who are the unsung professionals within the academy—unsung because their contribution to the academic enterprise is rarely recognized, and professionals because of their commitment, training, and adherence to high standards of performance and excellence in their areas of expertise (Rosser, 2000).

What We Know About the Work Life and Retention of Student Affairs Leaders

Midlevel administrator is a broad term that often depicts new professionals as well as supervisors who remain in the field and move on to positions such as directors, coordinators, associate directors, advisors, counselors, and other specialized staff positions. More specifically, the area of student affairs includes an impressive range of academic and academic support areas that help foster the goals and mission of the academic enterprise. More importantly, student affairs leaders who oversee the plethora of student support areas (e.g., freshman interest groups, first-year experiences, cocurricular activities, diversity support) strive to enhance the growth, development, and the social and academic engagement of students within an academic institution. Given the breadth of key positions these student affairs leaders oversee, it is only fitting that we examine the issues that inform their professional socialization and influence the quality of their work life, satisfaction and morale, and retention within the academy.

Even though numerous issues and themes constitute or even define administrative work life, six broad dimensions regarding administrators' work life seem to emerge consistently in the higher education literature as most important: career support, recognition for competence, intradepartment relations, external relations, working conditions, and perceptions of discrimination. These dimensions have been shown to influence the quality of higher education midlevel administrators' work life and their intended departure more generally (e.g., Johnsrud, 1996; Johnsrud & Rosser, 1999b; Rosser, 2004; Twombly, 1990; Volkwein & Parmley, 2000), and with student affairs administrators more specifically (e.g., Burns, 1982; Evans, 1988; Hirt, Esteban, & McGuire, 2003; Lorden, 1998; Rosser & Javinar, 2003; Ward, 1995).

The intent to stay in or leave one's position is a good indicator of actual turnover (e.g., Bluedorn, 1982; Lee & Mowday, 1987). Lee and Mowday suggest that job satisfaction, commitment to the organization, and job involvement explain individuals' intentions to stay or leave. Moreover, Bluedorn developed a conceptual model of organizational turnover that specifies a process that begins with five antecedents of job satisfaction: pay, participation in relationships, communication related to tasks, organizational communication, and participation in decision making. Based upon individuals' attitudes and perceptions within the organization, they will then react affectively, cognitively, and behaviorally according to their own definitions of organizational situations. Bluedorn's model provides a framework to study higher education administrators' perceptions of their work life leading to affective responses, such as individual satisfaction and/or organizational morale, which may have a direct impact upon the intent to stay in or leave the organization.

Affective responses or antecedents come together to produce mediating measures such as job satisfaction and/or morale that are built upon individuals' organizational experiences. Previous research on midlevel administrators within higher education has indicated the power of affective responses (i.e., satisfaction, morale) on work-life processes, and specifically the impact of these antecedents on turnover intentions (Johnsrud & Edwards, 2001; Rosin & Korabik, 1995; Rosser, 2004; Rosser, Hermsen, Mamiseishvili, & Wood, 2007; Rosser & Javinar, 2003). Even though theoretical development of *satisfaction* as a response to a series of work-life dimensions or determinants has been limited, Gruenberg (1979) defines satisfaction as the individual's emotional reaction to a particular job. Benge and Hickey (1984) identify job satisfaction as the combination of various attitudes held by an individual employee at a given time. Lawler (1994) suggests that satisfaction reflects components of drive theories and need theories and that satisfaction is directly related to want and need. As Lawler notes, according to drive theories, satisfaction and cessation of potential behavior are because of the satiation of primary drives (e.g., career support, recognition for competence, working conditions, intradepartment relations). The term *need* refers to clusters of outcomes that people seek as ends in themselves, such as the intent to stay in or leave one's position and/or career in this case. Lawler goes on to say that the majority of work on satisfaction has been in the context of the workplace and there is a continuing need to examine the factors that may influence job satisfaction.

Although the literature in higher education on *morale* is limited, Madron, Craig, and Mendel (1976) define morale as a group's psychological state characterized by confidence, enthusiasm, discipline, willingness to work, and related attributes. They argue that morale may be seen as a potential symptomatic attribute that might be used in examining organizational difficulties. More specifically, high morale is manifested when individuals show determination to do their best under any circumstance. Low morale implies that the individuals see themselves as powerless or socially unimportant (Doherty, 1988). Often associated as being an affective response to organizational work-life issues, or commonly referred to as a mediating social psychological variable, administrative morale refers to the level of well-being that an individual or group is experiencing in reference to his or her work life (Johnsrud, 1996).

Although much debate continues regarding the conceptual understanding of satisfaction and morale, both have been defined and measured as separate and distinct concepts. Johnsrud and Edwards (2001) note that satisfaction is most often related to an individual's feelings regarding his or her job, while morale is related to how one views or feels about the organization. For example, the overall dimension of satisfaction includes items such as individual freedom on the job, sufficient variety of work-related tasks, enjoyment of the work and job, trust and confidence of colleagues, satisfaction with work responsibilities, fair salary compensation, an overall indicator of the individual's job satisfaction, and having input on matters that affect one's work. However, morale depicts a common sense of organizational purpose that administrators as a group perceive the organization cares and values them, that administrators are proud, loyal, and committed to the organization, and the institution treats them fairly. Therefore and in this case, the work-life experiences of student affairs leaders are mediated by their (high or low) levels of satisfaction and morale, which in turn explain their intention to stay in or leave their career or position. We would be remiss if we didn't mention that a certain amount of turnover can be positive as it may allow us to reassess or reorganize administrative duties, responsibilities, and organizational or unit structures. Therefore, the close monitoring and assessment of what an acceptable turnover rate is or should be within a given unit or organization is critically important, and turnover should not be viewed simply as debilitating.

A national study conducted by Rosser and Javinar (2003) involved almost 1,200 student affairs leaders who were randomly selected from a total midlevel administrative national population of 11,300 from public and private institutions within five Carnegie classifications. The study identified six dimensions of the quality of work life that for student affairs leaders had a significant and/or direct impact on their morale and satisfaction. These work-life measures can potentially provide student affairs leaders or managers with approaches to identify areas to address on their own or with the support of their supervisor, and thus positively influence the morale and satisfaction of new professionals in student affairs in order to foster their retention in the profession. These measures and approaches are discussed in the next section.

Primary Work-Life Dimensions Most Important to Student Affairs Leaders

The first dimension of interest, *career support*, includes those issues regarding the student affairs leaders' professional and career development, opportunities for career enhancement, and job performance. This quality of work-life measure for midlevel student affairs professionals was found to have a significant and direct impact on their level of job satisfaction (Rosser & Javinar, 2003). The higher midlevel student affairs leaders' perceive support for their career, the higher their level of satisfaction or emotional regard for the job.

Just as midlevel student affairs leaders desire support for their continued development via opportunities for participation in professional activities, so too do new professionals need continuing support as they make the transition to professional status. Supervisors need to financially support, encourage, and perhaps even require new professionals to attend or enroll in career activities such as professional conferences, in-service training, relevant and current skill-set training, and career-enhancing professional development programs. Additionally, supervisors who encourage and structure work schedules of new professionals to enable their enrollment in advanced programs of study not only role model the profession's belief in lifelong learning, they also enhance the division's overall status in the academy with credentialed staff members who have themselves experienced the scholarly regimen of advanced study.

The quality of the work-life measure for career support also involved midlevel student affairs leaders' sense that promotion opportunities were available and that hiring practices within their unit were fair. In addition, this work-life measure included the midlevel leader's perceptions that job performance criteria were clear and distribution of the workload was fair. New professionals likewise may have greater levels of job satisfaction if they were clear about performance standards and could acknowledge equity in the workload. Midlevel managers would do well to structure opportunities for new professionals to engage in job hiring processes so that the new professional may witness the assessment of applicant qualifications in writing, the development of interview questions, the conduct of purposeful and/or behavioral-based interviews, and the subsequent evaluation of applicants recommended for hire. This career experience would enable new professionals to judge for themselves the fairness of hiring practices within their unit and expose them to other career opportunities for the future. In addition, midlevel student affairs leaders, desirous of engendering job satisfaction among new professionals must outline clear performance criteria for their new professionals (Winston & Creamer, 1997; see chapter 6 for more information about early setting of performance expectations). Some new professionals are from the millennial generation and are likely to have been sheltered and structured as young children (Howe & Strauss, 2000). Therefore, it behooves midlevel managers to articulate and role model appropriate professional behaviors and actions since millennials expect policies to be clearly communicated and consistently enforced with adequate due process (Labrecque, 2006; Martin & Tulgan, 2001). New professionals need to know what level of performance is expected of them and how to accomplish their goals and assignments (Labrecque). Doing so empowers new professionals to take control of their positions, which may lead to their increased sense of job satisfaction.

A second dimension, *recognition for competence*, involves the mentoring, trust, guidance, feedback, and the decision-making authority that student affairs leaders are granted by their supervisor, director, dean, or vice president. This quality of work-life measure for midlevel student affairs professionals was found to have a significant direct impact on their satisfaction and morale (Rosser & Javinar, 2003). The higher the midlevel leaders' perception that they were recognized for their expertise and given the authority to make decisions as a result of that expertise, the higher was their level of satisfaction or emotional regard for the job, and the higher was their level of morale or feelings about the organization. No doubt, new professionals in student affairs would respond likewise, if given appropriate and adequate recognition for their contributions and competence. For example, student affairs leaders often bring an expertise to the table regarding their functional areas and/or students. Perhaps appointing them to college task forces or university committees that coordinate initiatives such as strategic planning, budgetary challenges, overall campus recruitment or retention efforts, changing student characteristics, and so on would enable new professionals in student affairs to offer differing student-centered perspectives while simultaneously demonstrating their knowledge base and expertise to the broader college or university community.

Student affairs midlevel leaders can structure their one-on-one supervision meetings with new professionals by providing sufficient and specific feedback about employee performance. Also, supervisors should use these meetings as an opportunity for purposeful actions and mentoring aimed at promoting learning for the new professional. This approach creates yet another growth opportunity for the new professional. Supervision from this mentoring and developmental approach will not only convey a message of acknowledgment and recognition of the employee's professional worth to the organization, but it also operationalizes and fulfills the student affairs profession's raison d'être: to challenge and support the development of new professionals' knowledge, skills, and abilities throughout their career (see chapter 7 for further information about supervision and mentoring).

Midlevel leaders can develop growth contracts or learning plans, support the new professional's initial membership in relevant professional associations, encourage and support conference attendance, assist in developing and presenting educational sessions with new professionals, sustain the growth of a department resource library, give praise and encouragement, attend events or witness the administration of services organized by new professionals, write simple personalized notes saying "great job," or publicly acknowledge the new professional's efforts at a regular staff meeting or a celebratory luncheon (Hammond, 1998). Efforts such as these recognize and reward new professionals for their contributions and efforts. This, in turn, may positively influence their satisfaction and morale, and stem desires to leave.

Few areas are more important to student affairs leaders than the building and fostering of positive relationships within and outside their functional units. A third dimension, *intradepartment relations* involves those professional relationships with colleagues within the unit and often entails creating a strong sense of teamwork, providing effective means of communication, reducing staff turnover, and building a culturally diverse community. This quality of work-life measure for midlevel student affairs professionals has a significant direct impact on their satisfaction and morale (Rosser & Javinar, 2003). The greater the midlevel leaders' view that their units are characterized by positive interpersonal relations, positive group dynamics, and gender and ethnic diversity, the greater is their level of satisfaction or emotional regard for the job, along with their level of morale or feelings about the organization. Student affairs work, as one author notes, is about the "consistent and persistent emphasis on and commitment to the development of the whole person" (Nuss, 2003, p. 65). Midlevel student affairs leaders would do well to focus simultaneously on fostering the holistic development of students whom they teach or counsel, and the holistic development of staff members whom they supervise.

Dalton (2003) outlines four essential tasks that provide a conceptual framework for midlevel managers to organize their efforts when promoting development for new and experienced staff members. These supervisory tasks are aimed toward improving effective group and team dynamics within the supervisor's unit and include helping new professionals to (a) fulfill the responsibilities for which they were hired, (b) master the specific competencies needed to successfully carry out assigned duties, (c) understand, cope, and thrive in their work culture and environment; and (d) engage in continual learning and professional development or renewal. Midlevel managers need to work toward effective teaming with new professionals where communication is two way and open, where group goals are clarified and cooperatively structured, where participation and leadership are distributed among all staff members, and where interpersonal or intergroup skills are stressed for seasoned and emerging staff members (Johnson & Johnson, 2006). Midlevel student affairs leaders can create these opportunities through regular staff meetings and by encouraging cross-functional work teams that draw different staff members from throughout the supervisor's unit. New professionals who find themselves engaged in a work environment where their participation and ideas are valued and solicited may be more likely to remain within that environment more specifically or in the student affairs profession generally.

A fourth dimension, *building external relationships*, involves those constituencies such as students, faculty members, senior administrators, and the public who are external to the student affairs unit but interface with student affairs administrators either directly or indirectly. This quality of work-life measure for midlevel student affairs professionals was found to have a significant direct impact on their satisfaction: the higher the perception that their units developed and maintained positive relationships with external groups, the higher the level of satisfaction or emotional regard for the job (Rosser & Javinar, 2003).

Related to the third dimension of intradepartment relations, midlevel student affairs leaders should encourage new professional staff members whom they supervise to engage with the broader campus community and avoid getting organizationally stuck in the functional silo of student affairs. Introducing new professionals to different external parties of the campus community as part of their new employee orientation or continuing staff training should be critical steps (see chapter 6 for more information about new staff orientation). Having new professionals represent the unit and participate in such activities as campus college recruitment fairs, orientation programs for new and transferring students, parents' weekends, or new employee orientations for the campus will provide the new professional with the opportunities to interact with other non–student affairs staff members.

Because many of the decision-making processes in higher education revolve around institutional committees, task forces, and the like, encouraging new professionals to become active participants in institutional decision making or governance is another effective way to broaden the views of new professionals about their roles and the roles of others on campus, especially of those outside student affairs. Finally, student affairs professionals deal with many bread-and-butter issues of students. Because student affairs deals with students' most basic needs (e.g. housing, food service, financial aid, academic advising, and class availability) and deals with students often in crises as evidenced by tragedies at Virginia Tech, University of North Carolina at Chapel Hill, and Auburn University, the student affairs professional comes into contact with external campus and community groups. Additionally, not a week goes by without a college campus having to address hazing incidents by registered student organizations or the expectations from neighborhoods for the campus to curtail or control the actions of students who reside therein. Midlevel student affairs leaders would serve new professionals well by providing in-service training in dealing with the media, facilitating meetings of neighborhood representatives, presenting at meetings of the board of trustees, and lobbying the state legislature. This will help new professionals become more skillful in their role as liaisons between their units or campuses and external constituencies.

An area that tends to elicit strong positive or negative organizational perceptions from midlevel or student affairs leaders is the institution's *work environment or working conditions*, a fifth dimension that includes salary levels, health benefits, retirement plans, institutional resources allocated to the unit, and the physical work environment including access to parking. This quality of work-life measure for midlevel student affairs professionals has a significant, direct impact on their satisfaction and morale (Rosser & Javinar, 2003). The higher the midlevel leaders' perception is that various working conditions are adequate or meeting expectations, the higher their level of satisfaction or emotional regard for the job, along with their level of morale or feelings about the organization.

The literature on attrition in student affairs suggests the reasons for departure. These include low pay, lack of opportunity for advancement, and poor work environments (Evans, 1988; Hancock, 1988; Holmes, Verrier, & Chisholm, 1983; Lorden, 1998). Although student affairs midlevel leaders may not determine salary levels, health benefits, or retirement plans (which may be subject to collective bargaining and/or legislative negotiations), they are in a position to affect the compensation packages of new professionals, especially during their initial hire, upon their passing probation, and during their annual year-end reviews. Midlevel managers need to develop and use consistent and fair methods when calculating salary offers to extend to potential new hires, remaining mindful of the salary levels of existing staff members as well. They must carve out the required time to complete probationary evaluations and annual evaluations so that new professionals eligible for salary adjustments may qualify and stand for consideration. The promise and granting of professional development leave for the new professional to pursue advanced degrees, other educational studies, or research may compensate for lower salary levels. Finally, midlevel student affairs leaders need to develop and implement consistent and fair bases for the assignment of offices and parking spaces. These basic needs can have a significant impact on the morale and satisfaction of the new professional.

As one author noted, balancing work and nonwork activities influences the student affairs professional's morale or feelings about the organization (Boehman, 2006) and as a consequence the individual's commitment to stay or leave the institution or the profession. Beeny, Guthrie, and Terrell state that while today's professionals have experienced an increase in the number of hours spent at work (as cited in Boehman, 2006), the new professional in student affairs may not necessarily subscribe to the value of "getting the work done, no matter how long it takes" that professionals of the boomer generation may have been acculturated to. It behooves midlevel student affairs leaders, then, to remain mindful of systemic practices, supervisory expectations, and work activities that may impinge upon the new professional's ability to conduct his or her family life, social activities, and community work. Accommodating new professionals with flexible work schedules that give them opportunities to contend with sick children or elderly parents, revisiting our own supervisory expectations to gauge workload equity about new professionals' putting in hours during the evenings or weekends, and expanding definitions of relevant community service or professional service to enable new professionals to balance their work and nonwork activities may be some critical first steps that student affairs midmanagers can take to foster family-friendly work environments.

The sixth dimension, *perceptions of discrimination*, which student affairs midlevel leaders hold or more critically experience, has an inverse effect on

overall morale. The higher the midlevel leader's perception is that discrimi-
natory acts, subtle or overt, occurred in the workplace, the lower the morale
or feelings about the organization (Rosser & Javinar, 2003). The discrimina-
tory acts cited within the workplace environment include sexual stereotyping, harassment, and discrimination; and racial or ethnic stereotyping,
harassment, and age discrimination. No other dimension can have more of a
debilitating effect on individuals and the quality of their work lives. Previous
research confirmed our findings and revealed that student affairs leaders who
perceive or experience discrimination tend to possess lower levels of overall
morale, and that may ultimately have an impact on their intention of staying
in their position or at their institution (Johnsrud & Rosser, 1999a; Moore,
1983).

Because of their position in the organizational chart, midlevel student
affairs leaders manage people, money, information, and programs (Mills,
2000). Given the task of providing support services and other administrative
duties, midlevel leaders often assume a liaison role, linking vertical and horizontal levels of their organizational hierarchy (White, Webb, & Young,
1990). As such, midlevel administrators are pivotal to achieving a multicultural workplace environment where new professionals experience, feel, and
perceive fairness, openness, and sensitivity to diversity, and where differences
in thinking and approaches are welcome. At a minimum, this translates to a
commitment from the midlevel student affairs administrator to plan, exe-
cute, and evaluate preventive and corrective actions. This includes adherence
to elements of campus policy, supporting campus programs, and offering
staff training to prevent harassment and discrimination of all types. More
critically, midlevel leaders need to become multiculturally competent in the
broadest sense of the term *culture* (Pope & Reynolds, 1997).

Midlevel student affairs leaders often set the parameters in which new
professionals and others operate. Enjoying the privilege of holding and exer-
cising the power and the authority within their units, midlevel administrators knowingly or unknowingly construct an organizational culture for their
units. If the goal of a multicultural organization is to be realized, then the
larger challenge for midlevel student affairs leaders is to become reflective
practitioners (Klein, 2006) who are (a) aware of the voices of new professionals and others whom they hear and grant audience for or not; (b) knowledge-
able of the values, morals, ethics, and principles they promote or not at the
workplace through words and actions; and (c) skilled in interrogating their

own social constructions of the organizational culture and committed to employing alternatives or not. According to Barr and Strong, only then will the new professional enjoy an organizational culture that is

> genuinely committed to diverse representation of its membership; is sensitive to maintaining an open, supportive, and responsive environment; is working toward and purposefully including elements of diverse cultures in its ongoing operation; and . . . is authentic in its response to issues confronting it (as cited in Taylor & von Destinon, 2000, p. 160).

To attain a welcoming and inclusive organizational culture, midlevel student affairs leaders must endeavor to recruit a diverse work team that avoids the homosocial reproduction of the same or the similar. In addition, midlevel student affairs leaders must role model ways of communication that minimize exclusivity or a sense of hierarchy in language use by avoiding language that is derogatory or that creates and perpetuates negative social stereotypes. Using degendered terms rather than regendered ones (the *chair* rather than the chairwoman or the chairman), replacing occupational terms containing man and boy with other terms (e.g., *wait help* for waiter/waitress, *flight attendant* for stewardess, *yard staff* for yardmen), and recasting the masculine pronoun *he* into the plural or alternating the use of she and he are examples that serve to remind the profession and the academy of areas where language use may still discriminate and foster misunderstandings in daily conversations. New professionals situated in more welcoming environments may experience increased positive morale or feelings about their work environment.

Conclusion

Examining the perceptions student affairs leaders have of their professional and institutional work life has uncovered implications for their level of satisfaction, morale, and intent to stay in or leave their current position. Six broad dimensions of work-life quality emerged, which if addressed by midlevel student affairs leaders may potentially affect the job satisfaction and organizational morale of new and continuing individuals in the field of student affairs, and in turn, may influence the retention of practitioners. Therefore, if we are to reinforce the practitioner's passion for our work in student affairs, then we "must be willing to address the quality of work-life issues for our members of the profession" (Blackhurst, Brandt, & Kalinkowski, 1998, p. 31).

References

Benge, E., & Hickey, J. (1984). *Morale and motivation: How to measure morale and increase productivity*. New York: Franklin Watts.

Blackhurst, A. E., Brandt, J. E., & Kalinkowski, J. (1998). Effects of career development on the organizational commitment and life satisfaction of women student affairs administrations. *NASPA Journal, 36*(1), *19–34.*

Bluedorn, A. C. (1982). The theories of turnover: Causes, effects, and meaning. *Research in the Sociology of Organizations, 1,* 75–128.

Boehman, J. (2006). The impact of work/non-work interaction on organizational commitment. *NASPA Net Results*. Retrieved April 12, 2007, from http://www .naspa.org/membership/mem/pubs/nr/default.cfm?id = 1548

Burns, M. A. (1982). Who leaves the student affairs field? *NASPA Journal, 20*(2), 9–12.

Dalton, J. C. (2003). Managing human resources. In S. R. Komives, D. B. Woodard, Jr., & Associates (Eds.), *Student services: A handbook for the profession* (4th ed.). San Francisco: Wiley.

Doherty, J. (1988). Psychological morale: Its conceptualization and measurement: The Doherty Inventory of Psychological Morale (DIPM). *Educational Studies, 14*(1), 65–74.

Evans, N. (1988). Attrition of student affairs professionals: A review of the literature. *Journal of College Student Development, 29*(1), 19–24.

Gruenberg, M. M. (1979). *Understanding job satisfaction*. New York: Wiley.

Hammond, D. (1998). Mentoring helps us create true learning environments. *ACUI Bulletin, 66*(1), 14–15.

Hancock, J. (1988). Needs and reinforcers in student affairs: Implications for attrition. *Journal of College Student Development, 29*(1), 25–30.

Hirt, J., Esteban, R., & McGuire, L. (2003). The worklives of student services professionals at rural community colleges. *Community College Review, 31*(1), 1–13.

Holmes, D., Verrier, D., & Chisholm, P. (1983). Persistence in student affairs work: Attitudes & job shifts among master's program graduates. *Journal of College Student Personnel, 24*(4), 438–443.

Howe, N., & Strauss, W. (2000). *Millenials rising: The next great generation*. New York: Vintage.

Johnson, D. W., & Johnson, F. P. (2006). *Joining together: Group theory and group skills* (9th ed.). Boston: Pearson.

Johnsrud, L. K. (1996). *Maintaining morale: A guide to assessing the morale of midlevel administrators and faculty*. Washington, DC: College and University Personnel Association.

Johnsrud, L. K., & Edwards, R. L. R. (2001, November). *Mediating the intent to leave: The affective responses of midlevel administrators to their worklives*. Paper presented at the annual meeting of the Association for the Study of Higher Education, Richmond, VA.

Johnsrud, L. K., & Rosser, V. J. (1999a). Predicting and reducing mid-level administrative turnover. *CUPA Journal, 50*(1–2), 1–8.

Johnsrud, L. K., & Rosser, V. J. (1999b). College and university mid-level administrators: Explaining and improving their morale. *The Review of Higher Education, 22*(2), 121–141.

Klein, A. M. (2006). *Raising multicultural awareness in higher education*. Lanham, MD: University Press of America.

Labrecque, K. (2006). *Supervising student employees*. Retrieved from http://www.pacrao.org/docs/resources/writersteam/SupervisingStudentEmployees.doc

Lawler, E. E. (1994). *Motivation in work organization*. San Francisco: Jossey Bass.

Lee, T. W., & Mowday, R. T. (1987). Voluntarily leaving an organization: An empirical investigation of Steers and Mowday's model of turnover. *Academy of Management Journal, 30*(4), 721–743.

Lorden, L. (1998). Attrition in the student affairs profession. *NASPA Journal, 35*(1), 207–216.

Madron, T. W., Craig, J. R., & Mendel, R. M. (1976). Departmental morale as a function of the perceived performance of department heads. *Research in Higher Education, 5*, 83–94.

Martin, C. A., & Tulgan, B. (2001). *Managing generation Y*. New Haven, CT: HRD Press.

Mills, D. B. (2000). The role of the middle manager. In M. J. Barr & M. K. Desler (Eds.), *The handbook of student affairs administration* (pp. 135–153). San Francisco: Jossey-Bass.

Moore, K. M. (1983). *Leaders in transition—A national study of higher education administrators*. University Park, PA: Center for the Study of Higher Education, Pennsylvania State University.

Nuss, E. M. (2003). The development of student affairs. In S. R. Komives, D. B. Woodard, Jr., & Associates (Eds.), *Student services: A handbook for the profession* (4th ed.). San Francisco: Wiley.

Pope, R. L., & Reynolds, A. L. (1997). Student affairs core competencies: Integrating multicultural awareness, knowledge, and skills. *Journal of College Student Development, 38*(3), 266–277.

Rosin, H., & Korabik, K. (1995). Organizational experiences and propensity to leave: A multivariate investigation of men and women managers. *Journal of Vocational Behavior, 46,* 1–16.

Rosser, V. J. (2000). Midlevel administrators: What we know. In L. K. Johnsrud and V. J. Rosser (Eds.), *Understanding the work and career paths of midlevel administrators* (pp. 5–13). New Directions for Higher Education, No. 111. San Francisco: Jossey-Bass.

Rosser, V. J. (2004). A national study on midlevel leaders in higher education: The unsung professionals of the academy. *Higher Education: The International Journal of Higher Education and Planning, 48*(3), 317–337.

Rosser, V. J., Hermsen, J. M., Mamiseishvili, K., & Wood, M. S. (2007). The impact of SEVIS on U.S. international student and scholar advisors. *Higher Education: The International Journal of Higher Education and Planning, 54*(4), 524–525.

Rosser, V. J., & Javinar, J. M. (2003). Midlevel student affairs leaders' intentions to leave: Examining the quality of their professional and institutional work life. *Journal of College Student Development, 46*(6), 813–830.

Taylor, S. L., & von Destinon, M. (2000). Selecting, training, supervising, and evaluating staff. In M. J. Barr & M. K. Desler (Eds.), *The handbook of student affairs administration* (pp. 135–153). San Francisco: Jossey-Bass.

Twombly, S. B. (1990). Career maps and institutional highways. In K. M. Moore and S. B. Twombly (Eds.), *Administrative careers and the marketplace* (pp. 5–18), New Directions for Higher Education, No. 72. San Francisco: Jossey-Bass.

Volkwein, J. F., & Parmley, K. (2000). Comparing administrative satisfaction in public and private universities. *Research in Higher Education, 41*(1), 95–116.

Ward, L. (1995). Role stress and propensity to leave among new student affairs professionals. *NASPA Journal, 33*(1), 35–45.

White, J., Webb, L., & Young, R. (1990). Press and stress: A comparative study of institutional factors affecting the work of mid-managers. In Robert B. Young (Ed.), *The invisible leaders: Student affairs mid-managers* (pp. 56–71). Washington, DC: National Association of Student Personnel Administrators.

Winston, R. B., Jr., & Creamer, D. G. (1997). *Improving staffing practices in student affairs.* San Francisco: Jossey-Bass.

PART TWO

CONTEXTS THAT INFLUENCE
SOCIALIZATION OF NEW
PROFESSIONALS

3

THE INFLUENCE OF INSTITUTIONAL TYPE ON SOCIALIZATION

Joan B. Hirt

T he first two chapters in this volume have examined the nature of socialization and the importance of work-life issues on the socialization of new student affairs professionals. Certainly these two topics provide a general framework useful in understanding the impact of socialization. But context also plays a key role in shaping professional practice, and one context that influences socialization in powerful ways is the type of institution at which one works. Indeed, the American system of higher education is the envy of the world, in large part because of the array of different institutional types it encompasses (Carnegie Foundation for the Advancement of Teaching, 2000). Students can attend comprehensive institutions, community colleges, historically Black colleges and universities (HBCUs), or any of a number of other institutional types.

Many characteristics can be used to assort colleges and universities. The type of control (public versus private), proprietary status (not-for-profit versus for profit), number of students enrolled, types of degrees and/or certificates offered, or the school's athletic league are all ways to differentiate postsecondary institutions from one another (Barr, 2000). Beyond institutional characteristics, however, there is another way to distinguish colleges and universities—by their mission.

Institutional mission statements are public pronouncements about a campus. To those outside the college or university, the mission statement informs. It tells prospective students what types of degrees it offers. Public officials glean a college's or university's focus from what is said in the mission statement. Potential faculty can learn about the campus's academic priorities and staff can discover if there is a good fit for them at the institution. Members of the local community or region can ascertain how the campus serves their interests (Barr, 2000; Martin, 1982). In other words, to external groups the mission statement sets the boundaries of the college or university.

These same mission-driven boundaries serve those internal to the campus. A clearly defined mission statement helps institutional leaders develop a strategic plan and allocate resources to enact that plan. It allows faculty to develop curricular offerings that are aligned with the mission and permits staff to identify the types of support services needed to accomplish mission objectives. A well-crafted mission statement is particularly crucial in times of financial exigency when it can help leaders decide how to prioritize programs and where to cut support (Barr, 2000; Martin, 1982). For those in student affairs, understanding and appreciating the mission of the institution where one works is critical to professional success.

Finally, the mission of an institution identifies how it is like other campuses. Colleges or universities that share elements of mission likely share other characteristics—they can be considered a group. Collectively, they form an institutional type, and the type of institution where one works influences one's professional life in multiple ways that make a real difference in the daily lives of administrators (Hirt & Collins, 2005).

This chapter addresses the differences in professional life for student affairs professionals at different types of colleges and universities. I start by describing one typological framework through which to view colleges and universities. Then I discuss eight distinct institutional types—baccalaureate colleges (both secular and sectarian), master's institutions, research universities, HBCUs, associate's colleges, tribally controlled colleges, and Hispanic-serving institutions (HSIs). For each type, I talk about the mission, the nature of work for student affairs professionals, the relationships that are keys to success for professionals, and the rewards professionals garner. I describe how new professionals are socialized by the institutional culture, guided by the assumption that some institutional settings are better suited than others for the new professional's interests and skill sets.

An Institutional Typology: The Carnegie Classification System

Postsecondary education in the United States is markedly different from higher education systems around the world in one important way: namely, there is no single system of higher education in the United States. Most countries around the globe have national educational systems in which access to postsecondary institutions (or tertiary institutions, as they are often called) is driven by performance at primary and secondary levels of education. National achievement tests establish success rates and dictate which students move on to higher levels of learning (Altbach, 1998). In contrast, in the United States each state manages its own higher education program, rendering 50 different systems plus those in the District of Columbia, Puerto Rico, Guam, and other territories. Each state has its own system of governing colleges and universities, approving new institutions and programs, assuring quality, funding postsecondary education, and controlling costs. Indeed, in many states there are multiple systems. New York, for example, has the State University of New York (SUNY) system and the City University of New York (CUNY) system. In California, the University of California, the California State University, and the California Community Colleges are three distinct higher education systems. This kind of variation in systems renders it nearly impossible to draw cross-state comparisons.

In response to the need to understand more about the American higher education system, the Carnegie Foundation for the Advancement of Teaching created a typology of institutions that has guided research and practice for over three decades (Carnegie Foundation for the Advancement of Teaching, 2000). The Foundation has issued six editions of the classification. The 1973, 1976, 1987, 1994, and 2000 versions assigned colleges and universities to categories based on their mission: doctoral/research universities, master's colleges and universities, baccalaureate colleges, associate's colleges, specialized institutions (e.g., seminaries, schools of art), and tribal colleges and universities. As postsecondary education grew more complex, however, the Foundation determined that a more multidimensional model was warranted. In addition to assigning campuses by mission, the latest Carnegie classification system assigns each institution to multiple groups by undergraduate instructional program, graduate instructional program, enrollment profile, undergraduate profile, size and setting, and level of community engagement

(Carnegie Classification of Institutions of Higher Education, 2005). These new categories render a more textured landscape of the nation's higher education institutions.

In this chapter, I use the 2005 Carnegie framework, albeit in a modified format. I take from that model the following categories: baccalaureate colleges (modified to include secular and sectarian), master's colleges and universities, doctoral-granting universities, associate's colleges, and tribally controlled colleges. I add to these groups, however, HBCUs and HSIs. These latter groups are not Carnegie classifications, per se, but they represent important sectors of the nation's postsecondary system and merit the same consideration as other groups in the schema. My decision to add these two categories of institutions was driven by two factors. First, there are over 100 Black colleges and universities and, depending on which definition is used, several hundred Hispanic-serving campuses. To ignore these relatively large segments of the higher education system would be disingenuous. Second, these types of colleges and universities educate students whose access to higher education has been constrained in the past but whose presence in the postsecondary arena is increasing and will continue to grow in the future. As a result, there is a pressing need to understand the nature of work, relationships, and rewards for student affairs professionals who work on such campuses.

Baccalaureate Colleges

Baccalaureate colleges were the first type of institution of higher learning in America. The nation's founders realized early that the colonies would need to produce leaders and clergy in order to survive. To that end, they modeled the first colleges after Cambridge and Oxford in England (Brubacher & Rudy, 1997; Rudolph, 1962, Urban & Wagoner, 2000). Today, of the 4,388 total institutions in the Carnegie Classification (2005) system, 645 (14.7%) are considered baccalaureate (often called liberal arts) colleges. To be classified as a baccalaureate college, an institution must award a majority of its degrees in the traditional liberal arts and sciences disciplines (e.g., psychology, history, philosophy).

Although baccalaureate institutions have evolved over time (Breneman, 1990, 1994), their mission statements focus primarily on the holistic education of students, and their curricula revolve around the arts and sciences.

Most are small, enrolling 1,600 to 1,800 students, and the majority of students tend to be traditionally aged (18–24 years old). Initially, all these colleges were associated with religious groups (O'Grady 1969) but over time, they took one of two paths: some became secular while others retained their sectarian affiliation.

Secular Baccalaureate Colleges

In some instances baccalaureate institutions reduced or completely severed their sectarian ties and became secular colleges. Student affairs work at secular baccalaureate schools has certain hallmarks. To start, staffs tend to be small and many professionals have ancillary or dual job responsibilities (e.g., one might serve as a hall director and as assistant director of campus activities). One-person offices are common and professionals tend to supervise undergraduate student assistants as opposed to graduate assistants or professional staff members (Hirt, Amelink, & Schneiter, 2004). This means that daily work can be frenzied at certain peak times of the academic year, and evening and weekend work is common. Even though the pace of work might suggest otherwise, introducing significant change at these secular liberal arts colleges is difficult. They are steeped in customs that are difficult to alter. As a result, staff members have to be creative in introducing new programs while respecting time-honored traditions. Finally, campus politics can be powerful at these institutions. Differences among constituent groups can be stark, though discourse about those differences is typically very civil, probably because the small size of the campus makes rancor too disruptive to daily life (Hirt et al., 2004; Hirt, 2006).

The unique character and culture at secular liberal arts colleges shapes the relationships that student affairs practitioners form with others. To begin with, they have close, continuous contact with students and form bonds with students that are far more intimate than those between professionals and students at most other types of campuses. Those relationships often include the families of students and span all four years of the students' education. Because the number of professionals on campus tends to be limited, administrators work very closely with one another. They work so closely together that family-like relationships among professionals are common. Finally, professionals at secular baccalaureate colleges tend to know many faculty on their campus and work with faculty more frequently than their counterparts at other types of institutions (Hirt, Schneiter, & Amelink, 2005).

The rewards for professionals at secular campuses also can be tied to institutional type. Although salaries and benefits at the most selective of these colleges are relatively high, remuneration at less-selective campuses can be more limited. Many of these institutions are located in rural areas, however, where the cost of living is lower. For those who are married or have a partner, campus activities are abundant and offer unlimited opportunities to involve significant others and children in the life of the college. Finally, it is not uncommon for people to spend their entire career at a single campus. This means that advancement opportunities are more limited and it may take longer to achieve higher-level positions. Loyalty is rewarded on these campuses, however, so when jobs do open up, internal candidates are frequently promoted (Hirt et al., 2005).

In general, then, new professionals at secular baccalaureate colleges are socialized in ways congruent with the institutional culture. To succeed, they will develop a high degree of autonomy in order to manage a one-person operation but will also need to develop collegial relations to sustain close working ties with colleagues. They should enjoy establishing and nurturing close relationships with students and their families. Great care should be taken to learn about the history and traditions of the institution. Many a new professional unfamiliar with the norms of liberal arts colleges has attempted to introduce radical change, only to face staunch opposition and, at times, loss of professional face. Embracing the traditions of the institution will enable new professionals to appreciate the customs and conventions of campus life. This is important, as they may spend much of their professional life at a single college.

Sectarian Baccalaureate Colleges

A second group of baccalaureate colleges retained their sectarian ties over time. The Carnegie Classification system (2005) identifies 314 Special Faith-Focused Institutions (7.2% of 4,388 colleges and universities). Some of these are baccalaureate colleges, though others are seminaries and bible colleges. Since the Carnegie framework does not distinguish secular from sectarian baccalaureate colleges, the number of the latter is somewhat difficult to ascertain. Hunt and Carper (1988) identified 800 sectarian campuses, which would suggest that they represent over 18% of postsecondary institutions.

In some ways sectarian campuses parallel their secular counterparts. Most enroll traditional-aged students, and most are small, enrolling 1,800 or fewer students. Their curricula revolve around arts and sciences, and they too talk about holistic education (Lucas, 1994). There are clear, distinguishing characteristics of sectarian institutions, however. The most obvious is the mention of their religious ties in their mission statement, frequently accompanied by a focus on spiritual development among students (O'Grady, 1969; Martin, 1982).

Work for those at religiously affiliated colleges is similar to work at secular campuses in a number of ways. Ancillary assignments and one-person offices are widespread, professionals have a large measure of autonomy, weekend and evening work is common, and campuses are steeped in traditions that shape, and at times constrain, professional practice. There are two major differences for professionals at faith-based campuses, however. The first has to do with campus politics. Even though politics operate on all college and university campuses, at sectarian institutions both campus and church politics are active agents that shape professional life for student affairs administrators. On campuses with sectarian leaders, dissension among campus constituencies can be academically and/or faith driven. Religiously affiliated campuses with lay leadership can find themselves embroiled in political issues with church leaders. Either way, church politics are an integral part of campus life for professionals, so professionals must be sensitive to that second layer of politics in order to succeed (Hirt, 2006).

Professional relationships are also different in one important way. They are shaped by the administrator's personal faith. Those who work at sectarian colleges refer to their work as a "calling" or a "mission" and frequently mention how "blessed" they are to work with others on their campuses. Promoting spiritual development among students is second nature to them—simply an extension of their own beliefs. Likewise, their work with other administrators is often grounded in a shared belief system that enables them to work through differences fairly amicably (Hirt, 2006).

The rewards for student affairs professionals at sectarian institutions are similar to those of their colleagues at secular campuses. Salaries tend to be low and benefits restricted at all but the most selective colleges. Advancement opportunities can be even more limited than at secular institutions because clerics serve in some capacities, often for years if not decades. Therefore fewer upper-level jobs become available. There seems to be one redeeming reward for administrators on these campuses, however—the ability to incorporate their own faith into their daily work. For many, the opportunity to integrate personal faith with professional practice is such a powerful reward that other elements of the reward system are secondary (Hirt, 2006).

In summary, sectarian baccalaureate campuses tend to socialize professionals in many of the same ways their secular counterparts do. Professionals need to form close relationships with students and their families. Their work with colleagues requires them to form familial-like ties and they will learn to operate autonomously, as many manage one-person operations. But life at religiously affiliated campuses differs in two important ways. First, church politics are ever present and can highly influence what work gets done and how that work is accomplished. Second, the open expression of faith and expectation that faith will inform professional practice is a norm on sectarian campuses. These two elements make professional life at religiously affiliated institutions distinctive.

Master's Institutions

Some of the liberal arts colleges that were founded during the first 250 years of the nation's history evolved to new institutional forms, such as master's institutions. Master's colleges and universities differ from baccalaureate campuses in two important ways: they offer both liberal arts and applied (e.g., engineering, business) degrees at the undergraduate level and they offer graduate education, typically master's programs, though some offer a limited number of doctoral degrees as well (Cohen 1998; Lucas, 1994; Urban & Waggoner, 2000). Most master's colleges started out as liberal arts institutions and persisted until the 1970s when financial and enrollment threats prompted them to broaden their mission and curricular offerings. Others, however, started out as teacher training institutions. As enrollments expanded in the post–World War II era, they became state colleges and, in many instances, members of state university systems. California, Illinois, New York, and Texas, for example, all boast multicampus state university systems comprised of master's institutions. Most of the 665 (15%) campuses in this Carnegie group (2005) are midsized (4,000–8,000 students) and tend to serve their geographic region. They often educate undergraduate students from underrepresented groups, and their graduate students tend to be working adults who seek graduate degrees to advance their career.

These characteristics influence the nature of work for student affairs professionals. Offices tend to employ more than a single professional, so supervising other professionals as well as undergraduates is common. Because many campuses are members of state systems, they tend to be highly bureau-cratized. Change is often enacted at the system level after consultation with member campuses, so those who work at these institutions may hone strate-gic planning skills at the broadest level. New professionals can expect to work with colleagues across a wide spectrum of offices on campus, so they gain exposure to many functional areas of the profession. Unlike baccalaureate colleges, master's institutions are highly responsive to the needs of the region they serve, hence change occurs relatively quickly as regional circumstances dictate (Hirt, 2006). Change happens more readily because these campuses are not as steeped in tradition as many baccalaureate colleges.

Institutional type also influences relationships for new professionals at master's colleges and universities. The larger size of the institution means that administrators get to meet scores of students, but they do not establish close, personal relationships with many of those students. On the other hand, because these campuses educate undergraduate, graduate students, and adult students, practitioners become well versed in the very different needs of these three student populations. Professionals across campus tend to work together on committees and projects so administrators get to know col-leagues across the division. Finally, the pace of work at master's institutions tends to be more even, and administrators are able to sustain separate per-sonal and professional lives (Hirt, 2006).

Rewards for those at master's colleges and universities can be directly related to institutional characteristics. First, since many campuses are part of a larger system, and since campuses operate on systemwide policies and procedures, there tends to be a lot of career mobility for new professionals. This is particularly true if one is willing to move from one campus to another within the system. Indeed, the challenge tends to be securing an initial posi-tion within the system. From there, advancement opportunities for good performers are fairly abundant. Second, salaries and benefits tend to be more reasonable than at many baccalaureate campuses. Finally, those who work at master's campuses report that they reap enormous rewards by working with students who might otherwise not have access to higher education opportu-nities. Indeed, many master's institutions include in their mission their com-mitment to serving minority and economically disadvantaged citizens from their region. Serving undergraduates from underrepresented groups and working adults is a distinguishing reward for new professionals at these cam-puses, and one that they seem to cherish (Hirt, 2006).

Overall, master's colleges and universities are very different from bacca-laureate campuses, and those differences have some profound effects on life for new student affairs professionals. They engage in work across their own campus and are trained in systemwide policies and procedures that enrich their strategic planning skills. They do not develop many intense personal relationships with students but do gain an appreciation for undergraduate, graduate, and adult student services. They form collegial relations with administrators across campus and enjoy enacting change. Career mobility is far greater at master's institutions, and salary and benefits are relatively good. Perhaps most important, however, is the satisfaction new professionals derive from working with the diverse types of students who attend these distinctive institutions.

Doctoral-Granting Universities

Doctoral-granting universities are another unique group of institutions. The Carnegie System (2005) identifies 285 such campuses, representing 6.5% of the 4,388 colleges and universities included in the schema. These campuses educate nearly 28% of the 17.5 million students enrolled in postsecondary institutions in the United States. This means that most enroll large numbers of students—typically 20,000 or more. Doctoral (often called research) uni-versities have a relatively complex mission (Fincher, 1989). They offer under-graduate education, but a distinguishing element of these campuses is graduate education, both in the disciplines and the professions. Graduate education is closely linked to a focus on research and the creation of new knowledge, another hallmark of research universities (Anderson, 2001; Slaughter & Leslie, 1997). Finally, many doctoral campuses are land-grant institutions, with a particular focus on service to their state. That notion of service has expanded to include national and international service for many doctoral universities.

Life for new professionals who choose to work at doctoral universities is very different from that of new professionals at the other types of institutions discussed so far. For example, these are large campuses, so most offices employ multiple professionals. Most often, new professionals become experts in their chosen functional area and are not as exposed to other functional areas on campus. Work tends to be fast paced nearly all the time and there is a pervasive sense of competition on campus. New professionals meet this competitive challenge by being both creative and proactive. They are expected to stay on the cutting edge of the functional area and to offer new programs and services that reflect the most current thinking. Professionals at doctoral universities do share one thing in common with their counterparts at baccalaureate colleges, however. Both types of campuses have deeply entrenched traditions that are hard to change. Beyond that, professional practice is very different at doctoral universities (Hirt, Kirk, McGuire, Mount, & Nelson-Henley, 2003).

This holds true for the kinds of relationships new professionals at research universities form. To begin with, they tend to work with large numbers of students but do not get to know many of those students very well. The staff-student ratio usually limits how close new professionals can become with all but a small number of students. They also tend to work very closely with other professionals within their own functional area and with professionals in one or two other offices on campus. Relationships with colleagues across campus, however, are generally constrained by time and the size of the student affairs division. Finally, they are less likely to know or work with faculty than their counterparts at other types of campuses. In large part this may be because of the faculty's preoccupation with research (Hirt, 2006).

The unique nature of the doctoral institution leads to some unique rewards as well. First, salaries tend to be among the most lucrative of all campus types and benefits are among the most comprehensive. New professionals at these campuses often receive support for professional development opportunities. Indeed, most campuses offer in-house developmental programs to staff members, and practitioners are encouraged to participate in regional and national opportunities as well. Although the demands on a professional's time are extensive at research universities, these campuses are large and complex so they offer far more in-house opportunities for advancement. Recall that upward mobility at baccalaureate colleges can be limited by the small staff size and long-serving senior staff, and mobility at master's institutions often involves moving to another campus within a system. At doctoral universities, moving up on the same campus is more likely (Hirt, 2006).

In general then, the distinctive nature of the doctoral institution influences life for new professionals in some unique ways. They develop expertise in a single functional area of student affairs administration and are expected to stay at the forefront of that area. The competitive spirit that drives the research agenda of the institution extends beyond faculty to administrators.

A sense of competition among student affairs units often emerges, and new professionals need to learn how to appreciate that competition, yet balance it with collaborative endeavors when necessary. Close working relationships develop with colleagues within one or two offices but not beyond. The rewards, however, include good salaries, benefits, professional development opportunities, and advancement options.

Historically Black Colleges and Universities

Another group of institutions unique to the American system of higher education includes HBCUs, which represent a variety of institutional types, including baccalaureate colleges, master's institutions, doctoral universities, and associate's colleges (Coaxum, 2001). They share a common purpose, however: to educate a certain segment of the population (Allen & Jewell, 2002; Brown & Davis, 2001). By 1850, only 29 Blacks in the United States had earned a bachelor's degree (Humphries, 1995) and the end of the Civil War revealed an urgent need to provide more educational opportunities for newly emancipated slaves. Most HBCUs founded during this time initially offered elementary education and gradually increased their curricular offerings as demand for higher levels of learning increased. Today, 103 HBCUs enroll about 300,000 students (Brown, Donahoo, & Bertrand, 2001). Most HBCUs are relatively small, enrolling 3,000 or fewer students, but collectively they confer 28% of all bachelor's degrees earned by Blacks in the United States.

Because HBCUs encompass several institutional types, generalizing what work is like at these campuses is difficult. In many ways, work at baccalaureate HBCUs parallels work at baccalaureate colleges in general, and professional life at master's-granting HBCUs is like that at other master's institutions. There are two unique elements to work at an HBCU, however. The first relates to racial uplift. New professionals on these campuses frequently refer to the opportunity they have to support Black students who are striving to better their lives (Hirt, Strayhorn, Amelink, & Bennett, 2006). Cultural advancement is high on their priority list and working at an HBCU allows them to achieve that goal. Second, they are dedicated to protecting and preserving HBCUs as an institutional type. Many of these institutions operate with very limited resources, but the professionals who work there recognize and appreciate the unique educational setting that HBCUs offer Blacks, and they are committed to sustaining that setting for future generations.

Relationships for new professionals on HBCU campuses are also tied to institutional type (e.g., master's institution, doctoral university) in many ways. There is one distinct difference, however, and that has to do with their relationship with students. Regardless of institutional mission, those who work at HBCUs see themselves as surrogate family members for students. They refer to themselves as de facto parents, siblings, grandparents, aunts, and uncles to the students they serve. Guiffrida (2005) refers to this as *other-mothering*, an entrenched value in African American culture. It stems from the days of slavery when families were often torn asunder as parents and/or children were sold or traded. Women promised to raise others' children as their own. This commitment spread to other social systems, like schools, in the postbellum era, and there is ample evidence that it persists today on HBCU campuses.

The rewards for student affairs professionals at HBCUs are also tied to institutional type, but there is one overarching reward that those at all types of HBCUs discuss: the ability to pay back what was afforded them when they went to college. They talk about repaying the debt they owe to those who helped them through college and see this as one of the most significant rewards of working at an HBCU campus. For many their work brought them home. Hirt (2006) reported that 63% of student affairs professionals at HBCUs graduated from an HBCU, and 44% graduated from the HBCU where they worked.

In general then, the socialization process for new professionals at HBCUs is bifurcated. In many ways institutional mission drives socialization (e.g., baccalaureate college). There are some distinctive elements of life at an HBCU, however. First, new professionals have an opportunity to contribute to Black cultural advancement and to ensure the perpetuity of HBCUs as a niche in higher education. The surrogate role they assume in their relationships with students is another expression of Black culture available to new professionals at these campuses. These culturally specific elements of professional life are exclusive to the HBCU environment, and those who work on these campuses seek out these unique professional opportunities.

Associate's Colleges

Associate's colleges (often referred to as community colleges) are the most abundant type of institution in the Carnegie system (2005). Over 41% (1,811) of the 4,338 campuses included in the schema are associate's colleges. A good proportion of these (531) are proprietary (for-profit) institutions, one of the fastest growing sectors of the higher education enterprise in the United States. Since proprietary schools are the only institutional type that is driven by a profit motive, professional life at such schools may be very different, so the remainder of this section focuses on not-for-profit associate's colleges only. Even among the not-for-profit section, there is enormous variation. In fact, the Carnegie system lists 14 different types of associate's colleges (e.g., single campus suburban, multicampus urban, small rural). There are some common elements within these institutions, however. For example, community colleges are distinctive in that they serve a defined geographic region. Their mission typically includes vocational development, transfer education, remedial or developmental education, and continuing education. Most serve as a community resource and acknowledge their commitment to serving the interests of their local districts.

The nature of work for new professionals can vary considerably, depending on the type of community college where they work, but there are some characteristic elements. First, the student affairs staff at most of these campuses is small, so professionals serve a relatively large number of students. Additionally, community colleges tend to be highly bureaucratized (like master's institutions) with policies and procedures for nearly all actions. This translates to professionals who have to produce at an incredibly high rate with a high degree of accuracy, day in and day out. Like master's institutions, community colleges are very responsive to their local districts. Since those districts are smaller than the regions served by master's colleges, change comes about very rapidly at community colleges. This means that professionals need to be prepared to respond to changes in services quickly and efficiently (Hirt, Esteban, & McGuire, 2003).

The brisk pace of daily work is made more tolerable in many instances by the relationships that are formed on associate's campuses. For example, student affairs professionals work as closely with their students as their colleagues at baccalaureate campuses. They get to know students (and their families) intimately and take great pride in watching students succeed over time. They also work more closely with faculty and academic administrators than professionals at any other type of institution. This is important because turnover among staff is low; many professionals work at the same institution for years if not decades. Working with a consistent group of colleagues over a long period of time is a hallmark of life at community colleges (Hirt et al., 2003).

In terms of rewards, two stand out for those who serve at associate's institutions. First, professional life at these campuses can be balanced with personal life fairly readily. The amount of evening and weekend work is limited and predictable so professionals tend to work a normal work week. Second, most community colleges are public institutions hence there is a statewide salary and benefit system. Compensation tends to be good. Moreover, many community colleges are located in rural areas where these higher salary levels translate to a higher standard of living (Hirt, 2006; Hirt et al., 2003).

Overall, then, there are characteristics of associate's colleges that socialize new professionals in idiosyncratic ways. Administrators are expected to know large numbers of students well, to appreciate four very different curricular programs (i.e., vocational, transfer, remedial, continuing), and to interpret those curricular programs to students accurately in a fast-paced environment that can change relatively speedily. This requires new professionals who are quick studies, who are flexible, and who can adapt to externally imposed change on a regular basis. The relative stability of the people who work at the campus may make these challenges somewhat more manageable, but there is little doubt that life at community colleges is distinctive in many ways.

Tribally Controlled Colleges

Perhaps the least studied segment of the higher education enterprise is the tribal colleges. There is some information available about the history of these unique campuses (e.g., Carney, 1999) but other work is limited. The first college was founded in 1968, and 33 others have opened since then. Most offer associate's degrees and some offer baccalaureate and/or master's degrees. Tribally controlled colleges are small, enrolling fewer than 1,000 students (McClellan, Fox, & Lowe, 2005). They typically serve women, many of whom have children, are economically disadvantaged, and who see education as a means to a higher standard of living (Belgarde, 2002). Indeed, their missions tend to reflect their commitment to offer educational opportunities to improve the lives of individuals, families, and tribal communities. Because they are controlled by tribes not states, they serve as potent symbols of sovereignty for tribes.

Very little is known about the work life of professionals at these colleges. Cajete (2005) describes the seven foundations that serve as the bedrock for learning and development—the environmental, the mythic, the visionary, the artistic, the affective, the communal, and the spiritual—though these describe how services are delivered rather than the work professionals perform. The types of students who attend tribal campuses may suggest the types of services offered: child care, financial aid, and career planning seem essential, although more research is needed to explore the nature of work on these campuses.

Relationships, however, are at the crux of tribal cultures so it would seem reasonable to suggest that they are at the heart of work at tribally controlled colleges. The welfare of the individual is inextricably linked to the welfare of the community, or tribe. Knowing individual students then would seem essential to professional success. Beyond knowing students, however, understanding tribal values and customs, and developing close ties with the tribal community would be needed in order to link individual and tribal interests.

The rewards that professionals garner from working at tribal colleges are also somewhat difficult to discern. Because individual and community success and failure are inherently linked, there must be a commitment to tribal culture and values. Perhaps, like their colleagues at HBCUs, those at tribal colleges seek to advance the cultural interests of their students and their tribes through their work on these campuses. Likewise, working to protect the unique niche in the higher education landscape that tribal colleges represent might be another intrinsic reward that drives professionals at these campuses.

In general, while it is reasonable to suggest that tribal institutions socialize new professionals in powerful ways, exactly how they accomplish that is much less clear than the processes in play at other types of institutions. Some of this may be attributed to the unique culture of each tribe. Certainly the interplay between the individual and the community is a critical socializing factor. More research is needed, however, to understand professional life at tribally controlled colleges. Such work is long overdue.

Hispanic-serving Institutions

The most recent type of institution to emerge in American higher education has come to the forefront over the past three decades. The number of Hispanics in the United States has quadrupled in that time period; they now represent 13% of the population, and that number is expected to grow to 22% by the year 2015 (U.S. Census Bureau, 2002). HSIs are the result of these demographic changes (Benitez, 1998). As Latino students flocked to select institutions, typically those closest to Hispanic population centers, Hispanic leaders pushed for federal designations for these campuses. Recognition of HSIs in Title III of the 1992 and 1998 Higher Education Reauthorization Acts has confirmed their niche in the higher education landscape. HSIs are designated as such because they serve a high percentage of Latino students. That percentage, however, varies by agency so estimates about the number of HSIs range from 131 to 738 (Laden, 2001), depending on what threshold is used. Reasonable estimates suggest that enrollments at HSIs have increased 14% in the past decade, so there is little doubt that these institutions serve an important segment of the population (Gregory, 2003).

Like their HBCU counterparts, HSIs include several types of institutions—associate's colleges, baccalaureate colleges, master's institutions, and doctoral universities. The work of student affairs professionals is driven to a large extent by institutional type. There are, however, elements of work that are peculiar to those at HSIs. First, their work tends to be grounded in notions of social justice hence it is relatively proactive. Professionals at HSIs advocate for the interests of their students. Second, enrollments are burgeoning at these campuses, but additional resources often are not. This means that the pace of work is hectic most of the time and relief in the form of added staff is not likely. Change can occur rapidly, so staff members need to be highly creative in order to respond to those changes with limited resources (Hirt, 2006).

Relationships at HSIs also have some defining characteristics. Like their counterparts at associate's colleges, professionals tend to work very closely not only with students but with their families. Indeed, it is not at all uncommon for students to refer to the sentiments of family members when talking with administrators. In fact, many conversations with a student are followed by conversations with members of that student's family. When planning events, attendance estimates include not only students but their extended families—parents, siblings, grandparents, aunts, uncles, and cousins. These aspects of professional life are unique to HSIs (Hirt, 2006).

The rewards that professionals garner are linked to the type of their HSI (e.g., associate's, master's) to some extent. There are two rewards, however, that are irreplaceable to those at HSIs. The first has to do with respect. The work of professionals at HSIs is steeped with respect. They respect one another and their students. They respect what their institutions mean to Latinos and they are convinced their work is respected by those outside the institution. Second, professionals at HSIs profess to social justice ideals and believe their work enables them to enact those ideals on a daily basis. Many come from the area served by the HSI where they work, and they seek to give back to the community that raised them and to advance the interests of the underserved. This is a powerful intrinsic reward for HSI administrators (Hirt, 2006).

Overall, socialization for new professionals at Hispanic-serving campuses is driven in part by the type of HSI (e.g., baccalaureate HSI). There are, however, elements of professional life that cross all HSIs. They work not just with Latino students but with their students' families, and new professionals need to have an appreciation for the role that family plays in Latino cultures. They work at institutions that are morphing rapidly and attracting many more students but few additional resources. This means professionals need to thrive in an environment that demands creative approaches and problem-solving skills. Finally, professionals are likely to be imbued with notions of social justice, or if they already hold such principles dear, to have those notions reinforced in the HSI environment.

Conclusion

Many factors play a role in the socialization of new professionals, but institutional type sets the context in which that socialization occurs. The mission of an institution often dictates the programs and services offered by the campus. Those programs and services have a direct bearing on the work new professionals' conduct. The mission also often defines the types of students who are drawn to an institution, which in turn influences the kinds of relationships new professionals have with students. Likewise, campus type can affect the administrators who are drawn to the institution and that can affect relationships between new professionals and their colleagues on campus. The intrinsic and extrinsic rewards certainly vary by institutional type and can make the difference between a good and bad fit for a new professional and a particular institution.

Although there is little doubt that institutional type is an important influence in the socialization process for new student affairs administrators, there are a number of caveats that are critical to consider. First, the portraits of different institutional types painted in this chapter are just that—portraits. They paint a very general picture of what might be considered a prototype campus within each type. But prototypes overlook all the exclusive elements of campuses. There is really no such thing as a typical baccalaureate college or doctoral university; each one has its own history and traditions that create a unique campus culture and environment. HBCUs, HSIs, and tribally controlled colleges include several types of institutions but socialize new professionals in ways that transcend those types.

It is important, therefore, to keep the influence of institutional type on the socialization process in perspective. Most (70%) graduate preparation programs are housed at doctoral universities or master's institutions (30%), and new professionals are usually socialized to the values of the campus where they complete their graduate education. They often try to translate those values to their first job setting, even if that job is at a very different type of campus. Other new professionals take their first job and are quickly socialized to the norms of their new campus and assume that those reflect the norms of all campuses. The point is that socialization by institutional type can lead to limited thinking about student affairs professional practice. This can prompt professionals to assume that there is one "best" approach to professional practice, which will not serve them well if they move to another type of campus. In fact, such thinking can inhibit professionals from seeking jobs at other kinds of campuses, something that should be avoided at all costs. Cross-institutional professional moves bring fresh ideas and energy to a campus and allow new professionals to see their work in new perspectives.

One way to avoid these pitfalls is to recognize that some socialization issues transcend institutional type. For example, those who work at baccalaureate colleges, community colleges, and HSIs all work closely with students and their families. Rapid change is endemic at community colleges, master's institutions, and HSIs. Doctoral universities and baccalaureate colleges are steeped in traditions that make it difficult to introduce change. Creativity is a necessary skill at doctoral universities and HSIs. In short, the same skill sets and experiences can lead to success in multiple institutional settings. Rather than allowing the type of college or university to constrain professional mobility, new professionals would be well served to recognize how experience at one type of campus can prepare them for work at a very different type of institution. If they can accomplish this feat, then institutional context serves rather than constrains professional socialization.

References

Allen, W. R., & Jewell, J. O. (2002). A backward glance forward: Past, present, and future perspectives on historically black colleges and universities. *Review of Higher Education. 25*(3), 241–261.

Altbach, P. G. (1998). *Comparative higher education.* Norwood, NJ: Ablex.

Anderson, M. S. (2001). The complex relations between the academy and industry: Views from the literature. *The Journal of Higher Education, 72*, 226–246.

Barr, M. J. (2000). The importance of the institutional mission. In M. J. Barr & M. K. Dessler (Eds.), *The handbook of student affairs administration,* (pp. 25–36). San Francisco: Jossey-Bass.

Belgarde, W. L. (2002). History of American Indian community colleges. In C. Turner, M. Garcia, A. Nora, L. I. Rendon (Eds.), *Racial and ethnic diversity in higher education* (pp. 1–12). Boston: Pearson.

Benitez, M. (1998). Hispanic serving institutions: Challenges and opportunities. In J. P. Merisotis & C. T. O'Brien (Eds.), *Minority-serving institutions: Distinct purposes, common goals* (pp. 57–68). San Francisco: Jossey-Bass.

Breneman, D. W. (1990). Are we losing our liberal arts colleges? *College Board Review, 156,* 16–21, 29.

Breneman, D. W. (1994). *Liberal arts colleges: Thriving, surviving, or endangered?* Washington, DC: The Brookings Institution.

Brown, M. C., & Davis, J. E. (2001). The historically black college as social contract, social capital, and social equalizer. *Peabody Journal of Education, 76* (1), 31–49.

Brown, M. C., Donahoo, S., & Bertrand, R. D. (2001). The black college and the quest for educational opportunity. *Urban Education, 36*(5), 553–571.

Brubacher, J. S., & Rudy, W. (1997). *Higher education in transition: A history of colleges and universities* (4th ed). New Brunswick, NJ: Transaction Publishers.

Cajete, G. A. (2005). American Indian epistemologies. In M. J. T. Fox, S. C. Lowe, & G. S. McClellan (Eds.), *Serving Native American students* (pp. 69–78). New Directions for Student Services, No. 109. San Francisco: Jossey-Bass.

Carnegie Classification of Institutions of Higher Education. (2005). Retrieved March 8, 2007, from http://www.carnegiefoundation.org/classifications/index .asp?key=805

Carnegie Foundation for the Advancement of Teaching. (2000). *A classification of institutions of higher education.* Princeton, NJ: Carnegie Council for the Advancement of Teaching.

Carney, C. M. (1999). *Native American higher education in the United States.* New Brunswick, NJ: Transaction.

Coaxum, J. (2001). The misalignment between the Carnegie classifications and black colleges. *Urban Education, 36*(5), 572–584.

Cohen, A. M. (1998). *The shaping of American higher education.* San Francisco: Jossey-Bass.

Fincher, C. (1989, August). *The influence of British and German universities on the historical development of American universities.* Paper presented at the annual forum of the European Association for Institutional Research, Trier, Germany. (ERIC Document Reproduction Service No. ED443301)

Gregory, S. T. (2003). Planning for the increasing number of Latino students. *Planning for Higher Education, 31*(4), 13–19.

Guiffrida, D. (2005). Othermothering as a framework for understanding African American students' definitions of student-centered faculty. *The Journal of Higher Education, 76*(6), 701–723.

Hirt, J. B. (2006). *Where you work matters: Student affairs administration at different types of institutions.* Washington, DC: American College Personnel Association.

Hirt, J. B., Amelink, C., & Schneiter, S. (2004). The nature of professional life at liberal arts colleges. *NASPA Journal, 42,* 94–110.

Hirt, J. B., & Collins, D. (2005). Work, relationships, and rewards in student affairs: Differences by institutional type. *College Student Affairs Journal, 24*(1), 4–19.

Hirt, J. B., Esteban, R., & McGuire, L. (2003). The worklife of student service professionals at rural community colleges. *Community College Review, 31,* 33–55.

Hirt, J. B., Kirk, G., McGuire, L., Mount, T., & Nelson-Henley, S. (2003). How student affairs administrators spend their time: Differences by institutional setting. *College Student Affairs Journal, 23,* 7–26.

Hirt, J. B., Schneiter, S, & Amelink, C. (2005). The nature of relationships and rewards for student affairs professionals at liberal arts institutions. *College Student Affairs Journal. 25*(1), 6–19.

Hirt, J. B., Strayhorn, T. L., Amelink, C. T., & Bennett, B. R. (2006). The nature of student affairs work at historically black colleges and universities. *Journal of College Student Development, 47,* 661–676.

Humphries, F. S. (1995). A short history of blacks in higher education. *The Journal of Blacks in Higher Education, 6,* 57.

Hunt, T. C., & Carper, J. C. (1988). *Religious colleges and universities in America: A selected bibliography.* New York: Garland.

Laden, B. V. (2001). Hispanic-serving institutions: Myths and realities. *Peabody Journal of Education, 76,* 73–92.

Lucas, C. J. (1994). *American higher education.* New York: St. Martin's Griffin.

Martin, W. B. (1982). *A college of character.* San Francisco: Jossey-Bass.

McClellan, G. S., Fox, M. J. T., & Lowe, S. C. (2005). Where we have been: A history of Native American higher education. In M. J. T. Fox, S. C. Lowe, & G. S. McClellan (Eds.), *Serving Native American students* (pp. 7–15). New Directions for Student Services, No. 109. San Francisco: Jossey-Bass.

O'Grady, J. P. (1969). Control of church-related institutions of higher learning. *Journal of Higher Education, 40,* 108–121.

Rudolph, F. (1962). *The American college and university: A history.* New York: Knopf.

Slaughter, S., & Leslie, L. L. (1997). *Academic capitalism: Politics, policies and the entrepreneurial university.* Baltimore: Johns Hopkins University Press.

Urban, W., & Wagoner, J. (2000). *American education: A history* (2nd ed.). Boston: McGraw-Hill.

U.S. Census Bureau. (2002). Resident population estimates of the United States by sex, race and Hispanic origin: April 1 to July 1, 1999, with short-term projection to June 1, 2001. Washington, DC: Author.

4

CHANGING STUDENT CHARACTERISTICS AND SOCIALIZATION

Jerrid P. Freeman and Colette Taylor

As Denise Collins noted in chapter 1, socialization of new professionals involves the interaction of the individual and the organizational culture. To most effectively socialize student affairs professionals the multiple contexts inherent in organizational cultures need to be examined as was addressed in chapter 3. To be sure, new student affairs professionals need to integrate their individual goals with the mission and values of their college or university culture. Yet some socialization issues transcend differences in institutional type or particular college cultures. One of these transcendent issues is understanding students. Given rapidly evolving societal trends, it is increasingly important that new professionals expand their understanding of how student populations will be changing in the future (Smith, MacGregor, Matthews, & Gabelnick, 2004). In this chapter, we start by describing the characteristics and enrollment patterns of today's college students. Next we present trends that will affect current and future college students. Finally, we offer resources and strategies so that professionals can continue to understand generational and other attributes of students while remembering that students are individuals who cannot be fully understood only through generational characteristics.

Student Characteristics

The days are long over when the vast majority of students could be described as White, male, middle class, single, 18–22 years old, residing on campus, and working less than 10 hours a week (Levine & Cureton, 1998). Today's college students are more often racially and ethnically diverse, over 25 years of age, female, attending school part-time while working full-time, or commuting from off campus (Choy, 2002). It is important for new professionals to understand different groups of students who populate our campuses.

Traditionally Aged Students

Most of the dramatic enrollment growth between 2000 and 2013 will occur among traditionally aged students between 18 and 25 years old (National Center for Educational Statistics [NCES], 2002), yet those students will have attitudes and experiences different from previous generations. As a reminder, a traditional student is conventionally viewed as about 18 to 25 years of age, enrolled full-time in postsecondary education, enrolled directly following his or her high school graduation, dependent on parents, and someone who does not work or works only part-time during the school year (Herideen, 1998; NCES, 2002). Although commentary about generational differences may seem to reflect stereotypes, social demographers examine traits of numerous individuals within each age group to determine general descriptors of a cohort (Zemke, Raines, & Filipczak, 2000). Few generalizations are entirely accurate. However, generalizations—such as those about generations—may highlight important trends.

For example, generational characteristics may be a useful framework to understand potential conflicts or differences between students (or new professionals) and experienced staff members. The millennial generation (traditionally aged students born after 1981) are purported to have very different characteristics from Generation X individuals (born between 1965 and 1981; Daniel, Evans, & Scott, 2001). Supervisors from Generation X may tend to value diversity, technology, fun, informality, and pragmatism. They feel strongly that they do not need someone looking over their shoulders. At the same time, this generation expects immediate and ongoing feedback, and is equally comfortable giving feedback to others. Interestingly, 18% of all full-time and part-time faculty employed at institutions of higher education are from Generation X (NCES, 2002). In contrast, millennials are typically team oriented, work well in groups, and prefer group activities to individual endeavors. Millennials seem to expect structure in the workplace. They acknowledge and respect positions and titles, and want a relationship with their boss (Daniel et al.; Howe & Strauss, 2000). These attitudes and values may conflict with Generation X's love of independence and hands-off style.

The projected enrollment boom, birth rates, and immigration patterns reveal that the millennial generation will make up 75% of higher education enrollment by the year 2012 (Coomes & DeBard, 2004). DeBard (2004) stated that millennial college students "are the most racially and ethnically diverse in this nation's history" (p. 33). The following trends illustrate this point:

- According to the 2000 U.S. Census, 39.10% of those under 18 years of age are people of color (Asian, Black, Hispanic, or Native American), as compared to 28.02% of people 18 and over (U.S. Census Bureau, 2001, 2002).
- Millennial students are far more likely to be biracial or multiracial than previous generations. Biracial or multiracial people made up 3.95% of the under 18 population in the 2000 U.S. Census, while they made up just 0.95% of the 18 and over population;
- Enrollment of women has increased by nearly 5% since 1980, bringing female enrollment to more than 56% of all those attending higher education (DeBard, 2004);
- Since 1980, the Asian American enrollment has grown by 33%, whereas overall enrollment has grown by only 22% (DeBard, 2004);
- One in five millennials is a child of immigrants (Howe & Strauss, 2003), and the number of children speaking a language other than English at home has doubled since 1979 (Broido, 2004);
- According to Mason and Moulden (1996 "one-fourth of all children born in the U.S. in the early 1980s will live with a step parent before they reach adulthood" (p. 11), and at any given point roughly 25% live with only one parent.

In general then, new professionals can expect to work with traditional-aged students who are more likely to be female and people of color. Characteristics of nontraditional-aged students will present other challenges for student affairs administrators.

Nontraditional Students

Beyond the issue of age, three-quarters of all undergraduates are nontraditional, according to the NCES (2002). Nontraditional students are defined as having one or more of the following characteristics:

- Delayed enrollment—did not enter postsecondary education in the same year they graduated from high school
- Attend school part-time for all or part of the academic year
- Work full-time—35 hours or more—while enrolled
- Financially independent as defined by financial aid
- Have dependents, other than a spouse, which may include children or others
- Single parent, having one or more dependent children
- Lack a high school diploma (Horn & Carroll, 1996; NCES, 2002).

Horn and Carroll (1996) grouped nontraditional students into three categories: highly nontraditional (4 or more characteristics); moderately nontraditional (2 or 3 characteristics); and minimally nontraditional (1 characteristic). The percentage of undergraduates in higher education who are highly nontraditional is 28%, those moderately nontraditional represent 28%, and students considered minimally nontraditional are 17% (NCES, 2002). What is most staggering about these statistics is that there are more highly nontraditional students in higher education than there are traditional students (27%). The three groupings developed by Horn and Carroll identify prominent characteristics of each distinct nontraditional student group and are important because students who possess a greater number of nontraditional characteristics are less likely to persist or graduate from college (NCES, 2002).

Financial independence, working full-time, and attending college part-time are major characteristics that must be addressed for the nontraditional population. Of the minimally (1 characteristic) nontraditional students, 36% attend part-time, 23% have delayed enrollment and work full-time, and 15% are financially independent. Among the moderately (2–3 characteristics) nontraditional students, 68% are financially independent, 64% are part-time, 52% work full-time, and 42% have delayed enrollment. Nearly all (99%) of the highly (4 or more characteristics) nontraditional students are financially independent, 80% attend part-time and have dependents, 76% delay their enrollment, and 75% work full-time (NCES, 2002).

Special Needs of Highly Nontraditional Students

The highly nontraditional students may be the most challenging for new professionals. These students have greater obstacles to overcome and require more pathways for access to postsecondary education as well as institutional support to obtain the knowledge, skills, and technological ability needed in today's economy (Freeman, 2006).

Because highly nontraditional students often have a history of academic skill deficits, economic disadvantages, and racial and/or ethnic oppression, some start college with a significant risk of academic failure or attrition. Furthermore, higher education institutions have traditionally not served this population as effectively as more traditional students (Cohen & Brawer, 2003). When Levin (2003) studied highly nontraditional students in American community colleges he called them "beyond the margins." This group falls outside the mainstream of college students and includes many students who are in "non-credit courses and programs, those who are or have been on welfare, those who suffer from long-term unemployment or underemployment, and those who are physically disabled, mentally challenged, immigrants, and often minorities" (p. 3). Many of these highly nontraditional students in noncredit courses are not tracked by their institutions; therefore, the actual number of students in noncredit courses across the country is only an estimate (Levin). In the aggregate, highly nontraditional students are less likely to have a sufficient understanding of how to effectively navigate societal expectations and roles, the education system, or the job market (Freeman, 2006). In practice, this population is often ignored and invisible, hence it is important for student affairs professionals to understand the needs and characteristics of highly nontraditional students (Levin, 2007; Smith, 2004).

Adult Learners

Another group within the nontraditional category, the adult learner population, has also received considerable attention from scholars. The adult learner is typically younger than 40 years of age, has completed high school or more, enjoys an above-average income, works full-time and in a white-collar occupation, is married and has children, and lives in an urban area (Bash, 2003; Merriam & Caffarella, 1999). Adult learners are succeeding, or at one point in time had succeeded, in the job market. Because of their past success, they have more external agencies concerned about their continued development and success in the new economy (Merriam & Caffarella). Yet they can also pose a challenge to student affairs professionals since they may be more difficult to connect with than traditionally aged students. The differences in life knowledge and experience may pose a challenge for new professionals who provide guidance and support for adult students. Adult learners expect their experiences and knowledge to be used, the knowledge taught in class to connect to their current understanding and reality, and their specific academic and career goals to be taken into consideration by the professor (Merriam & Caffarella).

Underserved /Highly Nontraditional Students

Another population of nontraditional students that will expand in the future is underserved students. Underserved students bring such attributes as low socioeconomic status (SES), racial and ethnic diversity, inadequate preparation for postsecondary education, interrupted education, need for new knowledge or skills in their work, are confined to prisons, or are disabled (Cohen & Brawer, 2003). Many from underserved groups are unaware of or unable to enroll in higher education, and often of those who enroll do not receive the guidance they need to achieve their educational goals (Freeman, 2006).

For instance, career planning is an area where underserved students need special attention. They may not understand that full-time occupations and long-term careers are diminishing (Bridges, 1994; Castells, 1996; Rifkin, 1995) or that jobs are becoming more part-time, temporary, and have fluctuating responsibilities (Aronowitz & DiFazio, 1994; Carnoy, 2000; Jones & Weinberg, 2000). Therefore they must be educated about the changing job market trends, including being given information about predicted labor shortages in certain sectors (Goldstein, 2006). In the future economic forces will have a greater impact on most of today's college students, especially the underserved. New professionals can directly help underserved students navigate these forces by being aware of their possible impact on career planning. In addition a wide variety of policies and practices, such as definitions of academic progress, academic support, tutoring, and financial assistance, must be developed (or reworked) to support this growing subpopulation of underserved students (Boylan, Bonham, & Tafari, 2005; Freeman, 2007).

Enrollment Patterns of Nontraditional Students

Even though student affairs professionals must prepare themselves to educate all types of nontraditional students, the aggregate characteristics of undergraduate students vary markedly by type of institution (see Table 4.1). Public two-year (community colleges) and private for-profit institutions have much larger proportions of moderately and highly nontraditional students than

TABLE 4.1
Nontraditional Statistics

Type of Institution	Traditional	Minimally nontraditional	Moderately nontraditional	Highly nontraditional
Total	27.4	16.6	28.3	27.7
Public 2-year	10.5	14.3	35.0	40.2
Public 4-year	42.5	20.0	23.1	14.4
Private not-for-profit 4-year	50.0	14.7	16.4	19.0
Private for profit	11.3	14.7	38.5	35.4

Note. From *The condition of education*, National Center for Education Statistics, 2002. Reprinted with permission.

four-year institutions, and much smaller proportions of traditional students. Eighty-nine percent of the students in community colleges and private for-profit institutions are nontraditional, compared with 58% at public four-year institutions and 50% at private nonprofit four-year institutions (NCES, 2002).

Although all types of institutions will see an increase in nontraditional students, adult learners, and underserved/highly nontraditional students in the future, community colleges will see the greatest escalation. For highly nontraditional students, community colleges have been the primary providers of postsecondary education (Davies, Safarik, & Banning, 2003; Levin, 2003; Shaw & London, 2001; Shaw, Rhoads, & Valadez, 1999; Terenzini & Cabrera, 2001). An acknowledged benefit of community colleges is that they serve effectively students who are not well served by traditional institutions of higher education (Grubb, Badway, & Bell, 2003; Herideen, 1998; Shaw, 1999; Valadez, 1996).

Characteristically, nontraditional and underserved students bring to campus greater socioeconomic and family concerns. They may not be academically well prepared and are likely to have a greater focus on life expectations outside college. Many are more concerned about career preparation and do not share the values and priorities of the more traditional members of the college community. All of these traits may be difficult for new professionals to understand (Freeman, 2006). For example, underserved students with low SES are debt averse, often take much longer to complete their degree, cannot participate fully in the college experience, and have extraordinary problems coping with traditional class schedules and such pedagogies as group projects. In too many cases underserved students are not accorded the respect that full-time students are given and may be subject to open hostility from staff members and fellow students (Steinberg, 2006).

New professionals in traditional public and private four-year institutions should be prepared to serve these nontraditional populations as well. While most four-year public (elite and research-focused institutions) and private institutions will not see a majority of their students classified as nontraditional, these institutions will continue to see rising numbers of such students and will need to serve them.

Current and Future Trends Affecting College Students

To understand the college students who will attend our campuses in the near future, student affairs professionals must speculate about the intersection of student characteristics and societal trends. In this section we look at three trends and how they are likely to affect our student populations.

Technology

Technology has catalyzed many changes in society and hence the characteristics of college students (Carnoy, Castells, Cohen, & Cardoso, 1993; Castells, 1996; Levin, 2001). Technology is an integral part of most students' lives and heavily influences their expectations of higher education. Yet discrepancies can emerge since some students have limited access to and experience with technology based on low SES. New professionals may struggle to be high tech and high touch with students who may not have as much experience with and knowledge of technology as a socioeconomically privileged staff member might assume (Cavanaugh, 2006).

New professionals are also challenged to find ways to integrate themselves into students' technology-driven social networks while also helping students understand how to appropriately navigate these social networks. They may struggle to keep up with technological and student changes in and out of the classroom. Developing effective communication venues (e.g.,

Facebook, MySpace, streaming videos, Instant Messenger, cell phones, podcasts, YouTube) can be integral to staying connected with today's undergraduates. Traditional notions of professional behavior that revolve around respect for an individual's privacy may need to be revisited because of the ubiquitous nature of social networking where the prevailing norm is self-revelation. Technology, and in particular social networks, may require different professional approaches to meet students' developmental needs. Future generations of students will likely be even more "connected" in a virtual sense and concurrently more hungry for self-understanding and the ability to establish meaningful, fulfilling relationships. New professionals may be called upon to address these seemingly mutually exclusive needs.

Finances

State funding and federal spending for higher education are on the decline while operating costs are rapidly rising. If tuition continues to rise to make up for declines in other sources of revenue, access, especially for those who seek full-time enrollment, will become more limited (Goldstein, 2006). Rising tuition costs and debt load most negatively have an impact on economically disadvantaged students (Kirwan, 2006). This will impede attainment of postsecondary education for those with financial concerns, stereotypically nontraditional and underserved students. Even students from relatively privileged backgrounds are increasingly concerned about the cost of higher education and the long-term value of a degree. Concerns about finances are likely to affect even more students in the future.

To work effectively with these students requires that new professionals acknowledge that educational cost (time and money spent) is a realistic concern, especially as costs rise, debt load grows, and overall financial pressures on students and families increase. Student affairs professionals must recognize that students may not graduate in four to six years, that they might need to work more hours while in college, and that they need jobs that pay well in order to meet their debt obligations. Furthermore, since a greater number of students have meaningful work experience before attending college, they expect that their skills will be used and expanded upon while they are in college. For example, Ben, a 31-year-old nontraditional student, may be seeking a second career when he takes a general education class after working his way up to being a manager of a small food establishment. He will likely expect that his past experiences, knowledge, and skills will be recognized and connected to the class curriculum. A new professional advising Ben or help-ing him find leadership opportunities must determine how to most appropri-ately identify valuable experiences that will allow him to feel a sense of respect for and connection to the institution.

Throwaway Society

A third issue affecting the ability to serve students is the throwaway mentality of society. In general, people today do not act in sustainable ways and waste a great deal of energy and material resources. Many consider this an outcome of the industrial economy (Hawken, Lovins, & Lovins, 1999). This has stim-ulated a throwaway and wasteful culture characterized by consumers whose expectations revolve around convenience, service, quality, and affordability (Snyder, 2007). The throwaway society is evident in students' demands that institutions offer the latest technology or that offices maintain staff and resources to immediately help students at all times.

Higher education cannot accommodate these student expectations with the current resource structure, and many would argue that institutions should not make student convenience the sole criterion for resource deci-sions. Nonetheless the disconnect between what students expect and what institutions are able to provide will be problematic for students. New profes-sionals must be prepared to address these expectations and explain the rea-sons behind a structure that is focused on supplying a quality and cost-effective education for all students. Fortunately there are many grassroots and nationwide sustainability efforts that are cropping up on campuses throughout the country to assist professionals in this effort. This is demon-strated by the 2007 American College & University Presidents Climate Commitment, a high-visibility effort to address global warming by garnering institutional commitments to neutralize greenhouse gas emissions and to accelerate the research and educational efforts of higher education. This commitment has been signed by over 400 college and university presidents and chancellors who hoped the commitment to exert their leadership in addressing climate change will stabilize and reduce their institutions' long-term energy costs. In another example, American College Personnel Associa-tion (ACPA) has developed the ACPA Sustainability Institute (www.my acpa.org/task-force/sustainability/primer.cfm), which brings together a diverse group of professionals who serve higher education and are committed to sustainability. This institute seeks to ensure a future where the environment, social justice, and the economy are all in balance.

Strategies to Stay Current about Student Characteristics

New professionals and their supervisors have a variety of resources available to continue their education about changing student populations. In addition to gaining new facts or theories, however, new professionals must integrate this knowledge into their professional values and their day-to-day interventions with students. In this section we offer resources and strategies that can assist student affairs administrators to stay current with changing student characteristics and needs.

Millennials Who Are New Professionals

As student affairs professionals work to develop the skills necessary to meet the challenges of the changing student population in higher education, there may be one resource that has not been explored. The majority of new professionals entering the field today are themselves a part of the millennial generation. Millennial professionals may find themselves in a unique leadership role in their institutions. By better understanding the needs of this generation, new professionals may be called on to "explain" millennials to their supervisors and senior administrators who are often from three other distinct generations—silent, boomers, and GenXers. Millennials can be great advocates for students by influencing organizational decisions and serving as a bridge to connect institutional policies and priorities to students.

Spanning four generation groups, those differences can be marked. Those from the silent generation (born before 1945), for example, typically seek work that is interesting and ask that their work be recognized and that they be paid fairly for that work. Baby boomers (1943–60) often prioritize work life over personal matters to gain gratification. GenXers (1977–82), on the other hand, possess a strong desire for advancement and seek flexible work schedules, mentoring, and merit pay for good work rather than extra pay for seniority. Because silents, boomers, and GenXers do not always see things the same way, millennial student affairs professionals may need to adapt to a style that is different from what they might prefer.

It is important to remember, however, that respect for generations goes both ways. Older workers may benefit by embracing the fresh perspectives of their millennial counterparts. Indeed, new professionals from the millennial generation should be viewed as a resource; they can provide information about and insights into the changing characteristics of students.

Assess Locally, Learn Globally

In today's environment, institutions of higher learning must assess students and their families in order to understand individual needs and expectations. Colleges and universities are challenged by the different learning needs, preferences, requirements, styles, and methods of new generations of students. The way a new professional believes students learn is critical. For example, consider that today's students are members of the digital age and often find lectures boring and uninteresting. Faculty members may feel that a student's lack of interest in listening to an expert lecture is disrespectful or identifies a lack of intelligence or understanding; that can lead to inaccurate perspectives. If professionals' understandings are inaccurate or out of date, their ability to work with students may be impaired (Fried, 2006). "Our assumptions and past experiences may not serve us well if we import them into our current work and superimpose them on present day campus culture" (Borrego, Forrest, & Fried, 2006, p. 59).

Student development theories can still be helpful to student affairs professionals but they cannot be relied upon solely (Evans, Forney, & Guido-DiBrito, 1998). What students want and need changes so rapidly that professionals must rely upon their interactions and knowledge gained through conversations with each student to hone their skills. It is important that professionals take the time to have purposeful conversations with students to know them as individuals. If they seek continuous feedback from students they can make changes to professional practice based on that information. These conversations require careful listening, a willingness to reach beyond student leaders for information, and a desire to reflect carefully on what one learns.

Institutions can also use local data on their students and current assessment data from similar institutions to guide their efforts to educate and develop students. A regular time can be designated to share this type of data across the institution or during supervision sessions and departmental staff meetings. These sharing opportunities are particularly important for those staff members who may not have learned about student characteristics in a graduate preparation program.

Regardless of campus type or location, professionals should familiarize themselves with basic information related to the primary and minority student cultures on their campus. Simply reading the material about students from the Office of Institutional Research is one way to gain an overall view of the student population. The Office of Admissions or Enrollment Management often has a wealth of demographic information about currently enrolled students and trends that may affect recruiting in the future. Finally, administrators need to pay attention to the distinctive characteristics of the institution's location. For example, new professionals who work at colleges and universities located on or near military installations should be aware that programs, services, and course delivery methods might need to address the requirements of their students who have military affiliations. Since these institutions tend to enroll sizable numbers of active-duty personnel, their spouses, or dependants, they will need traditional services along with specialized types of support to meet the needs of "citizen-soldiers" (Moskos, 2002, p. 76).

Paying attention to emerging social or political trends is also important. For example, veterans from Iraq will be a new population for many colleges and universities. These individuals will likely enter the classroom with different characteristics than the traditional-age or other nonveteran students. Veterans represent 3.6% of undergraduate and 3.9% of graduate students enrolled in higher education. They return home with significant physical and emotional challenges and personal perspectives and experiences that are not easily understood by other students, faculty, or staff (DeRicco, 2007).

Listening for institutional priorities that have implications for student recruitment can also spur learning about changing student populations. Institutions that desire to increase the number of international students they enroll will likely be open to providing professional development opportunities to learn about this population.

There are several important sources of national data about students' priorities, goals, values, and achievements. Most prominent among these resources is the Higher Education Research Institute (http://www.gseis .ucla.edu/heri/index.php), which for more than 40 years has surveyed entering freshmen about their values, time use, and goals. The National Survey of Student Engagement (http://www.nsse.iub.edu/index.cfm) conducts research about the degree of college student engagement. More than 1,200 institutions have participated in the research since its inception in 2000. Both of these resources are easily accessible and offer a large amount of data as well as reasoned inferences about college students.

Practical Suggestions

The following suggestions summarize the primary strategies that evolve from this chapter. They can be used by new professionals individually, by supervisors as they work with new professionals, by graduate preparation programs that are educating future professionals, and by institutional leaders with responsibility for planning for student success.

New Professionals

- Maintain continuous learning about the changing students and challenge your mode of thinking and perspective.
- Treat each student as an individual and try not to stereotype based on identified characteristics.
- Develop an ethic of continuous informal assessment of your student population to stay abreast of student change.

Supervisors

- Use regular staff meetings as an avenue to discuss ever-changing student characteristics.
- Use generational differences, experiences, and perspectives to improve and enhance brainstorming sessions; leave no voice unheard.

Graduate Preparation Programs

- Develop courses or integrate material into all classes on changing student demographics.
- Expand lessons about diversity to include all differences, beyond race, gender, and age.

Institutional Leaders

- Understand special financial struggles of students and develop new avenues to address their needs.
- Develop other effective communications tools (e.g., Facebook, MySpace, streaming videos, Instant Messenger, cell phones, podcasts, YouTube).
- Continuously evaluate and update policies and procedures; ensure they do not impede retention of students regardless of their characteristics.

- Create a more in-depth orientation for new professionals that covers student characteristics.
- On a regular basis share institutional data about students and data from peer institutions with staff members

Conclusion

New professionals in student affairs need to be prepared to educate and connect with students who are different from previous generations (e.g., increased diversity, variant perspectives, increasing mental and physical issues, assorted socioeconomic levels). Additionally, institutions must continuously adapt policies, procedures, and initiatives and programs to effectively serve these students. As the number of millennial students on campus grows, especially at public and private four-year institutions, schools will see an increase in students with diverse ethnic and cultural backgrounds, greater numbers of females, students with alternate perspectives on family, greater technological expectations, and students who are more likely to be actively involved in community service and respectful of elders and rules. These students will be guided, taught, mentored, disciplined, and developed by professionals who likely have different perspectives on and values about life and the world.

Consequently, administrators need to continuously learn about rapidly changing student demographics and characteristics. Failure to stay up to date will result in frustration for students and professionals. Student demographics may vary greatly from institution to institution based on size, location, and type, posing additional challenges for professionals who assume new positions and change institutional affiliation. The current level of training and education about these matters is inadequate (National Center for Public Policy and Higher Education, 2006). New professionals can no longer view the world only from their own perspective but must understand multiple perspectives. The impact specific demographics and characteristics have upon each individual student's perspective is significant.

In summary, new professionals need to realize they can no longer rely on students' remaining more or less the same. They can no longer make basic generalizations about individual students based upon age. Although each generation of students may have shared experiences this does not mean they have the same values and perspectives or will act in similar ways. The challenge for new professionals is not only to understand the group dynamics of emerging populations of students but also to appreciate and acknowledge the unique characteristics of each individual student.

References

Aronowitz, S., & DiFazio, W. (1994). *The jobless future: Sci-tech and the dogma of work*. Minneapolis: University of Minnesota Press.

Bash, L. (2003). *Adult learners in the academy*. Bolton, MA: Anker.

Borrego, S., Forrest, C., & Fried, J. (2006). Enhancing professional development. In R. P. Keeling (Ed.), *Learning reconsidered 2: A practical guide to implementing a campus-wide focus on the student experience* (pp. 59–63). Washington, DC: ACPA, ACUHO–I, ACUI, NACA, NACADA, NASPA, & NIRSA.

Boylan, H. R., Bonham, B. S., & Tafari, G. N. (2005, Spring). Evaluating the outcomes of developmental education. In G. H. Gaither (Ed.), *Minority retention: What works?* (pp. 45–58). New Directions for Institutional Research, No. 125. Hoboken, NJ: Wiley.

Bridges, W. (1994) *Jobshift: How to prosper in a workplace without jobs*. Boulder, CO: Perseus.

Broido, E. (2004, Summer). Understanding diversity in millennial students. In M. Coomes & R. DeBard (Eds.), *Serving the millennial generation* (pp. 73–85). New Directions for Student Services, No. 106. Hoboken, NJ: Wiley.

Carnoy, M. (2000). *Sustaining the new economy: Work, family, and community in the information age*. Cambridge, MA: Russell Sage.

Carnoy, M., Castells, M., Cohen, S. S., & Cardoso, F. H. (1993). *The new global economy in the information age: Reflections of our changing world*. University Park: Pennsylvania State University Press.

Castells, M. (1996). *The rise of the network society*. Malden, MA: Blackwell.

Cavanaugh, R. E. (2006, October). Most young people entering the U.S. workforce lack critical skills essential for success. *Diverse Issues in Higher Education*. Retrieved October 3, 2006, from http://www.diverseeducation.com/artman/pub lish/printer_6436.shtml

Choy, S. P. (2002). Non-traditional undergraduates. In National Center for Education Statistics, *The condition of education* (pp. 25–39). Washington, DC: U.S. Department of Education and Office of Education Research and Improvement.

Cohen, A. M., & Brawer, F. B. (2003). *The American community college* (4th ed.). San Francisco: Jossey-Bass.

Coomes, M., & DeBard, R. (2004, Summer). A generational approach to understanding students. In M. Coomes & R. DeBard (Eds.), *Serving the millennial generation* (pp. 5–16). New Directions for Student Services, No. 106. Hoboken, NJ: Wiley.

Daniel, B. U., Evans, S. G., & Scott, B. R. (2001). Understanding family involvement in the college experience today. In B. U. Daniel & B. R. Scott (Eds.), *Consumers, adversaries and partners: Working with the families of undergraduates* (pp. 3–13). New Directions for Student Services, No. 94. San Francisco: Jossey-Bass.

Davies, T. G., Safarik, L., & Banning, J. H. (2003, October/December). The deficit portrayal of underrepresented populations on community college campuses: A cross case analysis, *Community College Journal of Research and Practice, 27*(9–10), 843–858.

DeBard, R. (2004, Summer). Millennials coming to college. In M. Coomes & R. DeBard (Eds.), *Serving the millennial generation* (pp. 33–45). New Directions for Student Services, No. 106. Hoboken, NJ: Wiley.

DeRicco, B. (2007, Summer). Military veterans on campus: Coordinated student services can ease the transition. *Leadership Exchange, 5*(2), 14–19.

Evans, N. J., Forney, D. S., & Guido-DiBrito, F. (1998). *Student development in college: Theory, research, and practice*. San Francisco: Jossey-Bass.

Freeman, J. P. (2006). Postsecondary education for the underserved in America: A study of highly non-traditional students in community colleges. *Dissertation Abstracts International,*

Freeman, J. P. (2007, April–June). Community colleges in higher education: The role of community colleges in serving the underserved student. *Planning for Higher Education, 35*(3), 56–62.

Fried, J. (2006). Rethinking learning. In R. P. Keeling (Ed.), *Learning reconsidered 2: A practical guide to implementing a campus-wide focus on the student experience* (pp. 3–9). Washington, DC: ACPA, ACUHO–I, ACUI, NACA, NACADA, NASPA, & NIRSA.

Goldstein, P. J. (2006). *The future of higher education: A view from CHEMA*. Washington, DC: Council of Higher Education Management Associations.

Grubb, W. N., Badway, N., & Bell, D. (2003, March). Community colleges and the equity agenda: The potential of noncredit education. *The Annals, 586*(1), 218–240.

Hawken, P., Lovins, A., & Lovins, L. H. (1999). *Natural capitalism: Creating the next industrial revolution*. Boston, MA: Little, Brown.

Herideen, P. E. (1998). *Policy, pedagogy, and social inequality: Community college student realities in post-industrial America*. Westport, CT: Bergin & Garvey.

Horn, L. J., & Carroll, C. D. (1996, November). *Non-traditional undergraduates: Trends in enrollment from 1986 to 1992 and persistence and attainment among 1989–90 beginning postsecondary students*. Washington, DC: U.S. Department of Education, National Center for Educational Statistics.

Howe, N., & Strauss, W. (2000). *Millennials rising: The next great generation*. New York: Vintage.

Howe, N., & Strauss, W. (2003). *Millennials go to college.* Washington, DC: American Association of College Registrars and Admissions Officers and Life Course Associates.

Jones, A. F., Jr., & Weinberg, D. A. (2000, June). *The changing shape of the nation's income distribution.* Washington, DC: U.S. Census Bureau.

Kirwan, W. E. (2006). Higher education: Meeting today's challenges and regaining the public's trust. In R. L. Clark & M. d'Ambrosio (Eds.), *The new balancing act in the business of higher education* (pp. 46–53). Northampton, MA: Edward Elgar.

Levin, J. S. (2001). *Globalizing the community college: Strategies for change in the twenty-first century.* New York: Palgrave.

Levin, J. S. (2003, November). *Beyond the margins: Community college students outside the mainstream.* Paper presented at the annual meeting of the Association for the Study of Higher Education, Portland, OR.

Levin, J. S. (2007). *Nontraditional students and community colleges: The conflict of justice and neoliberalism.* New York: Palgrave Macmillan.

Levine, A., & Cureton, J. S. (1998). What we know about today's college students. *About Campus, 3*(1), 4–9.

Mason, M. A., & Moulden, J. (1996). The new stepfamily requires new public policy. *Journal of Social Issues, 52*(3), 11–27.

Merriam, S. B., & Caffarella, R. S. (1999). *Learning in adulthood: A comprehensive guide* (2nd ed.). San Francisco: Jossey-Bass.

Moskos, C. (2002). Reviving the citizen soldier. *Public Interest, 147,* 76–85.

National Center for Education Statistics. (2002). *The condition of education.* Washington, DC: U.S. Department of Education.

National Center for Public Policy and Higher Education. (2006). *Measuring up 2006: The national report card on higher education.* San Jose, CA: Author.

Rifkin, J. (1995). *The end of work: The decline of the global labor force and the dawn of the post-market era.* New York: Putnam.

Shaw, K. (1999). Defining the self: Construction of identity in community college students. In K. Shaw, J. Valadez, & R. Rhoads (Eds.), *Community colleges as cultural texts* (pp. 153–171). Buffalo, NY: SUNY Press.

Shaw, K., & London, H. (2001). Culture and ideology in keeping transfer commitment: Three community colleges. *The Review of Higher Education, 25*(1), 91–114.

Shaw, K., Rhoads, R., & Valadez, J. (1999). *Community colleges as cultural texts.* Albany, NY: SUNY Press.

Smith, B. L., MacGregor, J., Matthews, R. S., & Gabelnick, F. (2004). *Learning communities: Reforming undergraduate education.* San Francisco: Jossey-Bass.

Smith, P. (2004). *The quiet crisis: How higher education is failing America.* Bolton, MA: Anker.

Snyder, D. P. (2007). Academia and access to knowledge in the 21st century. In W. J. Anderson, J. Dator, & M. Tehranian (Eds.), *Learning to seek: Globalization, governance, and the futures of higher education* (pp. 6–23). New Brunswick, NJ: Transaction Publishers.

Steinberg, S. H. (2006, December). Widening the door to higher education: The continuing growth in the number of part-time students challenges old notions about time to degree. *Diverse Issues in Higher Education, 23*(23), 45.

Terinzini, P. T., Cabrera, A. F., & Bernal, E. M. (2001). *Swimming against the tide: The poor in American higher education.* New York: College Entrance Examination Board.

U.S. Census Bureau. (2001). Census 2000 PHC-T01. Population by Race and Hispanic or Latino Origin, for all ages and for 18 years and over, for the United States: 2000. Retrieved September 8, 2007, from http://www.census.gov/popula tion/cen2000/phc-t1/tab01.pdf

U.S. Census Bureau. (2002). Census 2000 PHC-T01. Population by Race and Hispanic or Latino Origin; White Alone Not-Hispanic or Latino Origin Population; Population Other Than White Alone Not-Hispanic or Latino Origin, by Age and Sex for the United States: 2000. Retrieved September 8, 2007, from http:// www.census.gov/population/cen2000/phc-t08/tab08.pdf

Valadez, J. R. (1996). Educational access and social mobility in a rural community college. *Review of Higher Education, 19*(4): 391–409.

Zemke, R., Raines, C., & Filipczak, B. (2000). *Generations at work: Managing the clash of veterans, boomers, Xers, and nexters in your workplace.* New York: Amacon.

PART THREE

STRATEGIES TO ENHANCE SOCIALIZATION OF NEW PROFESSIONALS

5

GRADUATE PREPARATION PROGRAMS

The First Step in Socialization

Linda Kuk and Michael J. Cuyjet

The academic content of graduate preparation programs and the knowledge and competencies they instill in their graduates are critical to the quality and competence of student affairs practitioners within colleges and universities (Creamer, Janosik, Winston, & Kuk, 2001). Winston and Creamer (1997) found that a combination of good professional preparation and experience, plus a good fit between the staff member and the institution are the two primary criteria for sound hiring practices. Graduate education programs by the nature of their intended purpose as preparation programs play a major role in the socialization of their students to professional roles (Creamer et al., 2001; Evans & Phelps Tobin, 1998; Kuk, Cobb & Forrest, 2007).

This chapter explores a number of ways that student affairs professional preparation programs play a role in the socialization of new professionals and contribute to their readiness for the challenges they face during the first few years of employment. The chapter begins by describing ways various components of preparation programs help prepare students for the socialization that will take place as they make the transition to the ranks of professionals. The chapter then examines a number of the master's-level programs in the country to demonstrate how different program foci affect students' development toward professionalism. Next, the chapter demonstrates the use of standards from the Council for the Advancement of Standards in Higher Education

(CAS) as models for the identification of core competencies for new professionals, then cites some results from recent research depicting current practitioners' perspectives on the role of preparation programs in developing competencies among new professionals. We continue by discussing how students, faculty, and student affairs practitioners contribute to effective socialization of graduate students in student affairs preparation programs.

The social transition through a professional preparation program to full-time employment as a student affairs professional has its share of adjustments. Evers, Rush, and Berdrow (1998), described the transition from college life to the reality of the world of work as the "Humbling Effect." During this adjustment process, the reality of the world of work places new professionals in the humbling position of not knowing as much as they thought they knew. Stress, discouragement, and at times professional failure can result from not being able to easily address the situations and issues that are presented. One of the assumptions attributed to professional graduate education is that transitional stress and adjustment time to a new professional role are greatly reduced by the socialization of graduate students to practical and professional experiences that provide them with opportunities to apply their knowledge and skills in real worklike situations. Evidence also suggests that socialization within a graduate preparation program places the graduate in a stronger position to be successful as an entry-level professional (Creamer et al., 2001; Kuk & Hughes, 2003).

Weidman, Twale, & Stein (2001) broadly discussed the role of graduate preparation in the socialization of professionals. They defined socialization in graduate school "as the processes through which individuals gain the knowledge, skill, and values necessary for successful entry into a professional career requiring an advanced level of specialized knowledge and skill" (p. iii). Socialization to professionalism "requires changes in students' self-images, attitudes and thinking processes" (Egan, 1989, p. 210). It requires synthesizing knowledge and expectations about the role "into a coherent behavioral pattern" commonly associated with a field or profession (Knight, 1973, p. 4). Tierney described socialization as the "process of becoming aware of and indoctrinated to the norms, beliefs, and values of the organization" (as cited in Amey & Reesor, 2002, p. 22). This process is related to the development of social consciousness and long-term direction and purpose (Amey & Reesor, 2002).

Essentially, socialization is the integration process that is a central attribute of professional preparation (see chapter 1). The core socialization experience in a graduate degree program consists of (a) the institutional culture of the university, which includes the academic program and peer climate; (b) the socialization process, which includes interactions, integration, and learning; and (c) the core elements of socialization, including knowledge acquisition, investment, and involvement. The program has the most control over these elements of socialization (Weidman et al., 2001).

Socializing Components of a Student Affairs Preparation Program

Within the field of student affairs the socialization process can differ in relevance and in quality, depending on the nature of the core socialization elements that are present within the institution's culture and the type and quality of the cultural components that are present within a preparation program. These might include such elements as curricular components, the quality of peers, faculty interactions, levels of integration within the curricular offerings, intentionality and application of theory to practice, as well as the assessment and feedback mechanisms that are included within a preparation program.

The Curriculum

One of the most fundamental ways that students are professionally socialized is through the curriculum, both in terms of the program's overall philosophy and its content. The philosophy of the profession, its values, vision, and ways of seeing the world are manifested through the curriculum and serve as the foundation for what is taught and what is modeled in the preparation program. Students are taught to identify with and integrate certain values, ethics, and perspectives that serve as the basis for professional thinking within the field. Course content lays out a road map of knowledge and theory that enables students to systematically apply knowledge to practice. It builds their capacity for the transfer of professional knowledge to programs and services they will administer in their future professional roles. The curriculum as a whole defines what it means to be a professional within student affairs, and how the knowledge is applied and practiced. In this context it is critical that course content is integrated, meaningful, and directly tied to professional practice and is grounded in a sound, overall understanding of the profession.

Quality and Diversity of Peers Within a Program

Students arrive at student affairs preparation programs from a variety of backgrounds and entry points with varying knowledge, skills, cultures, talents, prior leadership experience, and student affairs–related experiences. The spectrum ranges from students' entering preparation programs from totally unrelated academic baccalaureate programs, such as business or engineering, to those who have already served as full-time practitioners in the student affairs field. Their varied expectations, contributions, and commitment to learning and growth within the program are key elements in their professional socialization and that of other members of their student cohorts.

Learning and professional socialization is a community-based process within most student affairs preparation programs. Peer attitudes, contributions to classroom discussions, social interactions, and experiences can greatly influence the attitudes and values that students adopt toward professional roles and responsibilities. Negative attitudes, withdrawal, loss of commitment, backbiting, unethical and/or risky behaviors on the part of peers can seriously undermine the positive socialization process for all the students in a preparation program, and if unchecked can be carried over into professional work behavior. At the same time, the opposite types of attitudes and behaviors can be supportive and enhancing for every student. Student cohorts who reflect a broad spectrum of worldviews and bring diverse prior experiences to the program greatly enrich the experience of all students and effectively challenge the faculty. Through sound advising and effective vigilance, faculty and students can monitor the effects of peer influence and act appropriately to manage and positively enhance peer influence.

Interactions With Faculty and Practitioners

The quality and quantity of positive interactions with faculty and other student affairs practitioners is a key element in the socialization of preparation program students. Socialization occurs through effective modeling of behavior and through the use of real-world examples and experiences. Through intentionally planned classroom and out-of-class interactions with faculty and other student affairs practitioners, students can integrate professional expectations and realities that cannot be gained in exclusively theoretical contexts. Faculty can bring real-world situations to the learning process through their own practitioner and research experiences. They can also engage practitioners in the instructional process and create opportunities for students and faculty to interact regularly with the practitioner world. Such exposure provides opportunities for unplanned, serendipitous learning that gives future new professionals real life experiences and reinforces the principles and theories learned in the classroom.

Availability of Quality Professional Practice Opportunities

The application of theory to practice is crucial to successful professional socialization in preparation programs. Students need to have access to a wide variety of professional settings to gain applied experience as budding professionals. These experiential opportunities can take many forms: paid or unpaid internships, required practica, volunteer activities, shadowing experiences, summer and part-time work, and so on. What is important is the exposure of the student to professional practice, the application of professional ethics, the use of theory in application, and the successful realization of planned goals and objectives, along with the integration of program assessment and evaluation processes. These experiences should enable students to actually dig in and get their hands messy in terms of professional engagement, and as a result, learn what it means to be a professional practitioner. While voyeuristic or simulated activities are helpful learning experiences, they are insufficient as the sole means of realizing high-quality professional socialization.

Potentially the most fruitful interactive opportunity that bridges the realms of professional preparation and professional practice is the internship experience. Many programs construct this experience so it combines a periodic (often weekly) seminar meeting with an instructor from the faculty. The reflective activities of the seminar enable students to analyze their experience and apply it to their own growth as practitioners. Moreover, faculty members and student affairs professionals serving as site supervisors can collaborate to ensure that the maximum learning benefit accrues from the internship experience by students. An added benefit from this instructional collaboration is the opportunity for faculty and practitioners to develop a relationship so they can work together on other cooperative ventures.

Not only is the type and nature of the professional practical experience important, the quality of the experience in terms of design and supervision is essential for effective professional socialization. Professional practical experiences are of little value unless they focus on students' gaining professional experience and provide students with quality coaching and feedback. Supervisors of practical experiences should be viewed as "experiential faculty," and they should be nurtured and rewarded as such. At the same time, they should be expected to provide an organized, focused, and professionally based practical experience for the students they supervise. They should be expected, along with the student, to set goals and outcomes related to the experience. These goals should align with program goals and standards and should ensure that the experience is engaging and stimulating for the student. Practical supervisors should also be expected to continue their own professional development and to remain current in the knowledge and skills related to student affairs practice.

Design and Assessment of Learning Processes

The curriculum should be more than an array of courses and experiential opportunities. In order to achieve effective professional socialization experiences, the curriculum should be focused, intentionally designed, and integrate the learning experiences it encompasses. Every aspect of the program, from admission and orientation through graduation, should be designed and implemented to meet the purpose of preparing highly competent student affairs practitioners and to ensure that the elements of the program create meaningful, coherent, and cogent learning experiences. Self-reflection and periodic advising sessions that focus on the learning experience and the overall goals of the student and the program are critical elements of the learning and feedback process.

Accountability is an essential part of professional socialization. The attributes, skills, and knowledge that new professionals bring to the profession are paramount to the success of the profession in fulfilling its role and responsibility to the larger community. Professional preparation programs will increasingly have to demonstrate learning and professional preparation outcomes that result from their efforts. These curricular learning outcomes must be noticeably linked to corresponding activities that students will likely encounter when they enter the profession. Most importantly, the outcomes must be clearly measurable using criteria similar to professional assessment tools. Programs should also contain ongoing, intentionally designed input and feedback mechanisms so that they can adapt and respond quickly to changes in skills and competencies necessary for work in student affairs and higher education. It is critical to know what works and what does not work in the preparation learning process.

Current Curriculum of Preparation Programs

Well over 100 master's-level student affairs graduate preparation programs are available throughout the United States. Among student affairs preparation programs there is no consistent approach to curriculum content, program pedagogies, or experiential foci. Some programs focus on counseling, some on student development, and others on management and administration. The number of required credits varies widely, and practical experiences differ in type, amount, and quality of supervision.

In an attempt to better understand the focus and content of student affairs preparation program curricula, 96 master's-level preparation programs listed in the American College Personnel Association (ACPA) Preparation Program Directory were reviewed to determine the nature and breadth of the curricular content. This review (Kuk, 2007) essentially addressed three questions:

1. What was the overall focus of the program in terms of content? Traditionally student affairs preparation programs have been found to have one of three professional foci:
    a. *counseling,*
    b. *student development*
    c. *administration*
2. Did the overall program meet the ACPA Professional Preparation Standards and did it also meet the CAS professional standards for student affairs preparation programs? Meeting these standards would indicate that the program's overall content closely matched existing professional standards related to professional preparation socialization.
3. What was the content of the courses within the master's programs that classify themselves as student affairs preparation programs? Are there any core elements of content that appear in nearly all programs and would serve as core to professional preparation knowledge content socialization?

In reviewing the mission statements and the overall nature of the curricula within the 96 master's programs, it became clear that the programs covered the full spectrum of possible foci. However, it was nearly impossible to delineate the programs into three distinct categories. Rather, the programs could better be depicted as a continuum with counseling at one end, through student affairs administration to higher education administration at the other end. Most of the programs contained student development–related courses along with either a counseling or administrative focus, and some programs actually contained curricula with a strong mix of all three content foci. Only a few programs appeared to have only a higher education administration focus. In these cases the curriculum content did not appear to include student affairs or student development content elements.

The programs were also reviewed to determine if they self-reported compliance with the ACPA professional preparation standards and the CAS standards for master's-level student affairs preparation programs. Eighty-six (89.5%) of the 96 programs indicated that they complied with the ACPA standards, while only 32 (33.3%) self-reported meeting the CAS standards. This latter finding suggested there may be some distinctive differences between the student affairs profession's established standards for the overall content of curriculum and the actual content and focus of many preparation programs. These differences likely result in graduates from various programs having very different professional socialization experiences.

The courses offered in student affairs preparation programs also appeared to cover a wide spectrum. Within the 96 programs reviewed, there were over 50 distinct courses. No single course or course content was offered across all the programs.

Only three course-content areas—Student Affairs Programs and Services, Methods of Research, Administration (Student Affairs and/or Higher Education)—were found in at least 70% of the preparation programs reviewed. An additional five course-content areas were found in over 50% of the reviewed programs. These included Multiculturalism and/or Diverse Populations, Student Development Theory, College Students, Law or Law and Ethics, Student Affairs or Higher Education Issues. Of the 96 programs that were reviewed, 85.4% offered at least two student affairs–related courses from within the content areas listed above.

Even though there were sharp differences in the preparation program curricular offerings, 95% of the programs did require some form of practical experience as part of their curricular requirements. These experiences varied in type of experience, with assistantships and credit-bearing practica being the most commonly reported. The programs also varied in the number of practical experience credits required within the programs and the number of required hours associated with these experiences.

The results of this review suggest that the curriculum within student affairs preparation programs is distinctively different across programs. However, there appears to be a general overall focus related to student affairs theory and practice that is common across most preparation programs. At the same time, the actual content and number of courses related to student affairs appear to differ from program to program. This suggests that what is defined as the knowledge and experience needed to succeed as a professional is considerably different across preparation programs. These differences are likely to result in differences in student professional socialization. It is not clear to what extent these differences have an impact on practice or success among new professionals. It is clear that further research in this area is needed. These findings also suggest the need for further conversation about the value of creating a core preparation program content that is strongly encouraged as the curricular base for all programs that are classified as student affairs preparation programs.

The CAS Standards and Professional Preparation

The transition from graduate student to new professional is smoother if both these aspects of the profession share a similar theoretical foundation. Garland and Grace (1993) suggest that the evolution of the student affairs profession calls for a closer alignment of the roles of preparation programs and practitioners in the field. But since student affairs professionals perform increasingly complex functions at a wide variety of institutional settings, it is highly unlikely that there could be a single way to prepare professionals or a definitive set of professional education standards. Carpenter (2003) feels that the work of student affairs is complex enough to rely on multifaceted theories; while Burkard, Cole, Ott, and Stoflet (2004), suggest that human relations, administrative/management, technological and research competencies, and individual personal attributes are all crucial to the success of entry-level professionals in student affairs.

Nonetheless, it would be helpful if student affairs professionals and preparation faculty could identify standards that link preparation program curricula to practice. Employers could expect new employees to come to the job equipped with certain identifiable skills and competencies learned as part of their professional preparation in graduate school. Such standardization could also allow nascent student affairs practitioners to share a common base of skills and competencies for them to build professional development opportunities that are extensions of what they learned in their graduate programs. A viable list of skills and competencies for new practitioners can be created from an examination of the standards and guidelines for college student personnel preparation master's degree programs produced by the CAS (Dean, 2006).

The CAS standards state:

> All programs of study must include: 1) foundational studies, 2) professional studies, and 3) supervised practice. Foundational studies must include the study of the historical and philosophical foundations of higher education and student affairs. Professional studies must include (a) student development theory, (b) student characteristics and effects of college on students, (c) individual and group interventions, (d) organization and administration of student affairs, and (e) assessment, evaluation, and research. Supervised practice must include practica and/or internships consisting of supervised work involving at least two distinct experiences. Demonstration of minimum knowledge in each area is required of all program graduates. (Dean, 2006, p. 350)

An examination of these CAS standards suggests a "list of competencies" that can be gleaned from the language of the CAS standards. These knowledge and professional practice content and skill areas form a basic set of understandings and skill development that might be expected of all new professionals to bring to their new position regardless of the functional area in which they work. In theory, if all graduate preparation programs adhered to the CAS standards, new professionals graduating from these programs would gain a competent, basic, working understanding of the issues in the areas mentioned by CAS. At the same time, supervisors of these new professionals could expect that the students they hire have acquired an operational level of the knowledge and skills outlined within the CAS-prescribed competencies, and would be capable of performing these skills in their new job (Cuyjet, Longwell-Grice, & Molina, 2009).

Practitioners' Views Regarding Preparation Programs

Komives (1998) and Upcraft (1998) argue that practitioners need to become more engaged in preparation programs and the student affairs curriculum should be aligned with and more directly related to practice. Yet there is very little evidence that practitioners have been actively involved in the design and creation of most preparation programs, although practitioners do serve as adjunct faculty in a large number of preparation programs and serve on preparation program advisory boards where they exist.

Scholars have identified a number of key competencies and experiences that practitioners believe are essential for new student affairs professionals to possess. Table 5.1 summarizes the competencies identified by researchers.

Kuk et al. (2007) found that there were significant differences in the perceptions between faculty, senior student affairs officers (SSAOs) and mid-level managers regarding which professional competencies were important

TABLE 5.1
New Student Affairs Professionals—Key Competencies and Experiences
Summary Review of Findings

Competencies	Researcher	Year
Working collaboratively with others	Ostroth	1981
Interpersonal skills	Pope & Reynolds	1997
Ability to work with a wide variety of people	Lovell & Kosten	2000
Leadership skills		
Goal setting	Hyman	1988
Consultation		
Communication		
Assessment and evaluation		
Environmental and organizational management		
Personal communications	Saidla	1990
Understanding of individual difference		
Ability to demonstrate caring		
Knowledge of ethics and legal responsibilities		
Relevant assistantship experience	Kretovics	2002
Demonstrated helping skills		
Personal commitment to diversity		
Computer skills		

for new practitioners to possess, and where entry-level professional competencies should be learned. There seemed to be closer agreement on the importance of professional knowledge competencies as outlined by the CAS standards (Dean, 2006), but significant differences in the perception of importance of practice-oriented competencies, such as those related to management, change, and the processes associated with their implementation. There also appear to be significant differences in the perceptions of where these competencies should be learned. The findings suggest there should be closer collaboration between practitioners and preparation faculty regarding the curriculum of preparation programs and the expected knowledge and skill competencies as they apply to new professionals.

Several other studies have examined the knowledge and skills competencies that new professionals felt they had learned in their preparation programs and that they needed in their jobs. Waple (2006) assessed the skills new professionals believed they had attained in their master's degree programs and the degree to which they were used in their first professional positions. Cuyjet et al. (2009) examined the perceptions about various knowledge competencies of recent graduates of college student personnel preparation programs and their supervisors. New professionals indicated they had received the highest level of preparation on the topics of (a) understanding student development theory, (b) how college experiences can enhance student development, and (c) ethics and standards of practice. They also indicated that the three competencies of most importance in their current places of employment were (a) ethics and standards of practice, (b) knowledge in their area of specialization, and (c) knowledge of how the college experience could enhance student development.

This study also examined the perceptions of the supervisors of new professionals concerning their training in various competencies and the use of these competencies on the job. Supervisors felt that new professionals had received the highest level of preparation in the areas of (a) how college experiences can enhance student development, (b) understanding student development, and (c) ethics and standards of practice. They held that the competencies, (a) ethics and standards of practice, (b) working in diverse populations, and (c) knowledge in their area of specialization were the most important competencies for their supervisees to possess in their present employment. It is interesting to note the level of agreement between new professionals and the supervisors. New professionals felt most prepared on the topic of student development—their knowledge of it and their understanding of how college experiences enhance it in students. In corresponding responses, the supervisors agreed that these were areas of strength for their supervisees. Ethics and standards of practice, which received the third highest mean response from the new professionals, also received the third highest mean response among supervisors. On the application of competencies to one's work, we can again see a fairly high level of agreement between new professionals and the supervisors. Supervisors agreed that ethics and standards of practice and working with diverse populations were critical competencies, as did the recent graduates. Supervisors also agreed with their recent graduates that knowledge of the history of higher education was not very important.

In examining the differences between the perceptions of new professionals and those of their supervisors, there were four items that showed significant differences: (a) how the program has provided a strong understanding of the history of higher education, (b) how the program has provided a strong understanding of how the college experience can enhance student development, (c) how the program has provided a strong understanding of quantitative research methodology, and (d) how the program has provided a strong understanding of qualitative research methodology. In each of these four areas, recent graduates had a higher perception of their knowledge than the supervisors perceived them to have. The researchers speculated two possible explanations (for which they propose further study): (a) recent graduates have an inflated opinion of their knowledge/skills/understanding or (b) supervisors lack an appreciation of the knowledge/skills/understanding their supervisees actually have.

Taking a somewhat different approach and sampling only new (less than 5 years) professionals, Waple (2006) found relatively similar results. He developed a list of 28 new professional skills "drawn from preservice preparation and student affairs assessment literature" (p. 1). Examining the congruence between attainment and use, his subjects identified their top seven congruent skills, selected by more than 65% of respondents, as (a) effective oral and written communication skills, (b) ethics in student affairs work, (c) multicultural awareness and knowledge, (d) problem solving, (e) effective program planning and implementation, (6) student development theory, and (f) student demographics and characteristics. Waple concluded that these skills (as well as seven other competencies identified as attained and used by a slightly lesser number of the subjects—by 50% to 57%) were attained at a moderate to high degree and were being used from a moderate to high degree in the subjects' first professional positions. The congruence demonstrated by Waple's study and some of the data from the study by Cuyjet et al. (2009) would seem to indicate that preparation programs, particularly those that ascribe to the CAS standards, are meeting the needs of supervisors and new professionals regarding the areas both of these groups see as important to the profession.

Burkard et al. (2004) and Herdlein (2004) approached this question of skills and competencies of entry-level professionals by assessing the perceptions of midlevel or senior student affairs professionals. These studies identify personal competencies that tend to be more specific than in the previously described research. In grouping these specific skills, Burkard et al. refer to three general competency areas described in Herdlein's study—management skills, human relations skills, and personal attributes (such as flexibility, interpersonal relations, critical thinking, problem solving, creativity, and assertiveness) They add two additional competency areas: skills relevant to technology and meeting the needs of culturally diverse groups. They speculate that this level of specificity may be "a reflection of changing practices in student affairs and more recent changes in expectations of new professionals" (p. 298).

Enhancing Socialization in Graduate Preparation Programs

Socialization is a key factor in the success of graduate education of new student affairs professionals. Fostering intentionally designed opportunities for professional socialization and aligning these opportunities with a rich and professionally focused curriculum are essential. While the faculty may bear the primary responsibility for fostering professional socialization, it is also the responsibility of the students and actively engaged practitioners to contribute to this process. Effective socialization of graduate students is a multifaceted process that requires active engagement of all participants.

Students play a key role in their own professional socialization. It is their responsibility to become self-directed learners and to seek out opportunities to learn and to practice the professional knowledge and skills they need to become competent professionals. Graduate students have a responsibility to become fully engaged in their academic and practical experiences and to maximize their access to the wealth of learning that is available to them. It is their responsibility to plan how they will balance the competing demands of academic study and practical experiences with their personal lives. They need to be open to participating in voluntary activities that will enrich their ability to apply theory to practice and seek out faculty and practitioners who can effectively mentor them in achieving their professional goals. Each student also brings a variety of skills and experiences that can be shared to enrich the socialization process. Serving as peer educators and fostering the professional development of one another can contribute to the overall learning experience of students and faculty.

Practitioners also play a vital role in the socialization process of graduate students. They can carve out time to be available to students to discuss issues and provide mentoring interactions. They can help students understand the professional world and guide them in their professional planning process. Most importantly, they can intentionally create opportunities for students to be involved in their unit activities through hosting assistantships, practica, and volunteer opportunities. They can also invite students to be part of staff development opportunities in their units and thereby help them make the connection between what they are learning in class and how to apply it in the field. Through these practical application experiences practitioners can provide feedback and support to graduate students as they learn what it means to be a competent and engaged professional.

Faculty plays a major role in the socialization of graduate students. It is their role to design the curriculum and to align it to professional competencies and outcomes that are needed for students to be successful professionals. Faculty can also contribute to the effective socialization of students by going beyond their roles as instructors and advisors within the academic program. They can seek out and intentionally design professional opportunities for students to engage in professional networks, professional associations, and in the practical experiences that will enrich the students' understanding and commitment to the profession. Faculty can help students manage and prepare for the transition as they graduate and move into their professional lives and help connect students to practitioners who can help guide them in their professional journeys.

The Future Knowledge and Skill Needs Within the Student Affairs Profession

As higher education and student affairs practitioners' roles within it change, the knowledge and skills that practitioners require will also change. A number of scholars (Bair, Keppler, & Phelps Tobin, 1998; Hirt & Creamer, 1998;

Kuk, et al.,2007; Woodard, 1998) stress that issues around changing student demographics, shifting economic conditions, increasing accountability, and demonstrated organizational effectiveness may require new knowledge and professional competencies, and as a result, new learning and socialization requirements within professional preparation programs.

The population of students who will access higher education in the future is expected to be vastly more diverse than at any previous time in history. This diversity will manifest itself in different forms including racial, ethnic, lifestyle, learning, religious, and political differences, as well as an increased number of students who require assistance to access the physical and learning environments within the institution. The ability to work within this diversity and to provide all students with the programs and services they need to be successful will require student affairs practitioners to develop core cross-cultural/multicultural competencies, community development skills within the content of diverse environments, and knowledge of underrepresented cultures and philosophies. They will also require knowledge of learning theory and its applications, as well as the ability to apply such a theory to traditional, underrepresented, and marginalized populations.

The old notions of the safe ivory tower are giving way to the realization of life-threatening vulnerabilities throughout campus environments, and a new form of in loco parentis is emerging. As the pathologies manifested in the greater society continue to play out on relatively open college campuses, issues of mental health, violence, and safety will increasingly become center stage for student affairs practitioners. Student affairs professionals, who are generally the frontline connection between students and the larger campus and community environments, will bear the brunt of increasing calls for protection from harm. These performance expectations will require new sets of knowledge and skills in the areas of crisis management, mental health and violence triaging, and safety prevention education, among others. Practitioners will also need enhanced skills in navigating "helicopter" parental involvement in the daily lives of students at all levels.

With the increasing amount of college costs, families will come to expect enhanced customized services and instantaneous problem solving regarding issues and concerns. Parents and students will increasingly demand individualized attention for the student's learning and educational needs. Student affairs practitioners will need to acquire greater skills in environmental theory and learning theory applications, and will need to effectively be able to at least triage with learning diagnostics tools. They will also need greater understanding of problem-solving techniques and be able to respond with "concierge-like" approaches to customer services.

As costs increase in the face of limited financial assistance, the focus on cost containment and program and service cost analysis will expand. Student affairs practitioners at all levels will be expected to be able to manage financial resources, effectively develop and implement cost containment initiatives, and also to generate new sources of revenue. This will require practitioners to develop enhanced financial management knowledge, skills, and tools.

As accountability makes its way into the everyday expectations and the lives of collegiate organizations, assessment, action research, and evaluation knowledge and skills will become necessary at every level within student affairs organizations. Not only will these skills be needed for program and service assessment, but the student affairs organization as a whole will likely be required to undergo regular organizational effectiveness assessments and to demonstrate the ability to respond organizationally to continuous change and environmental demands. This will require a sophisticated understanding of organizational behavior, change management, and organizational design applications, along with assessment and evaluation knowledge and tools.

While many of these new professional knowledge and skills will be learned or enhanced on the job, there will be expectations on preparation programs to at least address fundamental and entry-level knowledge and skill development in most of these areas. Administrators of preparation programs will be expected to at least socialize their students to these new expectations, knowledge, and skill competencies as they present the changing dynamics of the various roles that are attributed to the student affairs profession. It is also likely that organizers of preparation programs will be increasingly called on to retool and reorient existing practitioners related to some of these professional development and training needs that may be beyond the expertise and resources of many student affairs institutional organizations.

Conclusion

Student affairs preparation programs play a major role in the socialization of new professionals. The relevance and quality of professional socialization will vary depending on the nature of the program, including the focus and content of the curriculum, the quality and diversity of peers, interaction with faculty and practitioners, availability of professional practice opportunities, quality of supervision within internships and practicum, the learning and feedback processes within the program, and the methods of individual and program assessment. The nature and quality of the curriculum, faculty, and practitioners associated with professional preparation programs will continue to play important roles in the socialization of graduate students.

The future needs, expectations, and roles of student affairs practitioners are likely to change. These changes will require new knowledge and skills of student affairs practitioners at all levels within student affairs organizations. Administrators of preparation programs are likely to be expected to play a significant role in addressing these new and enhanced knowledge and skill requirements for entry-level practitioners, and may also be asked to assist in reeducating and retooling existing practitioners related to the changing roles and responsibilities within the profession of student affairs.

References

Amey, M. J., & Reesor, L. M. (2002). *Beginning your journey: A guide for new professionals in student affairs.* Washington, DC: National Association of Student Personnel Administrators.

Bair, C. R., Keppler, W. M., & Phelps Tobin, C. E. (1998). In N. J. Evans & C. E. Phelps (Eds.), *The state of the art of preparation and practice in student affairs* (pp. 21–46). Washington, DC: American College Personnel Association.

Burkard, A., Cole, D. C., Ott, M., & Stoflet, T. (2004). Entry-level competencies of new student affairs professionals: A delphi study. *NASPA Journal, 42,* 283–309.

Carpenter, D. S. (2003). Professionalism. In S. R. Komives, D. B. Woodard, Jr., and Associates (Eds.), *Student services: A handbook for the profession* (4th ed., pp. 573-591). San Francisco: Jossey-Bass.

Creamer, D. G., Janosik, S. M., Winston, R. B., & Kuk, L. (2001). *Quality assurance in student affairs: Role and commitment of NASPA.* Washington, DC: National Association of Student Personnel Administrators.

Cuyjet, M. J., Longwell-Grice, R., & Molina, E. (2009). Perceptions of new student affairs professionals and their supervisors regarding the application of competencies learned in preparation programs. *Journal of College Student Development, 50*(1), 104–119.

Dean, L. A. (2006). Master's-level student affairs professional preparation programs. In L. A. Dean (Ed.), *CAS professional standards for higher education* (6th ed., pp.

349–358). Washington, DC: Council for the Advancement of Standards in Higher Education.

Egan, J. M. (1989). Graduate School and the self: A theoretical view of some negative effects of professional socialization. *Teaching Sociology, 17*(2), 200–217.

Evans, N. J., & Phelps Tobin, C. E. (Eds.) (1998). *The state of the art of preparation and practice in student affairs.* Washington, DC: American College Personnel Association.

Evers, F. T., Rush, J. C. & Berdrow, I. (1998). *The bases of competence: Skills for lifelong learning and employability.* San Francisco: Jossey-Bass.

Garland, P. H., & Grace, T. W. (1993). *New perspectives for student affairs professionals: Evolving realities, responsibilities, and roles.* ASHE-ERIC Higher Education Report No. 7. Washington, DC: George Washington University, Graduate School of Education and Human Development.

Herdlein, R. J., III. (2004). Survey of chief student affairs officers regarding relevance of graduate preparation of new professionals. *NASPA Journal, 42*(1), 51–71.

Hirt, J. B., & Creamer, D. (1998). Issues facing student affairs professionals: The four realms of professional life. In N. J. Evans & C. E. Phelps (Eds.), *The state of the art of preparation and practice in student affairs* (pp. 47–60). Washington, DC: American College Personnel Association.

Knight, J. (1973). *Medical students: Doctors in the making.* New York: Appleton Century-Crofts.

Komives, S. R. (1998). Linking student affairs preparation with practice. In N. J. Evans & C. E. Phelps Tobin (Eds.), *The state of the art of preparation and practice in student affairs* (pp. 177–200). Washington, DC: American College Personnel Association.

Kuk, L. (2007). Review of Student Affairs Preparation Programs. Unpublished raw data.

Kuk, L., Cobb, B., & Forrest, C. (2007). Perceptions of competencies of entry-level practitioners in student affairs. *NASPA Journal 44*(4), 664–691.

Kuk, L., & Hughes, B. (2003). Bridging the competency gap for new professionals. *Journal of Student Affairs, 12*, 71–84.

Upcraft, M. L. (1998). Do graduate programs really prepare practitioners? In N. J. Evans & C. E. Phelps (Eds.), *The state of the art of preparation and practice in student affairs* (pp. 235–237). Washington, DC: American College Personnel Association.

Waple, J. N. (2006). An assessment of skills and competencies necessary for entry-level student affairs work. *NASPA Journal, 43*(1), 1–18.

Weidman, J. C., Twale, D. J., & Stein, E. L. (2001). *Socialization of graduate and professional students in higher education.* ASHE-ERIC Higher Education Report, Vol. 28, No. 3. San Francisco: Jossey-Bass.

Winston, R. B., & Creamer, D. G. (1997). *Improving staffing practices in student affairs*. San Francisco: Jossey-Bass.

Woodard, D. (1998). Societal influences on higher education and student affairs. In N. J. Evans and C. E. Phelps (Eds.), *The state of the art of preparation and practice in student affairs* (pp. 3–20). Washington, DC: American College Personnel Association.

6

ORIENTATION IN THE SOCIALIZATION PROCESS

Sue A. Saunders and Diane L. Cooper

New professionals entering the student affairs workforce start their positions with decidedly mixed emotions and myriad questions. Relief about finding a position, anxiety about whether one will fit into the institutional culture, questions about whether one is really competent enough to do the job well, and excitement about new possibilities are all part of the experience of new professionals in transition (Magolda & Carnaghi, 2004; Renn & Hodges, 2007). A well-constructed, intentionally planned orientation is one way to address these issues as well as to improve job performance, foster confidence, build organizational commitment, and reduce attrition from the field. This chapter (a) examines the research and scholarship that explores the efficacy of different types of orientation approaches, (b) provides strategies for an effective orientation curriculum, and (c) discusses informal, experiential learning strategies that can further the benefits of structured orientation over an extended period of time.

Orientation and New Professional Effectiveness: Empirical Support

Student affairs units and higher education institutions have traditionally provided some type of structured experience to introduce newcomers to their jobs, their colleagues, and the larger organization (Saunders & Cooper, 2003). There is a considerable amount of anecdotal support that effective orientations are correlated with important employee development outcomes.

In a variety of business organizations, orientation programs are commonly perceived to increase new employees' morale and productivity (Addams, 1985; Mechling, 1996), reduce stress about a new position (Lockwood, 2001), improve performance (Carmeli & Tishler, 2004), and increase job satisfaction for employer and new employee (Mechling). In the higher education milieu, orientation is viewed as essential for effective job performance and satisfaction for student affairs professionals entering their first positions (Rosen, Taube, & Wordsworth, 1980; Saunders & Cooper, 2003).

The empirical support for orientation leading to important employee developmental outcomes, such as organizational commitment, job satisfaction, intention to remain in one's position or profession, is less definitive (Wanous, 1993). First, the efficacy of new employee orientation programs has not been heavily researched by scholars in student affairs, human resource management, or organizational psychology. Second, the few studies that do exist paint a somewhat mixed picture.

One of the outcomes most examined is organizational commitment. In a well-controlled study by Klein and Weaver (2000), new clerical, administrative professional, and technical employees in a large education organization were given the option of attending an institution-wide, three-hour orientation program about the organization's history, traditions, and purpose. Those who chose to attend demonstrated a higher degree of organizational commitment or expressed loyalty as compared to nonattendees when surveyed 1 to 2 months following the orientation event. This study also explored socialization (understanding and adapting to the culture of an organization), a concept that has been associated with intent to remain in one's position and with effective job performance (Feldman, 1989). In the Klein and Weaver study, orientation attendees, as compared to nonattendees, had higher degrees of understanding about the organization's history, goals, and values, and an increased level of interaction with coworkers. Although this study did not explore attrition or employee attitudes over an extended period of time, it is significant that a short orientation about organizational culture can have such a demonstrable effect, especially on interaction patterns.

Another study (Hellman, 2000) found that the association between attending orientation about organizational culture and commitment to the employer is strong as long as the newcomers attended orientation during their first 60 days with the company. Those who attended formal orientation earlier in their tenure felt more positively about their employer than those who did not participate in the organization's initial orientation. This certainly supports the importance of early, well-designed interventions with new professionals about organizational expectations, history, culture, and values.

The fact that orientation processes are structured so differently across institutions and functional areas (Dean, Thompson, Saunders, & Cooper, 2008) may explain the dearth of well-controlled studies about the effects of orientation on performance and commitment in student affairs organizations. In addition, since structured orientation of some sort is ubiquitous in student affairs, finding a control group that does not participate is problematic when conducting quantitative research. A discussion of the elements that might be included in an orientation program may help address this conundrum.

Components of Effective Orientation Programs

Interestingly, some qualitative researchers have looked carefully at the processes used by business organizations judged to have highly effective orientation programs (Martinez, 1992; McGarrell, 1984). From these studies, one can draw conclusions that are applicable to student affairs orientation programs. In one such qualitative study, Winkler and Janger (1998) conducted in-depth interviews with the following three organizations: Texas Instruments, a leader in technology; KPMG Peat Marwick, a professional services firm; and Intercorp, a managed-care services company. These authors determined several principles that were particularly important to a successful orientation. Beginning orientation during the hiring and recruitment process was viewed as essential. Employees' perceptions of the organization's expectations and culture begin with their first contact. For this reason, these early contacts should be intentionally designed to demonstrate the values of the organization. The first day of work was also viewed as very important in socializing the new employee. All too often new employees spend their first day filling out forms and figuring out how to get themselves to lunch. In effective orientations the first day is carefully planned to shape optimal attitudes about the organization. Additionally, effective orientation experiences incorporate meaningful and intense support. This should incorporate three types of support: (a) the direct supervisor who coaches and communicates performance expectations, (b) a mentor (could be a colleague) for information about unwritten rules and norms, and (c) division or human resources training staff who provide information on policies, procedures, and benefits. Finally, it is important to offer an ongoing orientation process and formal orientation or training that explicitly communicates expectations, values, and ways of being and doing within the particular orientation.

The conclusions drawn from research about effective orientation in business organizations confirm the scholarship about orienting nascent student affairs professionals (Saunders & Cooper, 2003; Winston & Creamer, 1997; Winston, Torres, Carpenter, McIntire, & Peterson, 2001). Specifically, the scholarship about orientation in student affairs contexts affirms that new employees should be given clear expectations about job duties and the relevant performance standards used in position evaluations. Additionally, orientation for new student affairs professionals should address the implicit, unspoken expectations for staff and salient characteristics of the organizational culture.

Orientation Needs of New Student Affairs Professionals

Renn and Hodges (2007) conducted an in-depth qualitative study of student affairs professionals on their first job and found that these individuals desired considerably more early instruction about their responsibilities and performance expectations than they received from their supervisors and/or institutions. This lack of orientation or explicit training left many of these new professionals highly frustrated and uncertain about their capacity to do their jobs well.

Traditionally, we interpret the term *new staff orientation* as consisting of a structured event or series of activities that occur before and during the early weeks of being on the job. Often orientation is defined as formal classroom training sessions with experienced staff "teaching" such discrete concepts as crisis management procedures, harassment policies, or referral to community resources to a group of eager but tired new professionals. In this traditional scenario, the new professional trainees tend to function as passive recipients waiting to hear everything needed to be successful in their new job. Many of us have argued on our own campuses that new student orientation needs to be more than a one-shot program, yet we tend not to view new employees as also benefiting from more of a University 101 approach with an extended period of instruction, small groups, and active learning methods

Professional literature (Flion & Pepermans, 1998; Saunders & Cooper, 2003; Winston & Creamer, 1997) and common sense indicate that new professionals need to learn about procedures, culture, and expectations before they work directly with students or colleagues. The classroom-type approach is efficient, particularly when there is a group of new professionals all preparing to start working at the same time. Yet, this type of formal orientation is not without limitations. Newer research on transfer of learning (Sheckley & Keeton, 2001) showed that "information learning in classroom training programs 'evaporates' within six weeks or so after the end of the program—possibly because the information is not deeply processed and linked to information already in memory" (p. 75).

These studies demonstrate that new professionals desire and need more from an orientation to their positions and the organization than typically occurs in practice. New professionals want more time dedicated to the process, greater depth and breadth of information provided, and intense support as they begin this new phase of their career. Couple that information with the fact that we know there is a payoff for the organization for providing thorough orientation programs, and perhaps it is time to consider an intentional, formal orientation curriculum design for student affairs practice.

What Should Be Included in a Formal Orientation Curriculum?

On most campuses, hiring of new staff does not always occur at the same time of the year, making it difficult to devote resources to formal orientation programs. In addition, many would argue that even though we are all working toward student learning and development, we remain affiliated with specific programs or services that have specific training needs. For example, new professionals in residential life may need to become skilled in building safety procedures. On the other hand, career services professionals need to learn the computerized career guidance programs available on the campus. Orientation teaches specialized job skills and procedures as well as a general overview and introduction to the culture, traditions, values, structures, and language of the institution. Winston and Creamer (1997) cautioned that "new staff need to know how business is conducted [and not conducted] in

hidden as well as visible ways" (p. 173). The challenge in designing the orientation curriculum goes far beyond the ropes to know. To be truly effective,
it must also include information about the possible barriers, pitfalls, sacred
cows, and covert rules of operation.

It is important to plan the curriculum to be an ongoing process rather
than a one-time meeting or program. As new professionals interact with the
environment, new issues will emerge, and their perceptions of organizational
politics, culture, and relationships will become more complex. Good supervision will include processing time for questions and perceptions. For more
information about supervision, see chapter 7.

Supplying Positive Start-Up Information

Any formal curriculum must consider that orientation begins at the time of
hiring. Saunders and Cooper (2003) provided a comprehensive list of action
steps supervisors should consider prior to the arrival of a new professional,
including

- Creating a plan to send pertinent information to the new employee
  at various points during the period between selection and the first day
  at work.
- Allotting time for several telephone calls or e-mail conversations during this period.
- Constructing a first-week orientation schedule for the new employee
  including meetings with Human Resources, participation in any
  institutional orientation activities, meetings with colleagues and representatives from offices that work closely with the position, and
  attending any division or departmental welcome activities.
- Publicizing your new professional's selection to the campus information office and other appropriate media.
- Making sure that the office is ready for the first day and that the new
  employee knows the specific details for arriving on campus. (p. 28)

Supervisors need to be prepared to answer questions about everything
from finding a church or temple to how to find good day care providers. For
new professionals, this may be the first time they have faced decisions about
signing up for employee benefits, finding a physician, or buying a home.
Many of these issues are not directly work related, but creating a supportive

relationship before the new professional starts work will carry over to the first day on the job. How these start-up activities are handled (or not) establishes the concept of how employees are valued in the institution and begins the supervisory relationship on a positive note.

Structuring the Initial Orientation

When the new professional arrives on campus, a structured orientation program should begin. Winston and Creamer (1997) suggested a number of activities that a supervisor should put in place, most important of which is arranging meetings for the new professional with the key individuals they will work with on a regular basis. Getting acquainted with important staff, faculty, and students is essential in the early days of the structured orientation as is understanding the job tasks, institutional policies, work site environment, and organizational culture and traditions (Saunders & Cooper, 2003).

A study by Dean et al. (2008) indicated that new professionals may not experience these recommended activities. About 300 new professionals completed a survey that asked if certain topics were (a) important for success in their current job and (b) adequately addressed in the orientation of their current job. Table 6.1 highlights the results of this survey.

The results of this study showed a gap between many of the issues new professionals feel they need to know about or understand and the inclusion of those issues in the formal orientation process. Previous research noted the problems that result for the institution and new professionals when orientation does not include an adequate socialization process for the job. For example, Amey (1990, 1998) outlined problems related to role conflict or ambiguity, inadequate understanding of the scope of responsibility, and dissonance between perceived position opportunities and those that actually exist. Intentional curriculum development for orientation must include a method for addressing this information as well as a purposeful way to process the resulting affective responses.

Interpreting Organizational Culture

Orientation programs usually include the rules and policies related to a position provided typically in the form of handbooks and/or policy manuals. These programs may also include a series of meetings between the new professional and his or her supervisor to discuss the same topics but in the context of the position or department. A formal curriculum would also provide a

TABLE 6.1
New Professionals' Perception of Their Orientation

Topic	Important to Success in My Current Position %	Inadequately or Not Addressed in Position Orientation %
Detailed job expectations	96.4	16.9
Performance standards expected	96.4	24.1
Understanding "unwritten" expectations	97.1	32.7
Institutional culture	97.7	23.1
Office culture	97.3	25.0
Understanding office procedures	97.0	17.2
Anticipating real or potential problems	90.1	35.5
Understanding the role of student affairs on campus	84.23	2.1

Note. From *Efficacy of Orientation for New Student Affairs Professionals,* by Dean et al., 2008, Adapted with permission of the author.

mechanism for open discussions about organizational culture and unwritten norms, which can often cause stress and lead to job dissatisfaction and ultimately professional attrition (Tseng, 2004; Tull, 2006)

How do we look outside the organizational system to help new professionals interpret the traditions, language, structures, and values of our institutions? This is not an easy task by any means. Schaef (1981) wrote about the difficulty of being clear in our understanding of a system that one lives in daily. Those supervisors who have been in an organization for a period of time see things from their own experiences which are inextricably enmeshed in the environment and various relationships. Supervisors rarely have the luxury of the time it would take to disengage from a system long enough to really see what a person new to the system is encountering. This is why it is so important to have discussions about organizational culture set in a context where the new professional feels secure to talk about what he or she is experiencing and is able to question the traditions, structures, and values without fear of being ridiculed or minimized in any way.

Discussing Diversity

If new professionals are to understand the organizational culture, they need to participate in open discussions about values related to diversity. These discussions should go beyond institutional policies and should include attention to the value of diversity in our lives. El-Khawas (2003) noted that "college and university administrators, counselors, and faculty certainly try to recognize many aspects of difference among their students . . . yet there is probably more to understand, a deeper awareness awaits" (p. 45). Although we may be making inroads in our work with diversity issues on our campus with students, much work remains in supervision and in professional development activities for our staff on this topic. Freeman, Nuss, and Barr (1993) stated that "an effective orientation of new staff members will reinforce the expectations and values of diversity and multiculturalism within institutions, divisions, and functional areas" (p. 463). In all student affairs functional areas, new professionals need to work effectively with all students, faculty, and staff.

Supervisors cannot, and should not, assume that new professionals have had exposure to working with students from diverse populations prior to their employment, although most graduate preparation programs do have required course work such as theories of multicultural identity development. Some programs have gone further and added specific supervised practice experiences (practica, internships, etc.) that require students to work with diverse student populations (e.g., students of color, students with disabilities, adult students, international students, etc.). Additionally, the general character and needs of students at a particular type of institution may be quite different from those previously encountered by the new professional. For example, a new professional who comes with prior experience at doctoral institutions will likely need explicit information about the common characteristics of students at a liberal arts institution. See chapter 3 for more information about the ways institutional type affects new professionals' socialization.

Orientation to a new position needs to build upon the new professional's incoming level of knowledge, skills, behaviors, and beliefs about working with diverse people within the context of the students who are served by the place of employment. If additional or specific diversity education is necessary, it may be possible to begin that process prior to the new professional's arrival on campus through directed readings, Webinars, or workshop/conference attendance. Having a sense of the organization's values and traditions related to diversity will set a context for further learning, relationship building, and continuing professional development once employment begins. An orientation curriculum must devote time and attention to this topic.

Learning About Technology

There seems to be a growing assumption that new professionals are coming to the job with many years of experience working with technology (Arend, 2005). Supervisors need to consider learning about technology in the same way they approach learning office policies and procedures. Most graduate preparation programs are incorporating more professional uses of technology into their curriculum but some specialized technology functions will still require on-the-job training. This will be particularly true, for example, for in-house programs that address scheduling, billing, human resources, and assessment practices, to name but a few.

Orientation must include information about the formal expectations of technology use as well as guidelines about informal use. New professionals coming directly from the role of student may believe that e-mail, instant messaging, Facebook/MySpace, and Internet surfing are all part of the typical work day (Lloyd, Dean, & Cooper, 2007). If the institution has policies related to technology use, these need to be discussed with the new professional as soon as possible in the orientation process so that appropriate work habits can be established early on. For example, in many states, open record laws make all communication conducted on state-owned institutional equipment open to legal processes. Another conversation may be needed about the type of pictures and content the new professional should have on social Web sites such as Facebook or MySpace. The transition from student to employee may be particularly difficult when it comes to technology use, so supervisors would be well advised to have this conversation before any organizationally defined inappropriate uses occur.

Methods to Promote Continuous Organizational Learning

One way to minimize the evaporation of gains from formal orientation programs is to intentionally enhance workplace learning by using the results of relevant experiential learning research. Therefore the remainder of this section outlines some of the research about workplace learning and offers suggestions about how supervisors might incorporate these findings into ongoing, intentional strategies that complement formal orientation.

Using Principles From Experiential Learning Research

Some experiential learning researchers who advocate a situated cognition approach argue that understanding and experiencing the context where one solves problems is essential (Anderson, Reder, & Simon, 1996; Fenwick, 2003; Hansman, 2001). In other words, one cannot simply transfer complex learning gained in one problem situation to another, but one must participate in the culture and use the tools of the environment where the new problems will be addressed. This situated cognition perspective questions the assumption that meaningful, deep, complex learning—the type required of effective student affairs practitioners—can be acquired before one experiences the organizational culture, the working relationships, the values of the institution, or the tasks that are required. Further, expecting a new professional to transfer learning acquired in a formal orientation situation to the messy, ambiguous world of practice requires additional intentional interventions.

The interventions designed to augment formal orientation should address four employee development principles: (a) focus on providing experience with real-world problems, (b) encourage active reflection on experience, (c) incorporate the learning goals of the new professional, and (d) ensure that new professionals know what they are expected to learn and have a path to reach expectations (Sheckley & Keeton, 2001).

Real-World Experience-Based Strategies

The truism that experience is the best teacher is supported by a significant amount of research. Greater levels of experience enhance one's ability to find shortcuts in problem solving (Chi, Glaser, & Farr, 1988). Employees with more experience typically have more tacit knowledge—that type of practical wisdom that allows for seemingly intuitive problem solving (Reber, 1993). Finally, experience in solving complex, real-world problems leads to increased complexity of resolution strategies that can be generalized to new situations (Smith, Ford, & Kozlowski, 1997).

A simple but risky way to gain experience resolving problems is to assign tasks and assume that the new professional will develop expertise on the job.

This approach is fraught with peril, especially when new professionals are millennials and less likely to see mistakes and failures as learning experiences. A more prudent approach is to modify some elements of the cognitive apprenticeship approach (Brandt, Farmer, & Buckmaster, 1993).

The first step of the cognitive apprenticeship approach indicates that it is extremely helpful to provide opportunities for new professionals to observe an experienced staff member successfully resolving a problem. This is more effective if observation is of the entire activity and not just individual components. For example, before facilitating a career development seminar, a new professional should watch an experienced professional role model run the seminar and observe the model developing the lesson plan. To be effective, these observations should include debriefing, with the model explaining what he or she said, what activities were chosen, how unexpected situations were dealt with and why. The goal is for the new professional to develop a mental model of what successful career development seminars look like. Therefore it is important that the new professional function as an observer in several different career development seminars.

The next step of the model is approximating, in which the new professional completes the task with extensive coaching and scaffolding. Such coaching or scaffolding could include cofacilitating a career development seminar with the model and the new professional. The model would provide feedback and could actually conduct part of the facilitation. The goal for the new professional is to begin self-monitoring and self-correcting her or his own performance. Over time, the coaching should decrease and eventually fade away. To be successful, however, the cognitive apprenticeship approach must incorporate adequate reflection.

Active Reflection on Experience

The term *reflection* is ubiquitous in student affairs work. But the meaning of this process is often obscured. Active, meaningful reflection that improves learning includes the following elements: (a) slowing down and being open to multiple perspectives; (b) actively analyzing, synthesizing, and evaluating experience; and (c) critically examining underlying beliefs, personal goals, practices, and inconsistencies (York-Barr, Sommers, Ghere, & Montie, 2001). According to Merriam, Caffarella, and Baumgartner (2007), the "outcome of reflection is to gain deeper insights that lead to action" (p. 173). This type of deep reflection requires that new professionals and their supervisors allow for adequate time and structure to accomplish these complex aims.

Some authors believe that reflection occurs best in discussion with one or more individuals (Sheckley & Keeton, 2001). Further, reflection is best focused on a specific work-related event or problem. Those participating in the dialogue should have adequate trust to question and challenge their beliefs and assumptions, look for the discrepancies between beliefs and actions (Osterman & Kottkamp, 2004), and examine their feelings associated with the problem (Boud, Keogh, & Walker, 1996). Obviously this type of reflection requires time and emotional energy. It will not work to have a "reflection period" as a 10-minute addendum to a staff meeting. Also, no efficient staff team could afford to deeply reflect on every issue. This type of reflection is highly useful as a part of staff retreats and other extended meetings. Fostering reflective dialogues of this type will encourage individual staff members to reflect carefully on their own individual problems and tasks. It is essential that the critical questions that guide reflection be carefully framed. York-Barr et al. (2001) created a four-step process for reflection that included:

1. Picking an event and asking what happened.
2. Analyzing and interpreting the event by asking "Why did things happen this way?" "Why did we act the way we did?" "How did the context affect the experience?" "Did past experiences affect the way we reacted?" "How?"
3. Making sense of the event in terms of future performance by asking "What have we learned from this event?" "How can we improve?" "How might this event affect our future thinking, behaving, interacting?"
4. Thinking about implications for action by asking "What am I going to remember to think about the next time this situation comes up?" "How could I set up conditions to increase the likelihood of productive interactions and learnings?" (p. 47).

For many new professionals this type of reflection can be very intimidating. It might, however, be encouraged as a part of a mentoring program for new professionals or with a small community of practice (see Communities of Practice section, pp. 123–124).

Incorporating New Professional's Learning Goals

In work with students, many student affairs professionals have adopted the model of Baxter Magolda and King (2004) as a way to foster students' learning and development. These authors identified three principles of effective learning environments that are relevant to how we continue the learning initiated at employee orientation. Specifically Baxter Magolda and King recommend that educators should (a) validate learners' capacity to know by soliciting students' opinions, (b) situate learners' experiences by using students' knowledge as a basis for continued learning, and (c) mutually construct meaning by having the expert and learner develop knowledge together to arrive at a more meaningful understanding.

All three of these principles can be addressed by having new professionals create specific learning goals once the formal orientation period has ended. These learning goals should be specifically designed to help the new professional continue to learn how to effectively perform in his or her new position. Such goals could serve as the basis for structuring an effective mentoring program. It is essential that these goals are carefully constructed with outcomes that are measurable, realistic, and meaningful—to the organization and to the individual. The learning goals should not simply be a vehicle for the individual to enhance skill development, but should also attend to the prevalent issues or problems of the organization. The process of creating mutually beneficial learning goals has the corollary benefit of encouraging the new professional to learn about the organization's issues and goals. Learning goals are also an excellent vehicle for the new professional and mentor/supervisor to mutually construct knowledge.

Map the Process to Achieve Learning Goals

With professionals new to an environment, determining the feasibility of learning goals is nearly impossible to accomplish without guidance. New professionals will not know the culture, the campus politics, or the leadership styles of institutional decision makers. Because of this lack of knowledge, a new professional's individual attempts to learn can be seen as naive, insensitive, or at worst, arrogant. For example, Alexandra, a new counselor in career services wanted to learn more about employer relations, even though this was not one of her direct job responsibilities. When she quickly attempted to offer her services to the office coordinator of employer relations, she was

rebuffed. Why? The coordinator had built a very specific procedure of culti-
vating employer representatives and simply did not have the time to teach a
new professional. Careful guidance from a mentor about how to achieve this
goal could have prevented this problem.

The process by which a new professional can achieve learning goals
should be carefully mapped out with the active involvement of a mentor.
Often new professionals' frustration is associated with wasted energy pursuing goals that are not feasible. Sternberg (1994) argued that the key cognitive
task in problem solving is to separate the relevant information from the irrel-
evant. If the aim of structured and informal orientation is to encourage the
employee to learn the information and skills necessary for effective performance, then the path should be a detailed written document. That document
should identify the connections between learning goals and the activities that
will foster goal achievement.

Communities of Practice

Although the conceptual details of communities of practice (Wenger, 1998)
are beyond the scope of this chapter, the fundamentals of this approach have
merit for ongoing orientation. Wenger believes that individual learning and
skill development are best developed through the synergy of a community of
practice. The community of practice is not simply a social group that fulfills
affiliation needs or a committee that emphasizes task completion. Instead
this approach requires sustained interaction among a group of employees
with a shared "domain of interest" (Wenger, 2007). Further, in a community of practice, members share expertise and help each other learn how to
do their jobs better. Simple water-cooler conversations about what's happen-
ing on campus are not sufficient; there must be an intensity of interaction
that fosters creativity and further learning. A community of practice can be
more or less intentional. The staff team that gathers for lunch in the college
cafeteria having meaningful discussions about how to help students in academic difficulty is a community of practice, even though the members might
not initially acknowledge it as such.

Although this simple but powerful concept often happens naturally, it is
an important one to acknowledge when thinking about new professionals'
incorporation into their jobs. Supervisors can invite new professionals into
community of practice conversations if appropriate, thereby providing them
with powerful learning opportunities. New professionals can also create their

own communities of practice. These communities can be constructed with colleagues from a graduate program and the dialogue can continue online rather than face-to-face. The challenges of such powerful communities of practice are many. Without conscious attention to the purpose of the community of practice, it can degenerate into gossip sessions or complaining sessions. If the community consists of people at different levels of the organization, there may be issues of power and confidentiality that would need to be addressed. However, the ways in which this approach fosters tacit knowledge or administrative common sense are extremely valuable.

New Professionals Orienting Themselves

The bulk of this chapter has emphasized what supervisors and institutions can do to orient new professionals. Feedback from new professionals (Dean et al., 2008) suggests that in many cases supervisors do not provide a comprehensive, structured orientation nor do they initiate informal, ongoing activities to facilitate continued learning about the new position. What then is a new professional to do?

Many of the strategies suggested in this chapter can be accomplished with or without supervisor or institutional leadership. New professionals can create their own "curriculum" to learn about institutional expectations. They can request information from their supervisor rather than waiting for the supervisor to take the lead. New professionals could carefully read important institutional documents, such as strategic plans, goals, view books, admissions Web sites, and press releases, to get a sense of the institutional culture. Volunteering for committees where the new professional is in contact with staff who have a history at the institution creates a network that can provide valuable insight into the unwritten rules and values of the university culture.

Many of the strategies suggested to improve continuous organizational learning can easily be accomplished without supervisor leadership. In fact, reflection on experience and communities of practice are often informal strategies that operate without any supervisory involvement. Even if new professionals are not required to create learning goals, nothing prevents them from carefully constructing learning goals and documenting achievement with a colleague or even a mentor from outside the institution.

Comprehensive orientation as described in this chapter is a critical component of success in a particular position. More importantly, effective learning about a new position translates into ongoing commitment to the profession and growth as a new professional. If an orientation is not being provided, new professionals can take many steps to maximize their own learning.

Conclusion

This chapter is built on the literature regarding new professional orientation and provides a rationale for formal, structured orientation programs and processes for new professionals. A formal curriculum is necessary to ensure that all aspects of the job, relationships, and the organization have been addressed (Saunders & Cooper, 2003). It is necessary not only to consider the written rules and regulations but also to include the unwritten norms, traditions, and processes to ensure a smooth transition and to increase job satisfaction and performance (Roderer & Hickman, 2000; Winston & Creamer, 1997). Literature about workplace learning indicates that learning goals, active reflection, and experiential learning activities are useful complements to the traditional orientation (Sheckley & Keeton, 2001). Continuing to focus intentionally on new professional socialization will also help new professionals become part of larger communities of practice on campus (Wenger, 1998).

References

Addams, H. (1985). Up to speed in 90 days: An orientation plan. *Personnel Journal, 64*, 35–38.

Amey, M. J. (1990). Bridging the gap between expectations and realities. In K. M. Moore & S. B. Twombly (Eds.), *Administrative careers and the marketplace* (pp. 79–89). New Directions for Higher Education, No. 72. San Francisco: Jossey-Bass.

Amey, M. J. (1998). Unwritten rules: Organizational and political realities of the job. In M. J. Amey & L. M. Ressor (Eds.), *Beginning the journey: A guide for new professionals in student affairs* (pp. 13–30). Washington, DC: National Association of Student Personnel Administrators.

Anderson, J. R., Reder, L. M., & Simon, H. A. (1996). Situated learning and education. *Educational Researcher, 25*(4), 5–11.

Arend, B. D. (2005). New patterns of student engagement. *About Campus* (July–August), 30–32.

Baxter Magolda, M. B., & King, P. M. (Eds.). (2004). *Learning partnerships: Theory and models of practice to educate for self-authorship.* Sterling, VA: Stylus.

Boud, D., Keogh, R., & Walker, D. (1996). Promoting reflection in learning: A model. In R. Edwards, A. Hanson, & P. Raggatt (Eds.), *Boundaries of adult learning* (pp. 32–56). New York: Routledge.

Brandt, B. L., Farmer, J. A., Jr., & Buckmaster, A. (1993). Cognitive apprenticeship approach to helping adults learning. In D. Flannery (Ed.), *Applying cognitive learning theory to adult learning* (pp. 69–78). San Francisco: Jossey Bass.

Carmeli, A., & Tishler, A. (2004). The relationship between intangible organizational elements and organizational performance. *Strategic Management Journal, 25,* 1257–1278.

Chi, M. T. H., Glaser, R. I., & Farr, M. (1988). *The nature of experience.* Hillsdale, NJ: Erlbaum.

Dean, L., Thompson, G., Saunders, S., & Cooper, D. (2008). *Efficacy of orientation for new student affairs professionals.* Unpublished manuscript. University of Georgia, Athens.

El-Khawas, E. (2003). The many dimensions of student diversity. In S. R. Komives, D. B. Woodard, Jr., & Associates (Eds.), *Student services: A handbook for the profession* (pp. 45–62). San Francisco: Jossey-Bass.

Feldman, D. C. (1989). Careers in organizations: Recent trend and future directions. *Journal of Management, 15,* 135–156.

Fenwick, T. (2003). *Learning through experience: Troubling orthodoxies and intersecting questions.* Malabar, FL: Krieger.

Flion, I. A., & Pepermans, R. G. (1998) Exploring the relationship between orientation programs and current job satisfaction. *Psychological Reports, 83,* 367–370.

Freeman, M. A., Nuss, E. M., & Barr, M. J. (1993). Meeting the needs of staff diversity. In M. J. Barr (Ed.) *The handbook of student affairs administration* (pp. 455–467). San Francisco: Jossey-Bass.

Hansman, C. A. (2001). Context based adult learning. In S. Merriam (Ed.), *The new update on adult learning* (pp. 43–51). New Directions for Adult and Continuing Education, No. 89. San Francisco: Jossey-Bass.

Hellman, S. W. (2000). An evaluative study of the impact of new employee orientation on newcomer organizational commitment (Doctoral dissertation, Pepperdine University, 2000). *Dissertation Abstracts International, 61,* 678A.

Klein, H. J. & Weaver, N. A. (2000). Effectiveness of an organizational level orientation training program in the socialization of new hires. *Personnel Psychology, 53,* 47–66.

Lockwood, S. (2001). Enhancing employee development: Development and testing of a new employee orientation protocol. (Doctoral dissertation, California School of Professional Psychology, 2001). *Dissertation Abstracts International, 62* (03), 1627B.

Lloyd, J. M., Dean, L. A., & Cooper, D. L. (2007) Students' technology use and its effects on peer relationships, academic involvement, and healthy lifestyles. *NASPA Journal, 44*(3), 481–495.

Magolda, P. M., & Carnaghi, J. E. (Eds.). (2004). *Job one: Experiences of new professionals in student affairs.* Lanham, MD: University Press of America.

Martinez, M. N. (1992). Disney training works magic. *HR Magazine, 37*(5) 53–57.

McGarrell, E. J. (1984) An organizational system that builds productivity. *Personnel Administrator 34*(8) 56–60.

Mechling, M. (1996). Orientation and training of employees. Retrieved October 26, 2007, from http://ohioline.osu.edu/hrm-fact/0003.html

Merriam, S. B., Caffarella, R. S., & Baumgartner, L. M. (2007). *Learning in adulthood: A comprehensive guide.* (3rd ed.). San Francisco: Jossey-Bass.

Osterman, K. F., & Kottkamp, R. B. (2004). *Reflective practice for educators: Professional development to improve student learning* (2nd ed.). Thousand Oaks, CA: Corwin Press.

Reber, A. S. (1993). *Implicit learning and tacit knowledge: An essay on the cognitive unconscious* (Oxford Psychological Series, No. 19). New York: Oxford University Press.

Renn, K. A., & Hodges, J. (2007). The first year on the job: Experiences of new professionals in student affairs. *NASPA Journal, 44*(2), 367–392.

Roderer, P., and Hickman, S., (2000). Successful orientation programs. *Training and Development, 54*(4), p. 59.

Rosen, J. A., Taube, S. R., & Wordsworth, E. L. (1980). The first professional year: Interviews with new professionals at SUNY-Stony Brook. *NASPA Journal, 17*(3), 52–59.

Saunders, S. A., & Cooper, D. L. (2003). Orientation: Building the foundations for success. In S. M. Janosik, D. G. Creamer, J. B. Hirt, R. B. Winston, Jr., S. A. Saunders, & D. L. Cooper (Eds.), *Supervising new professionals in student affairs* (pp. 17–42). New York: Brunner-Routledge.

Schaef, A. W. (1981). *Women's reality.* NY: HarperCollins.

Sheckley, B. G., & Keeton, M. T. (2001). *Improving employee development: Perspectives from research and practice.* Chicago: Council for Adult and Experiential Learning.

Smith, E. M., Ford, J. K., & Kozlowski, S. W. J. (1997). Building adaptive expertise: Implications for training design strategies. In M. A. Quinones & A. Ehrenstein

(Eds.), *Training for a rapidly changing workplace: Applications of psychological research* (pp. 89–118). Washington, DC: American Psychological Association.

Sternberg, R. J. (1994). Intelligence. In R. J. Sternberg (Ed.), *Thinking and problem solving* (pp. 266–288). San Diego: Academic Press.

Tseng, W. (2004). A meta-analysis of student affairs professionals' job satisfaction. *Journal of Taiwan Normal University Education, 49*(2), 161–182.

Tull, A. (2006). Synergistic supervision, job satisfaction, and intention to turnover of new professionals in student affairs. *Journal of College Student Development, 47*(4), 465–480.

Wanous, J. P. (1993). Newcomer orientation programs that facilitate organizational entry. In J. Schuler, J. L. Farh, M. Smith (Eds.), *Personnel selection and assessment.* Hillsdale, NJ: Erlbaum

Wenger, E. (1998). *Communities of practice: Learning, meaning, and identity.* Cambridge, UK: Cambridge University Press.

Wenger, E. (2007). *Communities of practice: An introduction.* Retrieved September 28, 2007, from http://www.ewenger.com/theory/index.htm

Winkler, K., & Janger, I. (1998). New employee assimilation. *Executive Excellence Inc., 15,* 15–16.

Winston, R. B., Jr., & Creamer, D. G. (1997). *Improving staffing practices in student affairs.* San Francisco: Jossey-Bass.

Winston, R. B. Jr., Torres, V., Carpenter, D. S., McIntire, D. D., and Peterson, B. (2001). Staffing in student affairs: A survey of practices. *College Student Affairs Journal, 21*(1), 7–25.

York-Barr, J., Sommers, W. A., Ghere, G. S., & Montie, J. (2001). *Reflective practice to improve schools: An action guide for educators.* Thousand Oaks, CA: Corwin Press.

7

SUPERVISION AND MENTORSHIP IN THE SOCIALIZATION PROCESS

Ashley Tull

T his chapter, like others in part three, addresses effective socialization strategies—specifically the formation of critical relationships. Active engagement in supervisory and mentor relationships is important for effective socialization of new professionals in student affairs administration. Effective supervision and mentoring enable new professionals to be successful when they encounter issues on the job. Some of these issues include commitment to personal and professional life, developing values congruence, development of self and work-related identities, and encountering burnout and attrition (Marsh, 2001). This chapter addresses definitions, functions, and tasks associated with supervision and mentoring, types and phases of supervisory and mentor relationships, and outcomes and obstacles encountered in supervisory and mentoring relationships.

Definitions, Functions, and Tasks of Supervision and Mentoring

Supervision has been described as a method of establishing ongoing relationships to meet the goals of individual staff members, as well as goals of their unit, division, and institution. Supervision provides insight into the larger context of work and is a method for holding staff accountable and reinforcing what they are doing well (Arminio & Creamer, 2001). Supervision in student affairs is not an easy process and requires time and practice. It is one of the most complex activities leaders are responsible for, and knowledge about staff development is required for effective supervisory relationships (Tull, 2006; Winston & Creamer, 1997). When done right supervision can help individuals and groups meet their objectives, while increasing organizational performance. "Supervision is a management function intended to promote the achievement of institutional goals and to enhance the personal and professional capabilities and performance of staff" (Winston & Creamer, 1997, p. 42).

New professionals have identified what they seek in their supervisors: structure, autonomy, frequent feedback, recognition of limitations, support, effective communication, consistency, role modeling, and sponsorship (Winston & Hirt, 2003). Some new professionals may have unrealistic or incongruent expectations of the supervisory experience, however. Harned and Murphy (1998) reported that

> many new professionals assume their first professional positions expecting to be apprenticed to their supervisors, and may eagerly await directives for office operation, career advice, and involvement opportunities in the field. Given the limits of tangible validation and reward in our field, it is often the supervisor to whom the new professional looks for reinforcement and reassurance. (p. 51)

Attention should be given to supervisory relationships by supervisors and new professionals alike. Supervisory relationships hold great potential to influence self-image, job satisfaction, and professional development. For these reasons supervisors should take their responsibilities seriously. Many within student affairs may have had limited role models or have had little or no formal training or expertise in supervision. This can be problematic for both supervisors and supervisees (Harned & Murphy, 1998).

Unlike supervision, mentoring is a more elusive and difficult concept to define. It is situational and complex (Zachary, 2000). In order to be most effective, mentors should be equipped with the appropriate knowledge and skills important for professional practice. Mentors who reflect on professional and personal experiences are able to identify and discuss positive attributes with protégés (Cardwell & Corkin, 2007). While no common understanding of mentoring exists in student affairs or higher education, definitions have focused on a variety of themes, including networking and delegating (Hoffman, 2001), knowledge and skill acquisition (Cardwell & Corkin, 2007), career development and learning (Dixon-Reeves, 2003; Lawrie, 1987; Mavrinac, 2005; Tull, 2003c), and advising, role modeling, experience, and leadership (Cunningham, 1999; Tull, 2003c).

A number of functions of staff supervision and mentoring in student affairs have been discussed in the literature. Table 7.1 summarizes these functions and identifies the literature that has addressed them. Many are similar in nature for supervision and mentoring. For example, effective supervision and mentoring both involve communication of the unwritten rules of the organization and profession. Such activities help new professionals navigate political situations or pitfalls they may encounter. Supervision and mentoring both focus on career and skill development. Other functions, however, are more associated with either supervision or mentoring. For instance, team building is more closely associated with the former, while motivating and inspiring are more frequently discussed in the literature on mentoring.

In order to accomplish these functions, there are strategies associated with effective supervision and mentoring. Table 7.2 offers a fairly comprehensive list of these strategies and identifies the experts who have written about them, but several merit further discussion here. First, effective supervision and mentoring should provide new professionals with emotional support and guidance, particularly when obstacles are encountered in the socialization process. Some new professionals may seek emotional support more from their mentors, particularly from interorganizational or peer mentors. On the other hand, supervisors should be formally involved in the orientation and training of new professionals. Mentors, particularly peer mentors, may only provide informal support in the orientation and training processes. However, there is a role for supervisors and mentors in encouraging self-assessment by new professionals and providing constructive criticism in the socialization process.

An understanding of the definitions, functions, and tasks of supervision and mentorship is important for new professionals, supervisors, and mentors in the socialization process or those preparing for the socialization process. Some of the functions and tasks for supervision and mentorship are very similar. Each party in supervisory and mentor relationships should be clear about expectations of the other, recognize boundaries, be patient and conscious of time, and practice effective communication strategies. Through these activities supervisors and mentors can be beneficial to new professionals

TABLE 7.1
Functions of Supervisory and Mentoring Relationships

Function	Supervision	Mentorship
Communicating mission and unwritten rules	Arminio & Creamer, 2001; Winston & Creamer, 1997	Bova & Phillips, 1982
Interpreting climate	Dalton, 1996; Arminio & Creamer, 2001; Winston & Creamer, 1997	
Personal/professional development	Barr, 1990; Dalton, 1996; Winston & Creamer, 1997	
Skill and career development	Dalton, 1996	Dixon-Reeves, 2003; Cardwell & Corkin, 2007; Bova & Phillips, 1982
Promoting teamwork	Arminio & Creamer, 2001; Winston & Creamer, 1997	
Coordinated work activities	Winston & Creamer, 1997	
Leadership, role modeling, advising, and coaching	Arminio & Creamer, 2001	Dixon-Reeves, 2003; Cardwell & Corkin, 2007; Bova & Phillips, 1982
Values, ethics, and fairness	Arminio & Creamer, 2001; Dalton, 1996	
Active problem solving	Winston & Creamer, 1997	
Motivating and inspiring		Cardwell & Corkin, 2007

TABLE 7.2
Processes and Tasks of Supervision and Mentoring

Strategies	Supervision	Mentorship
Individual and group meetings	Arminio & Creamer, 2001	
Decision making and planning	Arminio & Creamer, 2001; Marsh, 2001	
Communication	Dalton, 1996; Arminio & Creamer, 2001	
Obtaining and using information	Barr, 1990	
Setting timely expectations	Barr, 1990; Arminio & Creamer, 2001	
Encouraging healthy lifestyles	Marsh, 2001	
Emotional support and guidance	Cardwell & Corkin, 2007; Cunningham, 1999; and Dixon-Reeves, 2003	
Orientation and training	Cunningham, 1999	Cunningham, 1999
Constructive criticism	Kram, 1980; Kram & Isabella, 1985	Kram, 1980; Kram & Isabella, 1985
Self-assessment	Cardwell & Corkin, 2007; Cunningham, 1999	Cardwell & Corkin, 2007; Cunningham, 1999
Making introductions to contacts	Cunningham, 1999; Dixon-Reeves, 2003; Kram, 1980; Wright & Wright, 1987	Cunningham, 1999; Dixon-Reeves, 2003; Kram, 1980; Wright & Wright, 1987

entering student affairs work. Often, they enact these activities through individual styles and/or phases.

Types and Phases of Supervisor and Mentor Relationships

Four types of supervision have been described in the student affairs literature: authoritarian, laissez-faire, companionable, and synergistic (Winston & Creamer, 1997). The authoritarian approach is based on the assumption that staff members require constant attention. Authoritarian supervisors view their staff as incapable or unmotivated, thus in need of monitoring and micromanagement. This is rarely true of new professionals, and this style becomes problematic when they encounter authoritarian supervisors (Winston & Creamer). The laissez-faire approach to supervision allows staff the freedom to use their own skills and talents to accomplish their job responsibilities. Laissez-faire supervisors subscribe to the "hire good people and then get out of their way" theory (Winston & Creamer, 1997, p. 195). They are in essence hands-off supervisors. This style can be difficult for new professionals who need more time with and attention from their supervisors, particularly new professionals who might struggle with obstacles such as role conflict, role ambiguity, and role stress. The companionable approach is philosophically and operationally based on friendships between supervisors and staff. Companionable supervisors seek harmonious relationships among staff and concentrate on being liked by their subordinates (Winston & Creamer, 1997). Problems arise for companionable supervisors when relationships are flawed, as they view positive relationships as the foundation of their success. In contrast to the first three supervisory styles, the synergistic approach to supervision is cooperative and requires joint commitment from the supervisor and supervisee. It is essentially "a cooperative effort between the supervisor and staff members that allows the effects of their joint efforts to be greater than the sum of their individual contributions. Supervision . . . has a dual focus: accomplishment of the organization's goals and support of staff in accomplishment of their personal and professional development goals" (Winston & Creamer, 1997, p. 196).

Supervisors can assist new professionals in the socialization process by practicing a synergistic approach to supervision. While this may not be the most natural or most common practice for practitioners or their organization, supervisors should recognize the benefits to the new professional and the greater organization. Supervisors who practice a synergistic approach to supervision maintain close working relationships with new professionals they supervise, allowing greater opportunities for an exchange of information at a time when it is advantageous for both parties. They are able to provide important organizational information to new staff, while new professionals provide feedback to their supervisors on their successes and difficulties in the socialization process.

New professionals can assist their supervisors by fully participating in synergistic supervisory relationships. Through their participation they receive valuable feedback that will assist them personally and professionally. They can gain the support they need to be fully socialized to the organization that employs them, as well as the student affairs profession. In the synergistic supervisory relationship the supervisor and the new professional take on important gains that serve each party and the greater organization.

Since mentoring is a more elusive concept than supervision, a wider range of mentor types have been described in the literature, including formal/informal mentors, peer mentors, comentors; developmental alliances; situational or spot mentoring; mentoring up; team or group mentoring; e-mentoring; supervisor as mentor; intraorganizational mentors; interorganizational mentors; long-distance mentors; and cross-cultural mentors. In some cases a mentoring relationship may have characteristics of several of these types or may depend on the organization where the relationship occurs as well as personality factors of the mentor and new professional (Tull, 2003c).

Mentoring relationships are generally characterized as formal or informal, regardless of other characteristics that might describe them. Many mentoring relationships in student affairs are informal in nature, even though some verbal agreement or loose goals are established. On the other end of the spectrum are well-developed mentoring relationships that serve as learning opportunities. These relationships often involve written outcomes, objectives, and time lines (Zachary, 2000). Mentoring relationships can happen accidentally, be coincidental, or be deliberately planned. Whatever the case, the relationship must be authentic if personal, professional, or institutional outcomes are to be achieved (Moore, 1982).

Peer mentoring relationships are premised on the assumption that multiple mentors can benefit a protégé. In many cases peers can exert greater influence on new professionals. They encourage nonhierarchical relationships that may already exist in work settings (Mavrinac, 2005) and that can be beneficial, assuming peers provide adequate support and information to their new professional colleagues. Chapter 8 in this volume elaborates on the role of peer mentors. In general, they are advantageous, although they may not provide all critical functions associated with mentoring (Kram & Isabella, 1985). Peer mentoring is more inclusive, authentic, and democratic. It provides a forum for individual aspirations that is learner driven and more available, motivating, and mutual (Mavrinac, 2005).

For many new professionals, supervisors may take on the role of mentor in addition to their supervisory role. Mentor relationships between an employee and supervisor occur often in the student affairs profession (Kelly, 1984). The duration of these relationships may also extend beyond the supervisory relationship, once the supervisor or new professional leaves the organization or institution. Some supervisors in student affairs organizations may take on the role of mentor to their own supervisees or to others who may not report directly to them (Tull, 2003c).

Alternatively, new professionals may identify mentors other than their supervisor. The active use of intraorganizational mentors can complicate relationships. Roles can be blurred for all parties involved. New professionals who have mentors and supervisors within the same organization may encounter a truncated hierarchy that is superimposed on the existing organizational hierarchy (Evans, 1984). If this occurs, new professionals and their supervisors and mentors should be clear about expectations for each type of relationship and give priority to meeting the expectations of supervisors.

Interorganizational mentors are those who exist outside the new professional's unit, division, or institution. In many cases new professionals will retain mentors from their undergraduate or graduate preparation programs even while seeking new intraorganizational mentors. Some new professionals may also develop mentor relationships with experienced administrators at different institutions (Tull, 2003d). This is often done to explore new perspectives, gain exposure to other institutional types, or as a method of professional networking. "Long-distance mentoring is a geographically diverse mentoring relationship that takes place when it is not feasible, desirable, or convenient for mentoring partners to meet on a regular face-to-face basis. It is not unusual for a relationship to start out as a face-to-face partnership and to become a long-distance mentoring relationship at some point along the way" (Zachary, 2000, p. 31).

Cross-cultural mentor relationships also are advantageous for new professionals, as they enable mentees to examine their values in relation to their unit, division, institution, and the profession of student affairs. These advantages include (a) becoming culturally self-aware, (b) developing a working knowledge of and appreciation for other cultures, (c) improving communication skills, and (d) becoming attuned to other cultures (Zachary, 2000).

Mentors of any type can assist new professionals through formal and informal relationships. Mentors should take their role seriously, as new professionals may be relying on them for important information critical to their success at the organizational or profession-wide level. They can create important learning relationships for new professionals that are intentional and outcome oriented. While some supervisors serve as mentors to the new professionals they employ, those supervisors should be careful to establish boundaries for discussions about performance and for topics such as professional advancement.

New professionals have much to gain through the formal and informal mentor relationships they establish with other student affairs administrators. They should be willing to engage in learning-oriented mentor relationships that will prove beneficial to their development and socialization to student affairs work. No matter the type of mentor relationship, new professionals should be authentic and committed in their efforts. Participation in mentoring relationships can provide new insights into peers, supervisors, and other administrators in the organization.

While research on types of supervisors and mentors is rife, little exists in the student affairs, higher education, or management literature on the sequential phases of supervisory relationships. Rather, there is information about the functions of supervisory relationships. These functions arguably represent a sequential order to some extent and include (a) recruitment and selection, (b) orientation, (c) supervision, (d) staff development, (e) performance appraisal (Janosik & Creamer, 2003; Winston & Creamer, 1998), and (f) separation (Conley, 2001). These supervisory functions have been defined as interlinking and overlapping (Janosik & Creamer, 2003).

Recruitment and selection of staff rest on two commandments: hiring the right person and doing it the right way (Janosik & Creamer, 2003; Winston & Creamer, 1998). Orientation occurs through formal and informal channels in student affairs administration. It should indoctrinate new professionals with the educational and operational philosophies of the unit, the division of student affairs, and the institution, as well as set expectations for personal and professional success (Janosik & Creamer, 2003). Supervision is the linchpin of staffing practices and is best conceptualized through synergistic supervisory relationships, addressed earlier in this chapter (see pp. 134–135). Both staff development and performance appraisal are seen as attending to individual and organizational development and evaluation that should occur simultaneously for the new professional (Winston & Creamer, 1997). Separation is an important, and often overlooked, phase of supervisory relationships. Employees will eventually leave their position because of promotion, poor performance, or personal reasons (Janosik & Creamer, 2003). Supervisors must plan for this phase and prepare a smooth transition out of the organization for the departing staff member.

All mentoring relationships have phases that, whether formally acknowledged or not, move the relationship forward or signal the end of the relationship. Two four-phase models have been identified in the literature. They share many similarities, with the exception of the fourth stage. The first model includes (a) preparing, (b) negotiating, (c) enabling, and (d) coming to closure (Zachary, 2000). Awareness of each of these phases is a key factor in successful mentoring relationships because they provide guideposts. Stages that are taken for granted or bypassed can have a negative effect on the relationship (Zachary, 2000). In the preparing phase, mentors explore their motivations and readiness for the mentor relationship. "The mentor evaluates the viability of the prospective mentor-mentee relationship. A prospecting conversation with the mentee assists in making that determination. This initial conversation then sets the tone for the relationship" (Zachary, 2000, p. 50).

The negotiating phase is the business phase of the relationship and is a time when the mentor and mentee come to an agreement on the goals and processes of the relationship. More specifically, a shared understanding of the assumptions, expectations, and goals are agreed upon by the pair. Other topics covered by the mentor pair in this phase are confidentiality, and boundaries and limits with respect to what they are comfortable talking about (Zachary, 2000).

The enabling phase is the longest of the four phases and serves as the implementation phase. This is when the majority of learning and contact between the mentor pair occurs. Enabling is complex and offers the greatest opportunities for growth on the part of both parties in the relationship. It also presents obstacles that can hinder the relationship unless they are not successfully removed. Open lines of communication between the mentor pair and thoughtful, timely, candid, and constructive feedback can be affirming and nurturing (Zachary, 2000).

The coming to closure phase "is an evolutionary process that has a beginning (establishing closure protocols when setting up mentoring agreement), a middle (anticipating and addressing obstacles along the way), and an end (ensuring that there has been positive learning, no matter what the circumstances). All three components are necessary for satisfactory closure," (Zachary, 2000, p. 52). This final phase provides an opportunity to evaluate learning that has occurred and apply that learning to other situations and relationships (Zachary).

The second model includes the phases of (a) initiation, (b) cultivation, (c) separation, and (d) redefinition (Kram, 1983). The initiation phase includes a period of six months to one year when the relationship is getting started and has significance for both parties. The cultivation phase lasts between two and five years when the career and psychological aspects of the relationship are expanded. The separation phase includes a period of 6 months to 2 years, when a significant change in the structure of the relationship occurs. The final phase, redefinition, lasts for an indefinite period of time, when the relationship is ended or takes on significantly different characteristics. It in some ways morphs into a peer-like friendship (Kram, 1983).

It is important for supervisors, mentors, and new professionals to be conscious of the sequential phases of relationships so that they may identify needs at any given point in the supervision or mentor relationship. New professionals will seek out information and support differently depending on the phase of the relationship. If care is not taken to build firm foundations for these relationships, new professionals may find them to be less fulfilling or less helpful in the socialization process. While the boundaries for supervisory and mentor relationships are loosely defined, some awareness of the phases outlined above can help all parties achieve desired outcomes and avoid obstacles in their relationships.

Outcomes and Obstacles of Supervisory and Mentor Relationships for New Professionals

Numerous outcomes are associated with supervisory relationships, including orientation; understanding of vision, mission, goals, and organization; professional development; coordinated work activities and active problem solving; feedback and appraisal; goal attainment; and career advancement.

Orientation processes are formal and informal in nature and vary by institution and supervisory relationship. Supervisors who pay particular attention to staff through the orientation process familiarize their supervisees with information related to the educational and operational philosophies of the unit, student affairs division, and institution. This includes operating procedures and expectations for personal and professional performance. Supervisors should also spend ample time providing an introduction to the campus and community surrounding the institution (Winston & Creamer, 2002a).

Successful orientation activities assist staff in feeling comfortable in their new organization and make them more productive on the job. These outcomes often result in reduced turnover (Roderer & Hickman, 2000). Staff members attending orientation are significantly more socialized in dimensions of organizational goals/values, history, and people than those not participating in training. Such staff members also have significantly higher levels of affective and organizational commitment than those who do not participate (Klein & Weaver, 2000). Orientation activities are discussed with greater detail in chapter 6.

Supervisors are ultimately responsible for ensuring that those new to their organization develop a clear understanding of the vision, mission, and goals of their units (Winston & Creamer, 1997). This can occur partly through the orientation process but should be reinforced by supervisors in an ongoing fashion. Beyond the vision, mission, and goals, supervisors should actively transmit other important concepts such as values, ethics, and principles of fairness (Arminio & Creamer, 2001; Dalton, 1996); institutional history, policies, procedures, and a profile of student characteristics (Boehman, 2007; Dalton, 1996); a map of the work environment (Barr, 1990); and an orientation to institutional work life (Marsh, 2001). By establishing ongoing relationships, supervisors can ensure that the goals of the institution, division, the unit, and individual staff members are met (Arminio & Creamer, 2001).

Professional development is a critical and often overlooked outcome of supervisory relationships. Effective staff development should concentrate on individual and organizational improvement, be derived from individual development plans, focus on process and product, be multifaceted and flexible, and recognize each staff member's maturity level (Winston & Creamer, 2002b). While each new professional has his or her own unique professional development needs, several common skills and competencies should be emphasized, including basic communication, leadership, and time management skills (Dalton, 1996); financial management skills; healthy lifestyles; involvement in professional organizations and campus wide activities; and identifying mentors (Marsh, 2001). Staff development processes should be tailored to individual staff members based on their particular needs and the skills necessary to succeed in their specific role. They should also help new professionals develop personally (Dalton, 1996; Winston & Creamer, 1997) and enable them to grow beyond their current role (Barr, 1990).

Two other outcomes of effective supervision are coordinated work activities and active problem solving among staff. These outcomes help supervisors develop teamwork and work group capabilities (Winston & Creamer, 1997) and enable them to both integrate the individual needs of staff with the greater organizational needs and help staff master necessary job skills (Dalton, 1996). Supervisors can reinforce supervisory and institutional expectations through staff development and teamwork initiatives. Those who hold regular staff meetings with individuals and groups and involve them in planning processes are better able to provide insight into the larger context of their work within the organization and institution (Arminio & Creamer, 2001). Through active problem solving supervisors reinforce expectations for new staff members and illustrate how they will hold staff accountable. New professionals who are introduced to challenges are actively involved in obtaining and using information and translating theory to practice (Barr, 1990).

Formal and informal feedback and appraisal are important outcomes of any supervisory relationship but are particularly critical for new professionals. They are the most effective approaches for offering feedback to staff in student affairs (Winston & Creamer, 2002c) and serve several purposes. For example, feedback and appraisal reinforce what staff members are doing well, and teach and coach them on what they need to do better. These processes also assist supervisors in clarifying organizational and institutional values, ethics, and principles of fairness (Arminio & Creamer, 2001). Supervisors assist new professionals in monitoring and managing organizational and institutional climates (Winston & Creamer, 1997) and promote continuous professional growth (Barr, 1990). Finally, supervisors are well served to use face-to-face contact through individual and group meetings consistently, thoroughly, and often with new professionals (Arminio & Creamer, 2001).

Effective supervisory relationships in student affairs assist new professionals in attaining their personal and professional goals as well as prepare them to advance their careers. Supervisors and supervisees should discuss openly and regularly long- and intermediate-term personal and professional goals. This is important as it addresses psychosocial and intellectual development needs of the new professional (Winston & Creamer, 1998). Supervisors can ensure that the goals of the organization, division, institution, and the new professional are attained through regular and ongoing communication with new professionals (Arminio & Creamer, 2001). Fostering individual, personal, and professional development and renewal have been described as essential components of the supervisory relationship in student affairs (Barr, 1990; Dalton, 1996; Winston & Creamer, 1997).

Several outcomes can be achieved through mentorship relationships as well. These outcomes are perceptual in nature and based on individual participants, leaving crucial decisions about the experience up to the individual mentor and/or protégé (Young & Perrewe, 2000a). One such outcome is knowledge acquisition (Zachary, 2000). Mentors can serve as guides, professionals who work at higher levels in the organization and hence can assist new professionals in learning the ropes and offer advice on how to succeed (Anthony, Kacmar, & Perrewe, 2002). Mentors provide new professionals with important knowledge about the organization's goals, norms, values, and other information relevant to succeeding in their jobs (Mavrinac, 2005; Tull, 2003a). Knowledge acquisition, in the form of information sharing, is a positive outcome of mentoring relationships for new professionals (Kram & Isabella, 1985).

Social support is one of the most important outcomes of mentoring yet is often overlooked or taken for granted. While new professionals may receive social support from any type of mentor, those who develop relationships with peer colleagues within their unit, division, or institution reap benefits offered by the social support these relationships offer (Young & Perrewe, 2000b). A lack of social support can lead to attrition. Because it is so important in the mentoring process, social support should be emphasized in the early stages of employment (Tull, 2003d).

Job satisfaction is another important outcome of mentoring relationships. Studies of student affairs professionals have shown that unmet expectations can predict intentions to quit (Bender, 1980; Blackhurst, Brandt, & Kalinowski, 1998; Flion & Pepermans, 1998; Holmes, Verrier, & Chisholm,

1983; Nelson & Quick, 1991; Olson, 1993; Renn & Hodges, 2007). Mentors are able to assist new professionals with career-role discrepancies that can trigger problems in the transition to work within the unit, division, institution, and student affairs profession (Hatcher & Crook, 1988; Mavrinac, 2005).

Many practitioners would describe mentoring as a professional development activity, another positive outcome (Kram & Isabella, 1985; Mavrinac, 2005; Wright & Wright, 1987). It provides opportunities for mentees to discuss career advancement (Kram & Isabella, 1985; Mavrinac, 2005; Wright & Wright, 1987) and learn about opportunities for promotion while charting career paths with the assistance of mentors (Anthony et al., 2002; Fagenson, 1989; Scandura & Schriesheim, 1994; Schmidt & Wolfe, 1980; Turban & Dougherty, 1994). For some new professionals, this may include networking activities that are more intentional and aimed at preparing them for their future employment (Hoffman, 2001). While mentors may find talking about career advancement uncomfortable (particularly the supervisor/mentor), such discussions are important as new professionals often seek career advancement opportunities. Because some new professionals lack knowledge about opportunities in the profession, career advancement is a topic that should be addressed in an appropriate and timely manner (Lorden, 1998; Rosser & Javinar, 2003).

Positive outcomes can be achieved through supervision and mentorship in the socialization process for new professionals. As noted, outcomes are achieved through formal and informal means. Supervisory relationships, which are generally more formal, provide structured mechanisms for the accomplishment of outcomes. Mentoring relationships, which are generally less formal, provide less-structured mechanisms for the accomplishment of outcomes. The latter should not be overlooked, as some mentors (i.e., peer mentors) can be effective in their work with new professionals in the socialization process. Both types of relationships are valuable in the socialization of new professionals.

To this point, I have discussed the positive aspects of supervision and mentoring. However, supervisors and staff members should be aware of several obstacles that can exist for new professionals. There are aspects of professional life that supervisors and their staff members should work to remedy. Role conflict is the first of these obstacles. New professionals who find themselves torn by conflicting job demands, encountering differences with their supervisors, or faced with obligatory tasks they are unwilling or uncomfortable undertaking may be struggling with role conflict (Amey, 1990). Role conflict can occur when two or more incompatible expectations arise for a staff member (Ward, 1995). New professionals uncertain about the scope of their responsibilities or the expectations of colleagues may be struggling with role ambiguity (Amey, 1990). Role ambiguity may occur when the information needed to guide behavior, "is incomplete, insufficient, unclear, or absent" (Ward, 1995, p. 36) or "prescribed behaviors are unclear and . . . there is some need for certainty or predictability regarding means for accomplishing goals" (Zellars, Perrewe, & Hochwarter, 2000, p. 1573). Role conflict and role ambiguity have been positively associated with employee anxiety, job dissatisfaction, and intention to leave (Klenke-Hamel & Mathieu, 1990). Strategies for addressing role conflict should include talking about specific roles, clarifying expectations, reducing the number of individuals staff members are accountable to, and increasing autonomy and self-directedness for staff (Ward, 1995).

Role conflict and role ambiguity have been referred to as *role stress*. Role stress occurs when new professionals are confronted with incompatible or unclear expectations that do not allow them to act in prescribed ways (Ward, 1995). Role stress can include role conflict, role ambiguity, as well as role overload, and has been widely investigated as a correlate to burnout (Zellars et al., 2000), yet another obstacle for new professionals.

Staff who are not provided with adequate orientation to their role within the organization or division of student affairs often struggle with role orientation. Supervisors should clearly communicate information about roles early in the recruitment and selection phases and should reinforce this information upon the new professional's entry to the organization. By providing a better understanding of personal and organizational work-life issues, supervisors can directly affect new professionals' job satisfaction and morale (Rosser & Javinar, 2003). Role overload occurs when new professionals are expected to do more than time permits them to do (Zellars et al., 2000). When new professionals encounter role conflict, role ambiguity, role orientation, or role overload, the outcome can be burnout, low job satisfaction and morale and, ultimately, attrition (Tull, 2003a).

Regular feedback and appraisal are essential to effective supervisory relationships. This is particularly true as supervisory relationships commence, and expectations and assumptions about a position and organization are often tested against the realities of organizational work life. Gaps can exist between expectations and realities held by new professionals and their supervisors. This often is the cause of role ambiguity and poor role orientation. Avoiding these are important for new professionals and their supervisors.

As new professionals begin their work they often believe that they should be provided ample opportunities for personal and professional growth. While this may be a reasonable expectation, it is not always the reality that they encounter. On some occasions disparities arise between the opportunities thought to be available and the realities discovered once on the job (Amey, 2002). Some new student affairs professionals may choose to leave the field because of a perceived lack of prospects for personal and professional advancement (Tull, 2003b). Supervisors can readily communicate opportunities for development and career advancement to those they supervise and assist them in pursuing these opportunities.

Employing a synergistic supervisory relationship allows new professionals to focus on navigating the obstacles identified above. Synergistic supervision involves an open and trusting relationship between supervisors and supervisees, identification of career anchors, and identification of professional aspirations and the skills and competencies necessary for staff to advance professionally (Winston & Creamer, 1998). The inability of staff to participate in synergistic supervisory relationships and to navigate obstacles may lead to diminished job satisfaction and greater intention to leave their job or the profession (Tull, 2006).

Like supervision, obstacles exist for mentoring relationships as well. Certain types of mentees, as Zachary (2000) has noted, can be problematic. Each of these types, while aptly termed, should be carefully understood in order to avoid the challenges they can present. The mentee types include consume-you mentees, jealous mentees, peripatetic mentees, manipulative mentees, and apathetic mentees. Consume-you mentees assume an attitude of entitlement and have a user mentality. These mentees often exploit the mentor's time. Jealous mentees grow or advance beyond their mentors. This can lead to resentment as mentees perceive their mentors as holding them back. Peripatetic mentees seek advice from their mentor but show little follow-through or commitment in the mentor relationship. Manipulative mentees regularly seek favors from their mentors and control within the mentor relationship. Last, apathetic mentees are lacking in candor, good intentions, and follow-through in the mentor relationship.

Conversely, there are dangers for protégés relative to an academic setting: mentors could lose power or influence, protégés may gain limited perspectives, mentors could leave the institution, or protégés could become attached to poor mentors (Wright & Wright, 1987). Other dangers include mentors who are rejecting, extremely critical, or indifferent to new professionals (Hunt & Michael, 1983); mentors who live vicariously through their mentees; or those who attempt to mold mentees in their likeness, which can be counterproductive to facilitating mentoring relationships (Kram, 1983).

Problems may arise in the initial stages if mentors are exploitive or use the mentor to further their own career. This could also stifle the protégé's career by blocking opportunities for career advancement. The mentor could further feel threatened by the protégé who begins to make progress toward the mentor's own position within the unit, institution, or profession (Wright & Wright, 1987). The premature ending of a mentoring relationship because of these kinds of circumstances can lead to a decrease in the self-esteem and confidence of the protégé (Hunt & Michael, 1983).

Effective supervisory and mentor relationships are essential for new professionals to assist them in avoiding obstacles encountered in the socialization process. Those supervisors and mentors who maintain close and regular contact with their new colleagues are best able to identify approaching obstacles and to be actively involved in creating solutions to address them. Many of the obstacles new professionals encounter in the socialization process can be averted in the earliest stages of employment (i.e., recruitment, selection, and orientation). Supervisors and mentors should be sensitive to each new professional's experiences in the socialization process, as no two experiences will be the same.

Conclusion

New professionals in student affairs administration who participate in effective supervisory and mentor relationships should be able to successfully navigate the obstacles addressed in this chapter and reap the positive outcomes these important personal and professional relationships offer. Through supervision, new professionals should participate in orientation processes; develop a clear understanding of the vision, mission, and goals of their organizations and institutions; participate in staff development activities, coordinate work activities and engage in active problem solving; receive regular feedback and appraisal; attain their personal and professional goals; and advance their careers. Through mentoring, new professionals should gain knowledge and a firm understanding of organizational culture, receive social support, experience greater job satisfaction and retention, develop professionally, attain their professional goals, and advance their careers.

References

Amey, M. J. (1990). Bridging the gap between expectations and realities. In K. M. Moore & S. B. Twombly (Eds.), *Administrative careers and the marketplace* (pp. 79–89). New Directions for Higher Education, No. 72. San Francisco: Jossey-Bass.

Amey, M. J. (2002). Unwritten rules: Organizational and political realities of the job. In M. J. Amey and L. M. Reesor (Eds.), *Beginning your journey: A guide for new professionals in student affairs*. Washington, DC: National Association of Student Personnel Administrators.

Anthony, W. P., Kacmar, K. M., & Perrewe, P. L. (2002). *Human resource management: A strategic approach*. Orlando, FL: Harcourt.

Arminio, J., & Creamer, D. G. (2001). What supervisors say about quality supervision. *College Student Affairs Journal, 21*(1), 35–44.

Barr, M. J. (1990). Making the transition to a professional role. In D. D. Coleman & J. Johnson (Eds.), *The new professional: A resource guide for new student affairs professionals and their supervisors* (pp. 17–29). Columbus, OH: NASPA.

Bender, B. E. (1980). Job satisfaction in student affairs. *NASPA Journal, 18*(2), 3–9.

Blackhurst, A., Brandt, J., & Kalinowski, J. (1998). Effects of personal and work-related attributes on the organizational commitment and life satisfaction of women student affairs administrators. *NASPA Journal, 35*(2), 86–99.

Boehman, J. (2007). Affective commitment among student affairs professionals. *NASPA Journal, 44*(2), 307–325.

Bova, B., & Phillips, R. (1982). *The mentoring relationship as an educational experience*. (Report No. CE 034 712). Albuquerque: University of New Mexico. (ERIC Document Reproduction Service No. 224944)

Cardwell, P., & Corkin, D. (2007) Mentorship: The art and science. *Pediatric Nursing, 19*(4), 31–32.

Conley, V. M. (2001). Separation: An integral aspect of the staffing process. *College Student Affairs Journal, 21*(1), 57–63.

Cunningham, S. (1999). The nature of workplace mentoring relationships among faculty members in Christian higher education. *The Journal of Higher Education, 70*(4), 441–463.

Dalton, J. C. (1996). Managing human resources. In S. R. Komives and D. B. Woodward (Eds.), *Student services: A handbook for the profession.* San Francisco: Jossey-Bass.

Dixon-Reeves, R. (2003). Mentoring as a precursor to incorporation: An assessment of the mentoring experience of recently minted Ph.D.s. *Journal of Black Studies, 34*(1), 12–27.

Evans, M. G. (1984). Reducing control loss in organizations: The implications of dual hierarchies, mentoring and strengthening vertical dyadic linkages. *Management Science, 30*(2), 156–168.

Fagenson, E. A. (1989). The mentor advantage: Perceived career/job experiences of protégés versus non-protégés. *Journal of Organizational Behavior, 10*(4), 309–320.

Flion, I. A., & Pepermans, R. G. (1998). Exploring the relationship between orientation programs and current job satisfaction. *Psychological Reports, 83,* 367–370.

Harned, P. J., & Murphy, M. C. (1998). Creating a culture of development for the new professional. In W. A. Bryan & R. A. Schwartz (Eds.), *Strategies for staff development: Personal and professional education in the 21st century* (pp. 43–53). New Directions for Student Services, No. 4. San Francisco: Jossey-Bass.

Hatcher, L., & Crook, J. C. (1988). First-job surprises for college graduates: An exploratory investigation. *Journal of College Student Development, 29*(5), 441–448.

Hoffman, J. (2001, February). Recruiting tomorrow's leaders begins with mentoring today's young professionals. *Net Results.* Retrieved November 15, 2001, from http://www.naspa.org/membership/mem/pubs/nr/default.cfm?id = 143.

Holmes, D., Verrier, D., & Chisholm, P. (1983, September). Persistence in student affairs work: Attitudes and job shifts among master's program graduates. *Journal of College Student Personnel, 24*(5), 438–443.

Hunt, D. M., & Michael, C. (1983). Mentorship: A career training and development tool. *The Academy of Management Review, 8*(3), 475–485.

Janosik, S. M., & Creamer, D. G. (2003). Introduction: A comprehensive model. In S. M. Janosik, D. G. Creamer, J. B. Hirt, R. B. Winston, S. A Saunders, & D. L. Cooper (Eds.), *Supervising new professionals in student affairs: A guide for practitioners.* New York: Brunner-Routledge.

Kelly, K. E. (1984). Initiating a relationship with a mentor in student affairs. *NASPA Journal, 21*(3), 49–54.

Klein, H. J., & Weaver, N. A. (2000). The effectiveness of an organizational level orientation training program in the socialization of new hires. *Personnel Psychology, 53,* 47–66.

Klenke-Hamel, K. E., & Mathieu, J. E. (1990). Role strains, tension, and job satisfaction influences on employees' propensity to leave: A multi-sample replication and extension. *Human Relations, 43*(8), 791–807.

Kram, K. (1980). *Mentoring processes at work: Developing relationships in managerial careers*. Unpublished doctoral dissertation, Yale University, New Haven, CT.

Kram, K. (1983). Phases of the mentor relationship. *Academy of Management Journal, 26*(4), 608–625.

Kram, K. E., & Isabella, L. A. (1985). Mentoring alternatives: The role of peer relationships in career development. *Academy of Management Journal, 28*(1), 110–132.

Lawrie, J. (1987). How to establish a mentoring program. *Training and Development Journal, 41*(3), 25.

Lorden, L. P. (1998). Attrition in the student affairs profession. *NASPA Journal, 35*(3), 206–215.

Marsh, S. R. (2001). Using adult development theory to inform staff supervision in student affairs. *College Student Affairs Journal, 21*(1), 45–56.

Mavrinac, M. A. (2005). Transformational leadership: Peer mentoring as a values-based learning process. *Libraries and the Academy, 5*(3), 391–404.

Moore, K. M. (1982, Winter). The role of mentors in developing leaders for academe. *Educational Record,* 23–28.

Nelson, D. L., & Quick, J. C. (1991). Social support and newcomer adjustment in organizations: Attachment theory at work? *Journal of Organizational Behavior, 12*(6), 543–554.

Olson, D. (1993). Work satisfaction and stress in the first and third year of academic appointment. *Journal of Higher Education, 64*(4), 453–471.

Renn, K. A., & Hodges, J. P. (2007). The first year on the job: Experiences of new professionals in student affairs. *NASPA Journal, 44*(2), 367–391.

Roderer, P., & Hickman, S. (2000). Successful orientation programs. *Training and Development, 54*(4), 59.

Rosser, V., & Javinar, J. (2003). Midlevel student affairs leaders' intentions to leave: Examining the quality of their professional and institutional work life. *Journal of College Student Development, 44*(6), 813–830.

Scandura, T. A., & Schriesheim, C. A. (1994). Leader-member exchange and supervisor career mentoring as complementary constructs in leadership research. *Academy of Management Journal, 37*(6), 1588–1602.

Schmidt, J. A., & Wolfe, J. S. (1980). The mentor partnership: Discovery of professionalism. *NASPA Journal, 17*(3), 45–51.

Tull, A. (2003a, July). Mentoring of new professionals in students affairs: Part one— Introduction. *Net Results.* Retrieved November 21, 2008 from http://www.naspa .org/membership/mem/pubs/nr/default.cfm?id = 1103.

Tull, A. (2003b, September). Mentoring of new professionals in student affairs: Part three—Implications for attrition. *Net Results.* Retrieved November 21, 2008 from http://www.naspa.org/membership/mem/pubs/nr/default.cfm?id = 1152.

Tull, A. (2003c, September). Mentoring of new professionals in student affairs: Part four—definitions and characteristics. *Net Results*. Retrieved November 21, 2008 from http://www.naspa.org/membership/mem/pubs/nr/default.cfm?id=1169.

Tull, A. (2003d, October). Mentoring of new professionals in student affairs: Part five–benefits. *Net Results*. Retrieved November 21, 2008 from http://www.naspa .org/membership/mem/pubs/nr/default.cfm?id=1230.

Tull, A. (2006). Synergistic supervision, job satisfaction, and intention to turnover of new professionals in student affairs. *Journal of College Student Development, 47*(6), 465–480.

Turban, D. B., Dougherty, T. W. (1994). Role of protégé personality in receipt of mentoring and career success. *Academy of Management Journal, 37*(3), 688–702.

Ward, L. (1995). Role stress and propensity to leave among new student affairs professionals. *NASPA Journal, 33*(1), 35–42.

Winston, R. B., & Creamer, D. G. (1997). *Improving staffing practices in student affairs*. San Francisco: Jossey-Bass.

Winston, R. B., & Creamer, D. G. (1998). Staff supervision and professional development: An integrated approach (pp. 29–42). New Directions for Student Services, No. 84. San Francisco: Jossey-Bass.

Winston, R. B., & Creamer, D. G. (2002a, September). Improving staffing practices. *Net Results*. Retrieved November 21, 2008 from http://www.naspa.org/membership/mem/pubs/nr/default.cfm?id=724.

Winston, R. B., & Creamer, D. G. (2002b, October). Improving staffing practices: Part five—Staff development. *Net Results*. Retrieved November 21, 2008 from http://www.naspa.org/membership/mem/pubs/nr/default.cfm?id=769.

Winston, R. B., & Creamer, D. G. (2002c, October). Improving staffing practices: Part six—Performance appraisal. *Net Results*. Retrieved November 21, 2008 from http://www.naspa.org/membership/mem/pubs/nr/default.cfm?id=783.

Winston, R. B., & Hirt, J. B. (2003). Activating synergistic supervision approaches: Practical suggestions. In S. M. Janosik, D. G. Creamer, J. B. Hirt, R. B. Winston, S. A Saunders, & D. L. Cooper (Eds.), *Supervising new professionals in student affairs: A guide for practitioners*. New York: Brunner-Routledge.

Wright, C. A., & Wright, S. D. (1987). The role of mentors in the career development of young professionals. *Family Relations, 36*(2), 204–208.

Young, A. M., & Perrewe, P. L. (2000a). The exchange relationship between mentors and protégé: The development of a framework. *Human Resource Management Review, 10*(2), 177–209.

Young, A. M., & Perrewe, P. L. (2000b). What did you expect? An examination of career and related support and social support among mentors and protégé. *Journal of Management, 26*(4), 611–632.

Zachary, L. J. (2000). *The mentor's guide: Facilitating effective learning relationships.* San Francisco: Jossey-Bass.

Zellers, K. L., Perrewe, P. L., & Hochwarter, W. A. (2000). Burnout in health care: The role of the five factors of personality. *Journal of Applied Social Psychology, 30,* 1570–1598.

8

STAFF-PEER RELATIONSHIPS IN THE SOCIALIZATION PROCESS

Terrell L. Strayhorn

It seems like you never can know enough. . . .
like you're always learning. I learned a lot about
theory, research, and counseling strategies
from the CSP [college student personnel] program. But, I learned a lot about being an administrator, about *our own* [emphasis added]
students, and about the importance of stuff like
budgets [laughing] from my on-the-job experiences with my colleagues.

—Anonymous entry-level professional

T he above quote was drawn from an electronic message sent to me
from one of my former students. In this excerpt, she speaks to the
nexus between graduate and on-the-job training and also points to
the learning that results from positive interactions with one's professional
peers, hereafter referred to as *staff-peer relationships*. In essence, my former
student, who is now an assistant director of student life, alludes to the nature
of staff-peer relationships and their importance to the socialization of new
professionals. While prior research in the field of educational administration
offers tangential support for this conclusion, to date, few studies focus exclusively on the nature of staff-peer relationships and their relevance to the
socialization of new professionals in the field of student affairs. This is the
gap I address in this chapter.

The importance of staff-peer relationships is the focus of this chapter.
First, I briefly review the existing literature and theory about this topic. Next,

I introduce a study in which I surveyed new professionals about their interactions with others on campus. After summarizing the results of that study, I discuss strategies that should be promoted among new professionals to support each other on a personal and professional level. Attention is given to the development of strong peer relationships within the institution and among peers in the student affairs and higher education profession.

The Existing Knowledge Base

A considerable amount of research has been amassed to understand the socialization of individuals to various systems and subsystems of higher education (Austin & McDaniels, 2006; Blackburn, Bieber, Lawrence, & Trauvetter, 1991; Merton, 1968; Pascarella, Terenzini, & Wolfle, 1986; Strayhorn, 2009; Tierney & Rhoads, 1993; Van Maanen, 1976, 1983, 1984). For instance, Pascarella et al. studied how freshman orientation programs affect postsecondary student persistence by way of socializing new students to college life. Tierney and Rhoads examined the socialization of faculty by focusing specifically on graduate school and involvement in professional organizations as "anticipatory learning" periods during which prospective members begin to assume the values and attitudes of the group or organization they aspire to belong to. Other scholars have emphasized the importance of socialization as the process by which individuals acquire what is needed to participate effectively in organizational life (Brim, 1966; Dunn, Rouse, & Seff, 1994).

In general, socialization results in knowledge acquisition, which increases the probability of effective role performance. In addition, socialization is defined by two core elements (i.e., investment and involvement) that lead to identification with and commitment to a professional role (Blackhurst, Brandt, & Kalinowski, 1998; Stein, 1992; Thornton & Nardi, 1975). Professional socialization often occurs through graduate preparation programs (Komives, Woodard, & Associates, 1996; Sandeen, 1991), professional development workshops (Cuevas & Eberhardt, 2007), and interpersonal interactions or relationships with one's peers (Astin, 1993), to name but a few.

While prior research has contributed to our understanding of the socialization of faculty (Austin, 2002; Tierney, 1997; Tierney & Rhoads, 1993), instructors (Cuevas & Eberhardt, 2007), graduate and professional students (Austin & McDaniels, 2006; Strayhorn, 2009; Weidman, Twale, & Stein,

2001), and working-class students in higher education (Wegner, 1973), no studies were readily uncovered that focus on the socialization of new professionals in student affairs administration. This is surprising as new professionals encounter a number of challenges upon entering the field (Ellis, 2002; Hamrick & Hemphill, 2002; Marsh, 2001). For instance, some newly minted administrators face role ambiguity, role stress, and work overload (Berwick, 1992; Conley, 2001; Sandeen & Barr, 2006). Imagine a newly appointed hall director who must offer support and referral services to students but also has to serve as a disciplinarian; this may be an example of role stress or role ambiguity. Socialization is the process through which roles are clarified, stress is reduced, and work is understood. Socialization processes help new professionals adjust to their work environment and the institution's culture (Amey, 1990, 2002; Katz & Tushman, 1983) so it is important to explore new data that were recently collected on this topic.

Why Do We Need New Information?

This chapter represents *terra incognita* in a number of ways. First, "organizational researchers have over-studied relatively harsh and intensive socialization and under-studied socialization of the more benign and supportive sort" (Van Maanen, 1984, p. 238). In other words, current literature overlooks and obscures more implicit, routine, process-oriented activities that circumscribe how individuals are socialized to an organization.

Second, previous work on socialization tends to employ qualitative research methods (Austin & McDaniels, 2006) that are superior to quantitative methods in terms of "giving voice" to the lived experience of individuals in specific settings (Glesne, 2006) but are limited in their ability to estimate relationships among variables and outcomes. Understanding the connections among such factors may be instrumental in modeling the conditions in which student affairs work occurs. In addition, quantitative data may be generalized to larger populations, so findings can inform the student affairs profession writ large.

Finally, as Tierney (1997) concluded, "socialization is a concept that is much discussed but frequently misunderstood" (p. 1). Given the paucity of information on the socialization of new professionals in student affairs, our understanding of their experiences is severely limited. In the preparation of this chapter, I sought to gather new data that might address these issues.

To that end, I collected information about peer relationships and socialization among new professionals in student affairs. Specifically, I designed a survey that asked about new professionals' interactions with staff and non-staff peers, the nature of their relationships with such groups, and job-related outcomes such as job satisfaction and intent to leave their current position. To do this, I drew upon my own expertise about survey design, quantitative research, and student affairs. However, I coupled my own expertise with the prevailing theories about this topic.

Theories on Socialization

Two theoretical frameworks guided my thoughts on socialization. The first is based largely upon Merton's (1968) work. His theory assumes that there are specific ways in which new members acquire information about an organization and come to understand important knowledge, skills, and values needed to operate effectively in that organization (Bragg, 1976; Dunn et al., 1994; Tierney, 1988; Weidman, 1989a). Thus, "the new [member's] task is to learn the cultural processes in the organization and figure out how to use them" (Tierney, 1997, p. 4). Organizational learning is often facilitated through meaningful staff interpersonal interactions and staff-peer relationships (Van Maanen, 1976, 1983, 1984). In short, new professionals' acquisition of information and understanding of a given profession are shaped to some degree by their interactions with professional colleagues and staff peers, at least theoretically.

Second, because socialization has been linked with attrition in professional fields, I used theoretical explanations about leaving a profession as lenses through which to view the importance of staff-peer relationships (Bender, 1980; Currivan, 1999; Johnsrud & Rosser, 2002; Mobley, 1977). I settled upon this frame because it gave me the opportunity to examine the importance of staff-peer relationships in terms of a consequence; that is, at first I struggled to understand why we need to know more about new professionals' staff-peer relationships. The work of Johnsrud and Rosser helped me to see the importance of staff relationships in terms of attrition or departure from the organization and/or profession. More information about this matter is offered in chapter 2. From this vantage point, the topic is a critical issue in student affairs that has implications for new professionals and their supervisors (Sandeen & Barr, 2006).

Taken together, these theoretical underpinnings seemed to be promising scaffoldings as each allowed me to see in new and different ways what seems to be ordinary and familiar (i.e., new professionals, daily interactions, and staff-peer relationships). In other words, I found theory useful for exoticizing the ordinary (Besnier, 1995) and making the familiar strange (Jakobson, 1987).

The Study

I wanted to gather information about the daily interactions of new professionals, along with their commitment to the profession so I sought out select individuals. These were all nascent administrators who worked in one of the 34 functional areas defined by the Council for the Advancement of Standards in Higher Education (Miller, 2003). A total of 74 new professionals provided information that formed the basis of this chapter. By new professionals, I refer to individuals who have assumed their current position since 2004.

A large majority of the sample consisted of women (81%). Less than a third were African American or Black; nearly three-fourths had a master's degree. In terms of functional area responsibilities: 57% worked in general student affairs capacities, 16% in academic advising, 14% in career planning/placement, 8% in intramural/recreation sports, and 5% in residence life.

Survey

To elicit information about the staff-peer relationships of new professionals, I designed a survey that consisted of a demographics form, 15 items, and an open-ended section in which administrators could write personal reflections or additional comments. I asked these new professionals to tell me about the number of relationships they had with their peers and other professionals on their campus and to rate the quality of those relationships. Finally, I asked new professionals to reflect on their current position and institution when rating their level of job satisfaction in three areas: current job, office/unit, and employing institution.

Because I sought to examine staff-peer relationships from a quantitative perspective, I used statistical techniques (i.e., factor analysis) to group items into potential explanations about the frequency of staff and nonstaff relationships as well as the quality of a new professional's relationships with these two groups. On the survey, "nonstaff" peers referred to student affairs administrators who worked in areas outside one's immediate office or unit and other administrators on campus who did not work in student affairs (e.g., academic affairs, secretarial staff, etc.). For example, a sample question asked participants *how often* they interacted with others ("How often do you interact with [your direct supervisor] on a weekly basis?"). Response options ranged from 0 ("not applicable, do not interact at all") to 3 ("more than four times a week").

Finally, I wanted to understand the extent to which staff-peer relationships affected new professionals' socialization to the profession, their job satisfaction, and their intent to leave the profession. So, I added several questions regarding the extent to which new professionals (a) would accept their current position if they could start over again, (b) intend to stay in their current position at their employing institution, barring promotion to a higher position, and (c) feel satisfied with various aspects of their current position, office/unit, and employing institution. The latter items were developed based on a review of the extant literature and research instruments available in the public domain (Arminio & Creamer, 2001; Winston & Creamer, 1997). That is, Winston and Creamer point out that new professionals may grow dissatisfied or complacent with their job if they go unsupported or unchallenged; dissatisfied workers may leave for a more rewarding position. Armed with this information, I developed these items to measure new professionals' satisfaction, intent to stay, and commitment to their current position.

To make sense of these data, I conducted several analyses using a combination of descriptive statistics, correlations, and multivariate statistical tests. I summarize the findings below and discuss their implications for new professionals and their supervisors.

Frequency of Peer Relationships

New professionals have a lot of contact with coworkers and nonstaff peers. Most new professionals report interacting with others in their office or department at least four times a week. This would make sense in that they probably operate in the same physical location as their coworkers or at least have a common office where they retrieve mail and supplies. What is interesting is the extent to which new professionals report interacting with their supervisor and others outside their immediate office or department.

New professionals have frequent contact with their supervisors, often-times daily or more than once a day. In stark contrast, however, they rarely if ever interact with other senior leadership on campus. I did not find this too surprising as new professionals and senior administrators (e.g., dean of students, vice president for student affairs, provost) tend to operate in different arenas. New professionals are often considered those who work in the trenches with students and their families, while upper-level administrators may have little to no interaction with students and parents, for example.

Last, new professionals report very few interactions with their nonstaff peers—that is, new and midlevel professionals on campus who work in units outside one's own and/or colleagues at other institutions (i.e., student affairs administrators off campus). This may provide clues to an area that can be leveraged to support the socialization of new professionals. I will return to this point again later in the chapter.

Nature of Staff-Peer Relationships

Perhaps more important than how often new professionals interact with peers and others is the nature of those interactions. For the most part, the time new staff members spend with others in their own offices is work related. When they socialize, they do so with professionals from other offices or with people outside the student affairs profession.

Similarly, new professionals tend to interact with student affairs administrators off campus and senior administration on campus in highly professional ways as well. This is important information for supervisors to consider when working with new professionals. For instance, supervisors may need to create specific events that engender social interactions among new professionals and their peers (e.g., cookouts, holiday socials, breakfast talks) if they hope to promote closer relationships between new professionals and others on campus.

New professionals describe the nature of their relationships with various professional groups differently. Most describe their interactions with their supervisor and staff peers as very positive and supportive. On the contrary, few new professionals rate their relationship with senior administrators on campus (e.g., provost, chancellor) in that way. That new professionals tend to perceive their relationships with staff peers as generally positive and supportive may reflect the fact that they interact with such individuals more frequently than others. This is good news for new professionals—familiarity breeds pleasure. Supervisors of new professionals might consider this information when designing staff orientation activities and future staff development workshops. For example, supervisors should make time for peers to meet other staff members early. When I worked for a Division of Student Affairs, the dean of residence life introduced me to her staff on my very first day, took all new staff members to lunch as a group, and encouraged me to get to know staff members through face-to-face meetings. Not only did this help to make me feel like part of the team, but also it led others to invite me to attend group meetings, campus events, and after-work social activities.

Staff-Peer Relationships and Outcomes of Socialization

Quantitative analysis of the survey data allowed me to assess correlationally the impact of staff-peer relationships on two outcome measures: job satisfaction and intent to leave. Generally speaking, new professionals who interact frequently with staff peers are more satisfied with their work and work environment. It may be the case that new professionals derive satisfaction from their work when they work with colleagues who are friendly, supportive, and collaborative. Supervisors should consider this information when formulating work policies. Policies that facilitate staff-peer interactions (e.g., creation of work groups or teams) may increase satisfaction with one's work environment (i.e., staff peers, department, institution), which, in turn, can improve staff retention.

New professionals' satisfaction with the work environment also was highly correlated with the *nature* of staff-peer relationships. That new professionals who perceive their relationships with coworkers as positive and supportive are more satisfied on the job makes intuitive sense. But the correlational nature of these data point to an important problem for supervisors to consider. That is, it is also true that new professionals who describe their relationships with coworkers as negative or nonsupportive are more *dissatisfied* on the job. Supervisors should keep this in mind when responding to new professionals who report difficulties in working with other staff members or seem to resist the socialization process. Without attention to their concerns, new professionals are left to grow dissatisfied, which greatly increases the odds of their leaving.

Perhaps the most important finding from my research is the observation that new professionals who interact frequently with their supervisors and rate those interactions as very positive and supportive tend to be highly satisfied with their work. In fact, satisfaction with one's work and the nature of one's relationship with his or her supervisor was the most highly correlated relationship that I uncovered. This holds promise for new professionals and their supervisors. Indeed, it is important for supervisors to make time for new professionals. No matter how busy they get, supervisors should carve out room on their calendars for new professionals to talk about their experiences on the job, identify challenges they face, and set professional development goals with the advice of someone with more experience. Likewise, new professionals should make time to meet regularly with their supervisor. Using additional information from the survey, here is what new professionals gain from such interactions: knowledge about administrative practice (e.g., budgeting, supervising, resolving conflicts); communication skills, support for professional development, and a more nuanced understanding of the inner working of one's institution.

Finally, new professionals who feel their employing institution is a good place to work are highly satisfied with their job. In addition, those who perceive their employing institution as a good place to work are less likely to leave their current position within a year. Taken together, this information suggests that new professionals who feel a sense of belonging in their current work environment are generally more satisfied and much more likely to be retained. But the question is: How do you foster a sense of belonging among new professionals? Prior research may provide clues to strategies for promoting and sustaining a sense of belonging among new professionals. Indeed, other chapters in this volume, such as chapter 6 and chapter 7, may inform new professionals and supervisors. For example, supervisors would do well to encourage new professionals to become involved in purposeful activities such as professional staff associations and university committees. Many campuses have committees charged with designing staff development programs, task force groups charged with formulating institution-wide strategic plans, and governance teams whose principal activity is to represent the voice of staff on campus. Participating in these activities may prove effective in enhancing the socialization of new professionals.

Supervisors also might encourage new staff to participate actively in national professional associations like the American College Personnel Association (ACPA) and the National Association of Student Personnel Administrators (NASPA). For instance, both groups host preconference workshops and receptions at their national conferences for new student affairs professionals. NASPA sponsors several knowledge communities, one of which is devoted to new professionals and graduate students. Similarly, new staff members might be advised to join regional associations. The Southern Association for College Student Affairs sponsors an annual New Professionals Institute—an intensive, 5-day workshop that brings together new professionals to discuss their experiences openly and to network with other new professionals and a team of seasoned faculty members. Through involvement in such activities, new professionals may acquire the social capital necessary to feel connected to one's unit, campus, or the profession at large.

New professionals also need to assume responsibility for their own development. To this end, they might engage in a constellation of activities, such as volunteering to serve on search committees, presenting at national conferences, and even mentoring undergraduate students who aspire to enter the field of student affairs (Jablonsky, 1998). Attending campus events and participating in campus governance structures may assist new student affairs staff in understanding the organizational culture in which they operate.

Predicting Job Outcomes From Staff-Peer Relationships

Before turning my attention to a fuller discussion of how these results relate to the work of new professionals and their supervisors, I think it's important to summarize what I learned about the effect of relationships on job outcomes. Several factors influence the extent to which new professionals (a) rate their current institution as a good place to work, (b) would choose their current position again, and (b) find their job satisfying. I found substantial support for the fact that the frequency, nature, and quality of staff-peer relationships trump other effects (e.g., gender, level of education) thereby reifying the importance of this chapter's focus. This is important information supervisors may refer to; each of the former represent areas over which administrators have some degree of programmatic and policy control. Frequency, nature, and quality of staff-peer relationships are much more manipulable than generally fixed characteristics like gender and educational attainment. That is not to say that supervisors cannot invest in new professionals' earning advanced degrees, but it may be more important to ensure that new professionals are interacting with their coworkers in positive and supportive ways on a regular basis.

Implications for Policy and Practice

In this chapter I have presented new information on the frequency, nature, and quality of staff-peer relationships among new professionals in student affairs. It seems clear that staff peers and supervisors are well positioned to serve as socializing agents for new professionals. However, administrators outside one's immediate office and senior-level administrators on campus rarely, if ever, interact with new professionals. Creative strategies could be devised to co-opt such peers in the process of socializing new professionals to the department, institution, or profession. For instance, supervisors across units (e.g., dean of students, director of housing, and academic deans) might work together to sponsor combined training sessions for new staff members on issues that affect them all (e.g., assessment, working with parents, and programming). This not only provides an opportunity for new professionals to acquire the knowledge and skills that make them effective administrators (Weidman, 1989a, 1989b) but also provides an opportunity for new professionals to interact socially with others who might share their expectations and experiences but work outside of their immediate office or unit.

That staff peers and supervisors may serve as powerful socializing agents has implications for new staff orientation. In other words, these results provide clues to strategies that hold promise for successfully socializing "outsiders" to become "insiders" (Bullis & Bach, 1989). Supervisors might devise staff-peer mentoring programs in which experienced staff members are paired with new professionals to serve as role models, coaches, or guides, similar to how some faculty members serve as mentors to students (Brown, Davis, & McClendon, 1999; Green & Bauer, 1995; Strayhorn & Terrell, 2007). Such relationships might serve as mechanisms for acclimating new staff to the division, facilitating the "continuing conversation" that is characteristic of effective organizations (Komives, 1998), or teaching new professionals the written and unwritten codes that often guide professional practice day to day.

Second, the nature of new professionals' relationships with their supervisor(s) and other senior-level administrators on campus is more professional than social. New professionals tend to have social relationships with those who work outside student affairs; however, such interactions are quite infrequent, if available at all. On the surface, this information may reflect the mere state of affairs—that is, new professionals interact professionally with their coworkers and socially with those who do not work in the field (e.g., nonprofessional staff, students, etc.). However, more information is needed as it may allude to a sort of work-life imbalance that prevents new professionals from interacting with their coworkers socially. One of my recent master's advisees explained it best: "Well, it's just that I see them so much at work and even sometimes in the evening. I don't want to see them again until the next morning. My time is my time and I usually spend it with my *real* [emphasis added] friends and family."

Supervisors might consider these points if work-life balance is the goal. For new professionals to experience balance between their work and life roles, there is a need to reconcile the professional and the social. The real take-home message is for supervisors to remember that new professionals are both workers and *people*. While investing in their professional development, do not forget to facilitate their social adjustment.

Third, new professionals in this study rated their relationships with supervisors and staff peers as generally positive and supportive. Their relationships with senior-level administrators on campus tended to be neutral or generally negative and unsupportive. This may be related to the fact that new professionals rarely interact with such groups; as a result, they may perceive senior-level administrators and off-campus professionals as unfamiliar, unwelcoming, unfriendly, and unsupportive. In the absence of face-to-face interactions, individuals form and rely on stereotypes (Sigelman & Tuch, 1997) based on limited information from other sources (e.g., perceptions, opinions, rumors, etc.). This can be problematic as new professionals who perceive other staff as unfriendly may be hesitant to work with them, which in turn may affect how work gets done or prevent potentially rewarding collaborations.

To ameliorate these potentially negative effects, supervisors can take steps to introduce new professionals to other administrators on campus and vice versa. For example, supervisors might distribute electronic announcements via e-mail that introduce new hires to other professionals on campus. Alternatively, Web-based videos can be used to introduce new professionals when they first start the job. Here's a fictitious example of an e-mail that can be written and shared across campus:

Colleagues, it gives me great pleasure to introduce our new Coordinator of Student Activities, Ms. Kimberly Jones. Ms. Jones' "first day" on the job is tomorrow. Kimberly joins our staff after serving as the assistant coordinator of orientation at the University of Niagara Falls for 7 years. She holds a bachelor's degree in sociology and a master's in college student personnel from the University of Tennessee (Go Vols!). Indeed, we are pleased to have Kimberly join our staff of highly qualified professionals. Please join me in welcoming Ms. Jones to our team. She can be reached at (865) 900–3232 or kjones@fakemail.edu. Her office is located at A316 Claxton.

Notice the celebratory language used in this example—"great pleasure," "pleased to have [her]," and "join me in welcoming." Supervisors are encouraged to use this language when crafting such announcements. Positive words of this sort engender positive responses from staff. Including words or phrases that hold significance to new staff—like "Go Vols"—may help new professionals feel at ease and smooth their transition to a new environment.

Fourth, participants indicated that relations with supervisors and staff peers yielded the most impact on their knowledge, skills, and understanding of student affairs work within their office or unit. This makes sense as student affairs work tends to be highly decentralized, especially on large campuses such as research universities (Hirt, 2006). While the general nature of academic advising is common across campuses, how work gets done, the pace of work, and the role of relationships is best understood, perhaps, by those who work in a *specific* office on a *specific* campus. Thus, supervisors may want to use experienced staff members to provide in-house training to new professionals in addition to what they might receive at regional and national conferences.

In addition, these findings underscore the relevance of socialization theory to the study of staff-peer relationships in a student affairs context. Frequent, positive, and supportive staff-peer relationships produce clear and unambiguous increases in understanding student affairs work, commitment to the field, and satisfaction with one's work environment. Not only does this suggest that socialization theory is an effective tool for supervisors who struggle to understand the challenges that new professionals face and the ways such challenges can be reduced, but also new professionals might consult this chapter when thinking about their own development. For instance, if I were a new professional who wanted to learn more about the role that theory plays in making decisions, I would identify learning opportunities (i.e., workshops, training sessions, and conversations) that would expose me to frequent, positive, and supportive interactions with individuals who specialize in using theory to make decisions, such as my supervisor, other senior administrators on campus, or faculty in graduate preparation programs.

The frequency and nature of staff-peer relationships affect new professionals' satisfaction with their job and work environments. New professionals who interact with their staff peers frequently and in positive, supportive ways are more satisfied with their work than those who interact infrequently and in negative, unsupportive ways. This is critically important for us to understand, as satisfaction with work is related to whether new professionals would choose their current position again and to their intent to leave (Rosser, 2004). Indeed, results point to possible linkages between socialization theory and work turnover models posited by others (Bean, 1980, 1983; Price & Mueller, 1981). This information is important for supervisors, as it suggests multiple policy levers that can be used to increase staff retention and may inform future hiring decisions.

Finally, new professionals whose interactions with staff peers are very positive and supportive are more likely to choose their current position if they had to do it over again. This is good news for supervisors and managers who may consult these findings when formulating policies that guide professional conduct. Apparently, positive, supportive staff-peer relationships facilitate integration into one's department or office that can lead to a sense of membership, belonging, commitment, or feeling "stuck to" an office (Hirschman, 1970). As such, integration increases satisfaction, thereby reducing the odds of attrition (Bean, 1983). It is important to note that the reverse also is true; dissatisfaction is reduced by frequent, positive, supportive staff-peer interactions. This may provide clues to strategies that can be leveraged to retain staff members who are currently dissatisfied. For example, managers might encourage and support such professionals to interact with their peers by introducing work teams, staff learning communities, or staff retreats. Dissatisfied professionals might be encouraged to talk with their peers openly to air their concerns and recommend solutions to problems.

Relationship With Prior Literature and Chapters in This Volume

My findings reflect previous research on the important role that experienced, organizational members play in the socialization of new members. Van

Maanen (1976) argued that organizational socialization consists of "long standing rules of thumb . . . somewhat special language and ideology that help edit a member's everyday experience. . . . [It also] models . . . social etiquette and demeanor, [and] certain customs and rituals" (p. 1). Given the degree of specificity involved in understanding and transmitting organizational values and dispositions, perhaps socialization to an organization is best done by current members of that organization. New professionals report learning most about student affairs and the work of their office/unit from their interactions with staff peers and supervisors.

The success (or failure) of new professionals has been attributed to support received from those in their work setting during the socialization process (Amey, 1990, 2002; Katz & Tushman, 1983; Scher & Barr, 1979). Findings from my study suggest that new professionals' satisfaction with their job, perception of their employing institution as a "good place" for new practitioners to work, and their intent to leave/stay is predicated upon the nature (i.e., positive and supportive) of their relationships with staff peers and supervisors. So, not only is the success (or failure) of new professionals attributed to such support, but their subjective evaluation of their work-related experiences is tied to the nature of their staff-peer relationships. Thus, staff-peer relationships hold importance in and of themselves; new professionals and their supervisors should view them as critical to their success.

Professional preparation is important for individuals in fields such as student affairs (Bloland, 1992)—aspiring and new professionals are socialized to the values, beliefs, and knowledge of the field through such preparation (see, for example, chapter 5 in this volume; or Hesburg, Miller, & Wharton, 1973). Findings from this study highlight the important role that staff-peer relationships play in facilitating the socialization of new professionals to student affairs work. Faculty in graduate preparation programs should consider these findings when designing curricula. Faculty members would do well to include courses on interpersonal communication and conflict resolution, for example, as such skills are important in forming and negotiating meaningful interpersonal relationships with one's staff peers.

National professional associations play an important role in the socialization of new professionals (see chapter 10). For instance, most professional associations (e.g., ACPA, NASPA, etc.) sponsor annual conferences and professional development workshops that offer new professionals an opportunity to expand their knowledge, develop new skills, and network with peers across the country. However, it is important to note that participants in my study report few interactions with off-campus colleagues. It may be the case that new professionals are less likely to be members of professional associations and therefore unlikely to attend national conferences and meetings. Professional associations should study this issue in depth; should further work provide evidence to support this assertion, association leaders would do well to provide incentives to encourage involvement among new professionals who, according to some, are "the most important people in any division of student affairs" (S. R. Komives, personal communication, September 19, 2006).

Recommendations for Future Practice

In light of my findings, I offer several explicit recommendations for those who are interested in improving the socialization of new professionals in student affairs. Indeed, these recommendations hold promise for future practice and can be justified by the results of the study this chapter is based on.

Supervisors must play a role in the socialization of new professionals in student affairs. Supervisors are encouraged to design opportunities for intentional and frequent engagement with their new staff. In addition to regularly scheduled all-staff meetings, supervisors might plan special sessions for new staff in which they discuss the values and dispositions of the profession and subtle nuances that may exist within the organization. For instance, last year I did consulting work for a small liberal arts college. During my visit, new professionals complained that they felt overworked and undervalued. Face-to-face time with their supervisor could have provided "place and space" to air their grievances; such meetings also give supervisors an opportunity to acknowledge the contributions of new staff members.

Supervisors can conduct meetings with new professionals in a variety of ways to achieve the goals outlined in this chapter. For example, supervisors might hold one-on-one meetings with new staff to recommend specific career development opportunities that fit individual goals or to identify knowledge deficiencies that are perhaps best discussed in private settings. On the other hand, supervisors might meet with new professionals periodically as a group. The former promotes quality and the latter promotes quality, quantity, and peer relationships.

Staff-peer relationships affect a number of important outcomes such as knowledge, skills, job satisfaction, and intent to leave. Therefore, student affairs leaders should strive to create work environments that are opulent with opportunities for teamwork and collaboration, where possible. The more effort new professionals expend in frequent, positive, supportive relationships with their staff peers, the more they benefit. To this end, I recommend consideration of work groups, staff retreats, staff-peer mentoring programs, new professional staff orientations, and cross-unit partnerships. There is one caveat to qualify this recommendation; team approaches should only be used when appropriate and necessary. It makes little (or no) sense to build a team to accomplish work that is more readily done by an individual.

Administrators should use nonstaff peers in socializing new professionals to the profession, institution, or department even if such individuals are less useful in introducing new professionals to their specific office or unit. In this study, new professionals rarely, if ever, interacted with other senior-level administrators, student affairs professionals in other offices on campus, and off-campus colleagues. Since socializing new professionals effectively is such a daunting time- and resource-consuming process, I recommend that supervisors and staff peers work with others to accomplish this goal. Sponsoring joint training sessions, using professional consultants, and attending national conferences sponsored by professional associations represent promising practices.

Finally, new professionals should take initiative for enhancing their own socialization. Throughout this chapter, I recommend several practices in which new professionals might engage to concertedly cultivate their own talent and adjustment to student affairs work. For instance, new staff members should request appropriate orientation to their new role if it is not automatically provided. Orientation activities should be designed to introduce new staff to administrators, faculty, students, and other key people with whom the new employee will work. New staff members are encouraged to take these "anticipatory socialization" (Dunn et al., 1994) activities seriously and to raise questions or concerns if they feel inadequately prepared to assume assigned responsibilities.

New staff often bring with them new perspectives and ways of thinking that may lead to creative solutions to old problems. However, far too often good ideas are quickly dismissed because the genius came from a newbie who failed to understand how new ideas are introduced in the division or because the idea was presented by a new, lone ranger. New professionals need to know how formal and informal communication occurs at work and how innovations are best presented (Winston & Creamer, 1997). By interacting with their staff peers and developing meaningful relationships with their supervisors, new professionals become respected members of the team whose ideas are more readily accepted and acted upon.

Conclusion

Some reports suggest a rapid increase in the number of new professionals in student affairs and provide evidence that there is substantial dissatisfaction among new student affairs professionals (Evans, 1988; Richmond & Sherman, 1991). Without adequate support, dissatisfied new professionals may face additional challenges that undermine their performance and in turn lead to departure from their position, unit, or the profession in general. Efforts to support new professionals should involve building or enhancing their relationships with staff peers and supervisors. It is essential to understand that *where* new professionals work makes a difference but perhaps more importantly *with whom they work* and *how* matter equally as much.

References

Amey, M. J. (1990). *Bridging the gap between expectations and realities* (pp. 79–89). New Directions for Higher Education, No. 72. San Francisco: Jossey-Bass.

Amey, M. J. (2002). Unwritten rules: Organizational and political realities of the job. In M. J. Amey & L. M. Reesor (Eds.), *Beginning your journey: A guide for new professionals in student affairs* (pp. 13–30). Washington, DC: National Association of Student Personnel Administrators.

Arminio, J., & Creamer, D. G. (2001). What supervisors say about quality supervision. *College Student Affairs Journal, 21*(1), 35–44.

Astin, A. W. (1993). *What matters in college: Four critical years revisited.* San Francisco: Jossey-Bass.

Austin, A. E. (2002). Preparing the next generation of faculty: Graduate school as socialization to the academic career. *Journal of Higher Education, 73*(1), 94–122.

Austin, A. E., & McDaniels, M. (2006). Preparing the professoriate of the future: Graduate student socialization for faculty roles. In J. C. Smart (Ed.), *Higher education: Handbook of theory and research* (Vol. 21, pp. 397–456). New York: Agathon.

Bean, J. P. (1980). Dropouts and turnover: The synthesis and test of a causal model of student attrition. *Research in Higher Education, 12*(2), 155–171.

Bean, J. P. (1983). The application of a model of turnover in work organizations to the student attrition process. *Review of Higher Education, 6,* 129–148.

Bender, B. (1980). Job satisfaction in student affairs. *NASPA Journal, 18,* 2–9.

Berwick, K. R. (1992). Stress among student affairs administrators: The relationship of personal characteristics and organizational variables to work-related stress. *Journal of College Student Development, 33,* 11–19.

Besnier, N. (1995). The appeal and pitfalls of cross-disciplinary dialogues. In J. A. Russell, J. M. Fernandez-Dols, A. S. R. Manstead, & J. C. Wellenkamp (Eds.), *Everyday conceptions of emotion: An introduction to the psychology, anthropology, and linguistics of emotion* (pp. 559–570). Dordrecht, The Netherlands Kluwer.

Blackburn, R. T., Bieber, J. P., Lawrence, J. H., & Trauvetter, L. C. (1991). Faculty at work: focus on research, scholarship and service. *Research in Higher Education, 32,* 385–413.

Blackhurst, A., Brandt, J., & Kalinowski, J. (1998). Effects of personal and work-related attributes on the organizational commitment and life satisfaction of women student affairs administrators. *NASPA Journal, 35*(2), 86–99.

Bloland, P. A. (1992). *The professionalization of student affairs staff.* Ann Arbor, MI: ERIC Clearinghouse on Counseling and Personnel Services. (ERIC Document Reproduction Service No. ED347495. Accessed November 23, 2008 from http://eric.ed.gov:80/ERICDocs/data/ericdocs2sql/content_storage_01/000001 9b/80/28/ee/51.pdf

Bragg, A. K. (1976). *The socialization process in higher education.* Washington, DC: The American Association of Higher Education.

Brim, O. G. (1966). Socialization through the life cycle. In O. G. Brim & S. Wheeler (Eds.), *Socialization after childhood* (pp. 3–49). New York: Wiley.

Brown, M. C., Davis, G. L., & McClendon, S. A. (1999). Mentoring graduate students of color: Myths, models, and modes. *Peabody Journal of Education, 74*(2), 105–118.

Bullis, C., & Bach, B. (1989). *Social turning points: An examination of change in organizational identification.* Paper presented at the annual meeting of the Western Speech Communication Association, Spokane, WA.

Conley, V. M. (2001). Separation: An internal aspect of the staffing process. *College Student Affairs Journal, 21*(1), 57–63.

Cuevas, F., & Eberhardt, D. (2007, November). *Community college faculty socialization.* Paper presented at the annual meeting of the Association for the Study of Higher Education, Louisville, KY.

Currivan, D. (1999). The causal order of job satisfaction and organizational commitment in models of employee turnover. *Human Resources Management Review,* *9*(4), 495–524.

Dunn, D., Rouse, L., & Seff, M. A. (1994). New faculty socialization in the academic workplace. In J. C. Smart (Ed.), *Higher education: Handbook of theory and research* (Vol. 10, pp. 374–416). New York: Agathon.

Ellis, S. E. (2002). Words of wisdom. In M. J. Amey & L. M. Reesor (Eds.), *Beginning your journey: A guide for new professionals in student affairs* (pp. 141–149). Washington, DC: National Association of Student Affairs Administrators.

Evans, N. J. (1988). Attrition of student affairs professionals: A review of the literature. *Journal of College Student Development, 29,* 25–29.

Glesne, C. (2006). *Becoming qualitative researchers: An introduction* (3rd ed.). Boston, MA: Pearson Education.

Green, S. G., & Bauer, T. N. (1995). Supervisory mentoring by advisors: Relationships with doctoral student potential, productivity, and commitment. *Personnel Psychology, 48,* 537–561.

Hamrick, F. A., & Hemphill, B. O. (2002). Pathways to success in student affairs. In M. J. Amey & L. M. Reesor (Eds.), *Beginning your journey: A guide for new professionals in student affairs* (pp. 119–129). Washington, DC: National Association of Student Personnel Administrators.

Hesburg, T., Miller, P., & Wharton, C. (1973). *Patterns for lifelong learning.* San Francisco: Jossey-Bass.

Hirschman, A. O. (1970). *Exit, voice, and loyalty: Responses to decline in firms.* Cambridge, MA: Harvard University Press.

Hirt, J. B. (2006). *Where you work matters: Student affairs administration at different types of institutions.* Lanham, MD: University Press of America.

Jablonsky, R. (1998). The state of the art: A new professional's perspective. In N. J. Evans & C. E. Phelps Tobin (Eds.), *The state of the art of preparation and practice in student affairs: Another look* (pp. 203–211). Lanham, MD: University Press of America.

Jakobson, R. (1987). On realism in art. In K. Pomorska & S. Rudy (Eds.), *Language in literature* (pp. 25–26). Cambridge, MA: Harvard University Press.

Johnsrud, L. K., & Rosser, V. J. (2002). Faculty members' morale and their intention to leave: A multilevel explanation. *Journal of Higher Education, 73*(4), 518–542.

Katz, R., & Tushman, M. L. (1983). A longitudinal study of the effects of boundary spanning supervision on turnover and promotion in research and development. *The Academy of Management Journal, 26*(3), 437–456.

Komives, S. R. (1998). Linking student affairs preparation with practice. In N. J. Evans & C. E. Phelps Tobin (Eds.), *The state of the art of preparation and practice in student affairs: Another look* (pp. 177–200). Lanham, MD: University Press of America.

Komives, S. R., Woodard, D. B., & Associates. (1996). *Student services: A handbook for the profession.* San Francisco: Jossey-Bass.

Marsh, S. R. (2001). Using adult development theory to inform staff supervision in student affairs. *College Student Affairs Journal, 21*(1), 45–56.

Merton, R. K. (1968). *Social theory and social structure.* New York: The Free Press.

Miller, T. K. (Ed.). (2003). *The book of professional standards for higher education.* Washington, DC: Council for the Advancement of Standards in Higher Education.

Mobley, W. (1977). Intermediate linkages in the relationship between job satisfaction and employee turnover. *Journal of Applied Psychology, 62,* 237–240.

Pascarella, E. T., Terenzini, P. T., & Wolfle, L. M. (1986). Orientation to college and freshman year persistence/withdrawal decisions. *Journal of Higher Education, 57*(2), 153–175.

Price, J., & Mueller, C. (1981). *Professional turnover: The cases of nurses.* New York: Spectrum.

Richmond, J., & Sherman, K. (1991). Student-development preparation and placement: A longitudinal study of graduate students' and new professionals' experiences. *Journal of College Student Development, 32,* 8–16.

Rosser, V. J. (2004). Faculty members' intentions to leave: A national study on their worklife and satisfaction. *Research in Higher Education, 45*(3), 285–309.

Sandeen, A. (1991). *The chief student affairs officer: Leader, manager, mediator, educator.* San Francisco: Jossey-Bass.

Sandeen, A., & Barr, M. J. (2006). *Critical issues for student affairs: Challenges and opportunities.* San Francisco: Jossey-Bass.

Scher, M., & Barr, M. J. (1979). Beyond graduate school: Strategies for survival. *Journal of College Student Development, 20*(6), 529–533.

Sigelman, L., & Tuch, S. A. (1997). Metastereotypes: Blacks' perceptions of Whites' stereotypes of Blacks. *Public Opinion Quarterly, 61*(1), 87–101.

Stein, E. L. (1992). *Socialization at a Protestant seminary.* Unpublished doctoral dissertation, University of Pittsburgh, Pittsburgh, PA.

Strayhorn, T. L. (2009). African American male graduate and professional students. In M. H. Hamilton, S. D. Johnson, & et al. (Eds.), *Standing on the outside looking in.* Sterling, VA: Stylus.

Strayhorn, T. L., & Terrell, M. C. (2007). Mentoring and satisfaction with college for Black students. *The Negro Educational Review, 58*(1–2), 69–83.

Thornton, R., & Nardi, R. M. (1975). The dynamics of role acquisition. *American Journal of Sociology, 80*, 870–885.

Tierney, W. G. (1988). Organizational culture in higher education: Defining the essentials. *Journal of Higher Education, 59*(1), 2–21.

Tierney, W. G. (1997). Organizational socialization in higher education. *The Journal of Higher Education, 68*(1), 1–16.

Tierney, W. G., & Rhoads, R. A. (1993). Postmodernism and critical theory in higher education: Implications for research and practice. In J. C. Smart (Ed.), *Higher education: Handbook of theory and research* (pp. 308–343). New York: Agathon.

Van Maanen, J. (1976). Breaking in: Socialization to work. In R. Dubin (Ed.), *Handbook of work, organization, and society* (pp. 67–130). Chicago: Rand-McNally College Publishing.

Van Maanen, J. (1983). People processing: Strategies of organizational socialization. In R. W. Allan & L. W. Porter (Eds.), *Organizational influence processes*. Glenview, IL: Scott, Foresman, & Company.

Van Maanen, J. (1984). Doing new things in old ways: The chain of socialization. In J. L. Bess (Ed.), *College and university organization: Insights from the behavioral sciences* (pp. 211–247). New York: New York University Press.

Wegner, E. L. (1973). The effects of upward mobility: A study of working-status college students. *Sociology of Education, 46*(3), 263–279.

Weidman, J. (1989a). Undergraduate socialization: A conceptual approach. In J. C. Smart (Ed.), *Higher education: Handbook of theory and research* (Vol. 5, pp. 289–322). New York: Agathon.

Weidman, J. (1989b). The world of higher education: A socialization-theoretical perspective. In K. Herrelmann & U. Engel (Eds.), *The social world of adolescents* (pp. 87–106). Berlin: de Gruyter.

Weidman, J. C., Twale, D. J., & Stein, E. L. (2001). *Socialization of graduate and professional students in higher education: A perilous passage* (pp. 25–54). ASHE-ERIC Higher Education Report, Vol. 28. No. 3. San Francisco: Jossey-Bass.

Winston, R. B., Jr., & Creamer, D. G. (1997). *Improving staffing practices in student affairs*. San Francisco: Jossey-Bass.

9

INSTITUTIONAL
SOCIALIZATION INITIATIVES

Stan Carpenter and Linda Carpenter

F amed sociologist Edgar Schein (2004), upon the occasion of receiving the Everett Cherrington Hughes Award for Careers Scholarship from the Academy of Management succinctly summarized some of his and others' earlier work on socialization thusly:

> We come into our careers with values derived from family, school and community and we seek . . . to find jobs and organizations that permit us to exercise those values. . . . however, as we evolve in our occupational communities, our values are influenced. . . . we are socialized into our occupations and have to learn the "idioms" of that occupation. (p. 262)

This familiar career anchors hypothesis was then extended by Schein's further statements concerning the nature of employing organizations, suggesting that while it is widely understood that organizations break themselves into "functional, geographic and other kinds of sub-systems" (p. 262) and that these subsystems develop distinct cultures, it is not as clearly understood that

> each of these differentiated units reflects an occupational culture and develops its own sub-culture based on (i) its view of its primary task, (ii) its perception of its primary stakeholders, and (iii) the realities of the particular environment in which it functions. With these views there also evolve moral principles that can be quite different from one occupation to another. (p. 262)

Given the complexity of colleges and universities and the many different occupations and, therefore, subcultures at work, there could hardly be a more compelling case for helping a new employee learn how to function in the environment. Not only do new professionals have to learn the mores and customs of their own profession, but they must also avoid the taboos of others that are equally or more powerful. To accomplish this, we must pay attention to easing the transition from newcomer to old hand. Simply knowing how to avoid land mines is not enough of course. The institution and its professionals in student affairs also are obligated to protect the interests of the "clients": the students (there are other clients, as well, but the principal clientele is students), to advance the goals of the larger organization, and to maintain integrity with the overall profession. Integrity includes the inculcation of values, professional development, and ethical responsibility (Carpenter, 2001, 2003). Indeed, the entire notion of professionalism requires a mechanism for socialization and regeneration (Carpenter & Stimpson, 2007), as well as a conception of community.

Of course, there is a more prosaic set of reasons why the organization, in this case the student affairs division and/or a subunit thereof, wishes to smooth the early tenure of a new professional. Recruiting is expensive, difficult, and time consuming. Unhappy or unsuccessful employees are drains on the entire system, often causing geometric problems rather than just additive ones. It should be axiomatic that every person wants to succeed at his or her job and that the organization wants the same thing. If the new person is going to fail or not like the new position, the sooner this is known the sooner a remedy can be introduced. All of these mind-sets require active monitoring and some notion of an intentional process.

Socialization efforts should be focused on three fronts: personal, unit/division, and institutional. The nature and content of each of these foci are treated in turn, followed by suggestions on how to implement a comprehensive socialization process.

Personal

Where do I park? Where do I get office supplies? Who needs to know what and when? Some of these and other early questions seem mundane or trivial and some are fraught with peril, but which are which? The trouble with naïveté is that one doesn't know even what to ask. Socialization in the early days of a new job is, of course, conflated with orientation, but is experienced more in the nuance, the tone, than in the actual lack of information. If the new professional is made to feel like the information should have been known or found, or if no one seems to know, these are powerful messages about (in)competence and (lack of) support. Early interactions build a picture of the organization and should be monitored by a supervisor or other person with a stake in the outcome—a well-adjusted employee. A few studies and publications point to things that should be attended to.

In the first year of employment, new professionals experience issues in the general categories of relationships, fit, and competence (Renn & Hodges, 2007). These concerns seem most easily characterized by stages Renn and Hodges name Preemployment and Orientation (lasting about one month into the job), Transition (about 2–4 months), and Settling In (usually beginning after the start of the second semester and lasting through the rest of the first year).

New professionals, according to the relationships facet of this schema, are wrestling with the normal aspects of moving into a new environment in terms of finding salubrious companionship, on and off the job. The socialization impact here is massive and immediate. The new professional has to learn what is appropriate in terms of relationships with supervisors, peers, other parts of the university, students, and outside (of work) people in the context of the new position and responsibilities. It is easy for organizational incumbents to forget or dismiss the level and importance of tacit knowledge that is hard won over a period of time. The Transition stage may be particularly tricky—it is easy for assumptions to be made on all sides about several serious issues. If, for example, the supervisor is not communicating regularly with the new employee, it may be assumed that everything is fine or that there is some level of distaste. If the job seems to be getting done, it may not be clear that accomplishment is at the cost of unsustainable 90-hour work weeks. The point is that the socialization process requires consistent monitoring for a long period of time. Settling In, as a stage, can have challenges also because relationship misconceptions may be on their way to becoming calcified and taken as fact. It is always good for the new professional to have regular relationship checkups for the first year or even longer because of the possibility and consequences of poor communication. Also successful professional practice at this stage should involve growing confidence and independence.

Fit is a difficult concept to define and is also subject to the vagaries of individual perception. Too, the quality of fit has a tendency to sneak up on

a new professional in the Transition stage because during the Preemployment and Orientation stages the new professionals are so busy and feel relief
at simply getting a job (Renn & Hodges, 2007). The new professional is
learning more about the organization and the culture(s) at the same time
that some notion of fit is emerging. This is a crucial time for active processing, and someone (probably the supervisor or other seasoned professional)
needs to reach out to ensure a positive or at least a well-considered outcome
because there is the possibility of the new professional's deciding to leave
the position. This is not necessarily a bad outcome for the person or the
organization, but it should not be based on incorrect information or unchallenged perceptions.

Hemmed in by perception, and even more so by trepidation, are discussions of competence. New professionals may feel well educated, but few
would argue that they are completely ready for professional practice on their
first day. Yet, student affairs jobs are typically quite demanding and every
person and position counts—there is no surplus! Hence the new professional
is expected to pull his or her weight almost immediately. Without attention
to socialization issues, this can lead to excessive work hours, unwarranted
self-criticism, and, ultimately, early attrition. Renn and Hodges (2007)
counsel a valuing of the competencies that the new professional possesses
and intentional development of those that are needed. They also strongly
urge that *supervisor* not be confused with *mentor*. Clearly, especially in interactions around competence, this could be frightening and such fear would
slow down needed growth. Chapter 7 in this volume elucidates the differences between supervision and mentoring.

In a study of competencies desired in entry-level employees, Burkard,
Cole, Ott, and Stoflet (2005) found that employers looked for what the
researchers deemed "personal qualities" (p. 293), such as flexibility, interpersonal relations, and the like, and what were called "human relations skills"
(p. 293), such as collaboration, teamwork/building, etc. To be sure, other
more theoretical and technical skills and knowledge are needed also, but personal qualities and human relations skills were very important to student
affairs practitioners surveyed. Obviously, this profession is a people business
and these personal traits and skills are critical. Equally clearly, many of these
traits are culturally defined and interpreted. It is essential that someone inter-
acts with new entrants to the organization to counter misperceptions and to
lend insight into how the new professional is coming across, intentionally or

otherwise. This someone should be sensitive and careful—ideally not in the new employee's immediate unit—and trained in ways to give feedback. Often, small adjustments can reap large dividends in perception. If the fit or these qualities are missing, there is little chance of success anyway; if there is a chance to salvage a shaky situation through dialogue or training, it should be taken.

Student Affairs Unit/Division

Beyond personal socialization to a new job is socialization in the context of the subculture(s) of the unit and division. Schein (2004) ascribes the status of moral idioms to some of the norms and practices of such units and suggests that they are crucial to socialization, so much so that rising in the organization or moving from job to job is akin to changing cultures so that one eventually becomes "morally relativistic" (p. 270) vis-à-vis the organizational subcultures. This notion of boundaries even within divisions implies that professionals must be vigilant to avoid dangerous conflicts arising from seemingly simple differences in perceived professional culture. Further, new professionals ought not be left to fend for themselves and be at the mercy of unknowing mistakes.

To illustrate this point, Hirt, Amelink, and Schneiter's (2004) study of student affairs work in the liberal arts college is instructive. The authors found that such practice was perforce collaborative and multifaceted, challenging, yet rewarding, team oriented, student centered, service oriented, creative, and personally visible, as well as political and community focused. Visibility is key as is participation and there is, quite literally, nowhere to hide at most liberal arts institutions. A recently hired professional who was not aware of or not picking up these values and practices quickly enough would need to be socialized and soon—there is little margin for error in a small staff. Nor is there room for quibbling. This environment calls to mind once more the importance of fit for the hiring organization and the individual, even though each, for different reasons, may feel some urgency to hurry along the hiring process, and a true judgment of mutual compatibility is tricky and time consuming.

Herdlein (2004) surveyed senior student affairs officers (SSAOs) regarding relevance of preparation for practice and found some predictable holes especially in the areas of administration, budgeting, and awareness of institutional environments among others. The purpose here is not to report the findings in detail but to give context to Herdlein's observation that even two intensive years, the length of most top professional preparation programs, was clearly inadequate to get entry-level professionals fully ready for their first employment experiences. This lends further credence to the idea that the student affairs division and unit have vested interests in continuing education in many different forms, including supervision, professional development, and intentional socialization, all of which should dovetail and certainly not be contradictory.

Clearly, the type of institution and postemployment training needs are two examples requiring divisional socialization, but there are also overarching values that need to be inculcated, ideas that are almost assumptions of the profession. These can be thought of as rooted in the more recent literature of the field and involve the nature and character of appropriate practice. One attempt at capturing these attitudes was Carpenter and Stimpson's (2007) analysis of professionalism, professional development, and scholarly practice. They end by noting four fundamental challenges for the profession, and these are offered here as axiomatic to proper socialization, especially that of entry-level practitioners:

1. Intentionality of practice as a challenge to intuition, "natural ability," and experience
2. Peer review of practice as a challenge to individual "initiative," isolation, and "privacy"
3. Consultation and community as a challenge to competition
4. Professional accountability as a challenge to "standards" (pp. 279–281)

The first of these suggests that practice according to tradition or any motivator other than research and theory is no longer good enough and cannot be tolerated. The socialization cue is to question everything—every program, every position, every expenditure—at every level. Only by example at the very highest levels will progress be made. The division and unit must be seen as committed to understanding why actions are taken and articulating the reasons for those actions.

The second challenge calls for a different and more demanding kind of professionalism than is currently practiced in most student affairs venues.

Professionals should evaluate one another and make suggestions. Professionals must be willing to be honest about failures equally as much, if not more so, than about triumphs. Each needs to be shared for the edification of all and for the benefit of students. Mistakes shouldn't happen twice—they must be challenged and corrected. Socialization takes place in the way that issues are addressed and in asking the new professional to evaluate others' work as appropriate.

Units within divisions and even divisions themselves should have the goal of serving students and the institutional mission at heart. There is no place for competition among units, only the discussion of how best to deploy resources. Competition and greed in whatever form are poisonous to professionalism, collaboration, and community. Professionals should be free to ask questions, to seek help without a thought of untoward motives or loss of advantage. Transparency, discussion, and honest analysis are the hallmarks of socialization here.

True accountability is as complex as the practice that it purports to measure. Suspicion should be aroused whenever simplistic indicators are proposed or used. The various popular ratings of universities and, for that matter, standardized entrance examinations are shot through with very difficult methodological and interpretation issues. This is widely known by experts yet they continue to be used as if they were reliable, let alone valid. Student affairs and other units within higher education institutions need assessment that is "not only ubiquitous, but also meaningful" (Carpenter & Stimpson, 2007, p. 281). What they don't need is more trivial data sets, collected in the name of efficiency but signifying nothing.

If the above assumptions seem theoretical and aspirational there is another set of socialization targets that are behavioral and practical. Every unit and every division has cultural norms in any number of areas.

To start, the discussion and use of theory and research generally, and "favorite" ones in particular, varies from office to office. This is subtly different from the challenge referred to above to begin basing every action on theory and research. Instead, what is meant here is whether or not "theory talk" is even welcome and if so at what level. Also, sometimes in some units, "pet" theories surface, depending upon the training and orientation of the positional incumbents. There are real issues around couching one's discussion in the "correct" ways.

Similarly, professional development at the divisional and unit level may mean a variety of things. In some places, it simply refers to traveling to conferences, while other divisions have elaborate professional development planning mechanisms built into annual evaluation schemes. The new professional needs to know what is available, what is valued, what is financially supported, and what is acceptable in terms of allocating time and effort. For example, it may be fine to take a class but only after one or two years on the job.

Some issues are quite prosaic. What are the dress codes for the division? For the unit? For meetings? For casual Friday? For student events? For conferences? For retreats? For evening and weekend work? These are not trivial questions and seem to be ever more important as the breadth of the fashion spectrum increases.

Also crucial are questions about the behavioral expectations surrounding alcohol. Obviously, drinking with underage students is forbidden but what about students who are of age? Is that problematic? Is it wise? Is it frowned on but tolerated? What about drinking and partying, not with students but where students are likely to be and see the new professional? Is that a problem or a positive? Depending upon the institutional mission, of course, public (or even private) alcohol consumption may be prohibited. Is there a different alcohol standard at conferences? Are there other conference expectations, things that are not done by professionals at a given institution?

Of course behaviors around alcohol are not the only boundary issues faced by new professionals, especially if they happen to be close in age to the students they serve. Formal institutional policies vary greatly, where they exist at all, concerning consensual romantic or sexual relationships among professional staff and students. However, every institution has a sexual harassment policy, and every relationship between staff and student, given the inherent power differential, is by definition suspect from the minute the relationship changes from professional to personal. Still, different divisions and units treat such issues differently, and part of socialization is to learn which behaviors are permitted and which are not. Someone in the unit should make sure to affirmatively address this particular topic very early in the employment of the new professional, since the consequences are potentially drastic.

Not all relationships that are personal are romantic of course, and yet they may look inappropriate from the outside. This is a tricky area for new professionals and should be the subject of careful discussion with peers, supervisors, and/or a mentor. As a guide, the professional should always be aware that he or she is in the position and the profession to promote the ethical education of students, and any interaction that puts that goal at risk is suspect.

Another very important normative question surrounds the interactions of divisional and/or unit colleagues. Ideally it is understood that disagreements and indeed all interactions are to be conducted courteously and professionally. However, there are all sorts of nuances in any organization. Are first names used for superiors? How far up? When students are around? How about for subordinates? Are faculty or other personnel from outside student affairs treated differently? Again, ideally, a standard of collegiality pervades, but if not, that is a clear occasion for socialization.

An important opportunity for socialization is one that is not so easy or pleasant. It should go without saying that interactions between and among colleagues who are culturally, ethnically, or otherwise different in ways that affect identity should be professional and nonjudgmental at a minimum. Ideally, a student affairs division and unit would have a culture of celebration of differences, but tolerance is requisite and nonnegotiable. Insensitivity in any form must be confronted, especially in new professionals, lest it ruin an otherwise promising career, as it has the potential to do. On a more positive and developmental note, modeling an organizational and personal commitment to diversity and its celebration can have a strong impact, not just on the targeted entry level employees but on all onlookers throughout the division and unit. The contagion of cultural collegiality will be noticed and emulated, if and only if the leaders of the division and unit are consistent in their own practice of it.

Institutional

Amey (2002) suggested that Tierney's (1991) elements of organizational culture could be useful in discussing the transition difficulties and considerations for new professionals. Her work is used here as the framework for examining some of the ways the new professional becomes socialized to his or her role in the institution as an individual and, more importantly, as a member of the student affairs division. The six elements are environment, mission, socialization, information, strategy, and leadership (Amey, 2002; Tierney, 1991).

Ideally all new professionals would have an in-depth understanding of the higher education institution where they are employed. However, since such an understanding is quite rare this is unlikely, especially given that all 4,300 (about) colleges and universities in the United States are unique in some, or many, ways. It behooves new professionals and those responsible for their socialization to spend as much time as necessary to obtain, provide, and facilitate an understanding of the internal and external constraints and opportunities attendant on the institution. Essential to this understanding are things such as institutional size, student demographics, selectivity, governance structure, and so on, but also and importantly, what the local political and decision-making structure is like, formally and informally. Are there financial difficulties among students or for the institution? Is there animosity between and among the faculty and the various support divisions of the university? Are student affairs workers thought of as professionals or service providers? As partners or support staff? For example, an increasingly prevalent role for student affairs is leadership in retention and other enrollment planning mechanisms. This is not necessarily a bad thing, as it can bring the division into the mainstream of campus power politics because of its inherent importance. However, if that is the only view of student affairs or if enrollment management is seen as simple consumer service, then the division and its participants need to know that and either embrace it or work to change it. Finally, Amey (2002) astutely points out that student affairs administrators always represent the division in every interaction on the campus and need to be good ambassadors because faculty, staff, administration, and even students frequently don't know what we do. Rule one: scan the environment.

Today, with the World Wide Web and information freely available, the new professional should have a pretty good idea of the mission of the institution before arriving on campus—or at least what a large group of people representing different campus constituencies agreed to call the mission. Sadly, or interestingly, depending on one's view of human nature, the mission of the institution is sometimes not reflected in all the activities of the university or college for several reasons. First, the mission statement, being by definition a compromise among competing interests, relies on superordinate images such as the "education of the whole student" that have very different meanings to different subunits of the organization (Birnbaum, 1988). Second, higher education institutions, even small ones, are almost unbelievably complex. Many different missions, goals, and objectives are all quite legitimately subsumed under the "larger" mission. Third, and most important to the new professional, while the global mission may be what the institution intends, it is actually the resultant of myriad smaller actions and reactions daily that define the institution, none of which may have a linear relationship to one another or to the mission. In other words, even if the university's goals are being achieved, it will be hard to see that in day-to-day interactions with students or with unit functions whose purpose may seem at variance with the larger goals but add up to something synergistic. Finally, beware of the institution in which the culture is so strong and reinforced by daily interactions that no deviation from the orthodoxy (usually based upon faith traditions, values, or heritage) is permitted. The new professional cannot always tell if she or he will be comfortable in such an organization until arriving and working there.

This entire chapter concerns socialization, so this section will only discuss Amey's (2002) and others' notion that every organization has rituals and traditions and that the new professional needs to become acquainted with them as soon as possible. This particular kind of socialization is not about the professional role exactly but really has to do with becoming a full-fledged organizational participant instead of being perceived as an outsider. The importance of this in most colleges and universities cannot be overemphasized—there is even a specialized language that grows up around widely known traditions, icons, and rituals (Birnbaum, 1988) and woe betide the individual who is not aware of the institutional saga(s). One can safely be "new" only for a little while in this sense.

Considerations around the use and misuse of information could easily fill this entire book and more. New professionals may believe that information will be freely available, in quantity and quality sufficient to do one's job. This is rarely so, in any complete sense. Two ways to look at this question are instructive. First, how does one get the information necessary to do one's job in the best way possible? The answer begins with handbooks, policies, missions, goals, reports, and other overt publications, but it also includes the campus newspaper, divisional rumors, the Board of Regents' (or equivalent) minutes, local and national court cases, cable television news networks, students, colleagues, offices across the campus, professional associations, and on and on. There is seemingly no limit to the information needed to conduct a student affairs program that involves such a complex organization as a college or university and such a complex goal as student development and learning. Also, so much information is available electronically that accuracy and filtering are issues that require experience, skill, and judgment (Amey, 2002).

A second set of considerations ensues once one has information that may be needed by other units or the larger organization. How does one share information and with whom? Schein's (2004) address, alluded to earlier in the chapter, principally concerned the moral idioms having to do with withholding or even lying about information, based solely upon occupational customs and sanctions. In the real world, the new professional needs at a minimum to know what is being risked when using or sharing information.

Much of what Amey (2002) addresses under the category of strategy has been covered in this chapter at the unit level. Strategy in this sense really means putting all the foregoing socialization to work in order to accomplish personal, unit, or divisional goals. Learning how to influence decisions and directions means being willing to abandon the illusion that high-stakes, value-laden choices in complex organizations are made in simple or linear ways. New professionals who pay attention to all the cues around them soon learn that they are by turn more powerful or less listened to than they should be based on their expertise and/or effort. Certainly, competence and hard work are the place to start one's strategy considerations and they will win out frequently. But strategy, intentionally planning how to plant seeds and have ideas heard, can be learned and practiced.

Leadership is not something that is possessed only by nominal leaders (Birnbaum, 1988). This has been the message of virtually every self-help or management book for the past two decades, but it must be learned in every new organizational context. Even in very hierarchical organizations, the secretary or the assistant to the nominal leader holds important gate-keeping power, for example. Institutional memory or contacts across the campus can be used like a scalpel or a cudgel as necessary but only by those who possess them. For new professionals, leadership opportunities will follow hard work, willingness to serve in many different (sometimes underappreciated or menial) roles and capacities, and consistent participation in unit, divisional, and institutional events. In Amey's (2002) words, "there is a close connection between effective leaders and effective followers" (p. 25). Apart from these strategies to gain leadership experience, new professionals should look for good role models of leadership at all levels of the institution to emulate.

Another important aspect of socialization at the institutional level is explicated by Hirt (2007) who examines the contrast between and among the dominant narratives of what she calls the "academic marketplace" (p. 245) and the narratives that are accepted by student affairs professionals as descriptive of their work. Hirt summarizes the former:

> These four narratives, then—the knowledge regime, consumerism, higher education as a manufacturer, and the public versus private benefits of higher education—have dominated the discourse of academicians during the past 25 years. Additionally, it is important to note that these narratives are not confined to those at large, public, research universities. The same notions have infiltrated the ways that other types of campuses see their work. (p. 251)

Hirt's take on student affairs narratives, on the other hand, is couched historically and is "collapsed into three basic narratives: *in loco parentis,* student services, and student development" (p. 252), which branches into a "subplot [in which] student affairs professionals can (and should) collaborate with academicians to offer seamless educational experiences. . . . [and] . . . student affairs administrators are educators whose work with students is as valuable as that of faculty instructors" (p. 253).

Hirt (2007) points out the gross discontinuity between the (student- and learning-centered) student development narrative and any of the four institution- and knowledge-production-based ones and then uses the *Principles of Good Practice for Student Affairs* (American College Personnel Association & National Association of Student Personnel Administrators, 1997) to illustrate how the seven principles (a proxy for student development) could be "recast" (p. 258) to more closely reflect the narratives that academic administrators and faculty have adopted. She suggests that the corporate university is already with us and will be for a long period. If student affairs as a profession wishes to thrive or even to accomplish its work with students, then it must fit into the dominant discourse, that of the academicians.

Hirt's (2007) article is a cogent and sophisticated yet accessible treatment of higher education politics in a macro context and should be required reading for all student affairs professionals but certainly for new professionals who are not hidebound in their thinking yet. However, that is not the reason it is introduced and summarized here. Rather, the intent is to show there are many different ways of looking at the various divisions, units, offices, functions, goals, missions, and activities in any organization, especially complex ones like universities. The goal is to showcase one attempt at determining the dominant narratives of groups on campus. The new professional needs to develop the ability on a smaller, institutional scale to map the institutional landscape in a similar way by talking to participants in the various divisions and units, by reading, by observing, and by trial and error. It is far easier to talk to people—and get them to buy in or help with activities—when one knows what they want, or need, to hear. If this seems manipulative, the reader should understand that nothing unethical is intended, nor should any student affairs goals be sacrificed. Simply put, there are ways to use narratives and language that are efficient in their pragmatism, as Hirt (2007) so elegantly shows.

One other aspect of institutional socialization needs to be addressed here, that of institutional citizenship. Just as student affairs professionals want students to be committed to and involved with the university or college, so too should new professionals become part of the life of the institution. This is accomplished in many of the ways detailed above, but it also should involve intentional activity aimed at involvement across the campus and in many venues and ways. Boehman (2007) applied the Meyer and Allen (1997) model to student affairs professionals, noting that institutional commitment (not quite the same as institutional citizenship, but related) is composed of "affective, continuance, and normative" (Boehman, p. 309) aspects. Normative refers to the moral or loyalty-based obligation (which is hoped for in divisional and institutional contexts), continuance involves the costs of changing organizational affiliation, and affective is mediated by job satisfaction, organizational support, organizational politics, and work/nonwork interaction or balance. Boehman conducted a study of the components of affective commitment, concluding (among other things) that, as expected, perceived organizational support was positively related and that perceived level of organizational politics was negatively related to affective commitment. The components of organizational politics were identified as (a) "competition for control of the agenda and policies of an organization, usually for the benefit of an 'in group'" (p. 311); (b) "an environment where compliance with group norms is expected and valued" (p. 311); and (c) "individuals who are politically active will get promotions and other incentives at the expense of others" (p. 312). Boehman showed once more that perception is reality and can have a disturbing impact, especially among the newly or incompletely socialized.

Of course perception is not necessarily reality, and part of socialization is to demythologize such beliefs. The definition of organizational politics detailed in this chapter is certainly ugly and would result in a negative organizational climate and poor decision making if it were applied as described. But, studied carefully, it is clear that there are advantages to having healthy dialogue around agendas and policies, even though there can be winners and losers in such battles. There is a fine line between spirited debates, in which one point of view more frequently comes out ahead (mission? vision? culture?), and negative politics. Losing one discussion is not a reason to quit talking; quite the contrary, the only way to really lose is to quit. The second point of the definition obviously turns on a question of degree and nature of the expected compliance. Again, culture consists of such norms, and while diversity should be valued, opting to ascribe conformity in small things to corrosive politics is simply whining. The third aspect of the definition is equally open to interpretation. If one word is left out, the phrase becomes "those who are . . . active will get promotions and other incentives," a situation that could readily be construed as appropriate unless someone has an ax to grind. This is not to deny the existence or even the occasionally poisonous nature of organizational politics—they exist and can be nasty. However, the new professional should be particularly careful, thoughtful, and patient before labeling complex organizational dynamics, especially on the word of a small number of participants. After all, as Newman and Carpenter (1993) put it:

> demystifying politics is the best way to take power away from the manipulative, egocentric employees and give it back to those who understand that organizational success enhances personal success. But the sad fact is that many people in student affairs think of themselves as "above" politics. The result is that the most skilled politicians in student affairs (and other fields) are often the least scrupulous employees. In short, professionals who fail to understand politics are at the mercy of those who do. (p. 223–224)

Good institutional citizens then are those who voluntarily participate in extra-unit governance, in professional development opportunities, in committees across the campus and across the division, taking the time to add their voice and their energy to decisions large and small. This attitude of activity, of civic obligation reflects well upon the unit, upon the division, and upon the person. It is possible that some will see this activity as political and it is, in the sense that polity simply refers to the way a group makes decisions. The only real question is whether the new professional wants representation at the deliberations for the unit, the division, and even the self. The answer is self-evident.

Making It Happen—Characteristics of the Process

Socialization of new professionals should be persistent and consistent. It starts with the hiring process, with treating applicants fairly and humanely, with valuing them and their time and effort. Once the hiring decision has been made, the socialization pressure should increase by sending materials and Web links, newsletters, divisional communications, and so on to make the new professional feel like part of the team. When the new employee arrives on campus (actually in town), he or she should be made to feel like family, literally. They should be contacted regularly and even fed occasionally. Orientation is treated in chapter 6, but the content of orientation is less important than the tone and the message, in the sense of brand messages. These should be consistent and recognizable from the application through orientation and beyond. All employees should be getting regular and intentional communications from the division that inform, translate institutional news and priorities into divisional information, and evoke a point of view, a professional message. Special attention should be paid to the new professional for at least 18 months to make sure that he or she is getting the messages that are aimed at all, not just the new. Finally, professional development opportunities should be folded into the mix in such a way that socialization shortcomings that have been noted by either the employee or the supervisor or mentor are addressed in a formative, positive way.

The program of socialization most purely targets new professionals of course, but it should be aimed at everyone in the division as a cultural booster shot if nothing else. After all, a dynamic culture should be ever changing, and subtleties in the message need to be inculcated frequently. The socialization process, as all student affairs programs and functions, should be overt and intentional. This is far too important to be left to chance, as has so often been the case in the past. There should be a well-thought-out program, with goals, milestones, and assessments for every group of new employees and perhaps for every individual. The process of developing this program and its goals should be transparent and inclusive, involving as many units as possible and specifically involving recent new employees. The program should be easy to change and open to modification. It should be responsive to the nature of the preparation of the new professionals and the needs of the affected units. There should be continuing dialogue among the supervisor(s) and those administering the program, who should engage in careful and regular training and development for the purpose. Finally, of course, the program should be evaluated regularly for effectiveness, with the bulk of the feedback coming from new employee participants.

Making It Happen—Mechanisms

Socialization, like any educational process, is ultimately the responsibility of the person being socialized. However, it has been shown that the person needs help in the form of expectations, ideas for activities and avenues, and mentoring. A carefully constructed program, such as the one described in this chapter, will help the person understand what is to be achieved, and hence the process can become a collaboration, especially if a mentoring relationship can be established that is completely outside of the supervisory one. Having a safe ear is critical in this process, because socialization can be quite risky and the stakes are high for the person and the unit/division.

Professional development, again with the cooperation, consent, and enthusiasm of the socializee, can be used to augment socialization, but carefully. To the extent that educational activities such as training or required readings are used, they should not be part of the evaluation process except in a very formative and positive way. Training is not the same thing as socialization, despite the fact that each influences the other. Supervision is covered in chapter 7, but its role in socialization should be gentle and carefully considered.

Opportunities for growth and experience, such as membership on institutional committees or being a division representative to some high-level activity, should be meted out with the greatest of care and with adequate support to guarantee success to the extent possible. It is possible to get too much, too fast in socialization, as in most things.

Finally, the best kind of socialization, the kind that makes the most sense and leaves the best impression, is modeling. Having finished-for-now exemplars to look up to is critical for new professionals and can do more for motivation than any set of readings or program goals. Much is accomplished by the simple dint of fostering professionalism in word and deed across the unit and the division. Socialization, after all, aims to help the person become an active organizational participant. Care must be taken that actions speak as loudly as words.

Conclusion

Two articles published some time ago show that the ideas discussed here are not new concerns. Hyde and Carpenter (1992) considered the problem of "aliens . . . trespassing" (p. 149) in a new culture. They talked about several possible missteps using the idea of the Aristotelian mean. The errors were inappropriate or false enthusiasm for the new place, failure to fit into the system, making inappropriate comparisons between the new and the old, failure to define success, failure to deal with failing, and listening without learning. They concluded,

> Recognizing the value of bridging the gap from alien to citizen, outsider to insider, and stranger to colleague is a start. . . . [since in many] . . . major dialects, the word "stranger" means "enemy." . . . [so] . . . the organization might benefit from directing energy toward avoiding, on both sides, the trespasses described. (p. 152)

Whitt (1997), also in a metaphorical vein, winds up her consideration of encountering a new culture, as the new professionals discussed here are doing, by giving a series of "Travel Tips":

1. Read the guidebooks before you leave home.
2. Identify your own cultural "baggage."
3. Get to know the natives.
4. Find a guide.
5. Experience local color.
6. See the sights.

7. Take side trips.
8. Learn the language.
9. Seek storytellers
10. Ask for directions.
11. Phone home.
12. Travel with an open mind.
13. Don't expect to change the culture. (pp. 518–522)

Similarity and congruence between these succinct and metaphorical statements and this chapter are of course obvious and intentional. Perhaps there should be one more, as the process of socialization is considered in the context of beginning one's career in student affairs: Have fun!

References

American College Personnel Association & National Association of Student Personnel Administrators. (1997). *Principles of good practice for student affairs.* Washington, DC: Author.

Amey, M. J. (2002). The unwritten rules: Organizational and political realities of the job. In M. J. Amey & L. M. Reesor (Eds.), *Beginning your journey: A guide for new professionals in student affairs* (Rev. ed., pp. 13–30). Washington, DC: National Association of Student Personnel Administration.

Birnbaum, R. (1988). *How colleges work.* San Francisco: Jossey-Bass.

Boehman, J. (2007). Affective commitment among student affairs professionals. *NASPA Journal, 44*(2), 307–326.

Burkard, A., Cole, D. C., Ott, M., & Stoflet, T. (2005). Entry-level competencies of new student affairs professionals: A Delphi study. *NASPA Journal, 42*(3), 283–309.

Carpenter, D. S. (2001). Student affairs scholarship (re?)considered: Toward a scholarship of practice. *Journal of College Student Development, 42*(4), 301–318.

Carpenter, D. S. (2003). Professionalism in student affairs work. In S. Komives & D. Woodard (Eds.), *Student Services: A handbook for the profession* (4th ed., pp. 573–591). San Francisco: Jossey-Bass.

Carpenter, S., & Stimpson, M. (2007). Professionalism, scholarly practice, and professional development in student affairs. *NASPA Journal, 44*(2), 265–284.

Herdlein, R. J., III. (2004). Survey of chief student affairs officers regarding relevance of graduated preparation of new professionals. *NASPA Journal, 42*(1), 51–71.

Hirt, J. B. (2007). The student affairs profession in the academic marketplace. *NASPA Journal, 44*(2), 245–264.

Hirt, J. B., Amelink, C. T., & Schneiter, S. (2004). The nature of student affairs work in the liberal arts college. *NASPA Journal, 42*(1), 94–110.

Hyde, S., & Carpenter, D. S. (1992). No trespassing: What every alien should know. *NASPA Journal, 29*(2), 149–152.

Meyer, J. P., & Allen, N. J. (1997). *Commitment in the workplace: Theory, research, and application.* Thousand Oaks, CA: Sage.

Newman, B., & Carpenter, D. S. (1993). The nature of organizational politics. *NASPA Journal, 30*(3), 219–224.

Renn, K. A., & Hodges, J. P. (2007). The first year on the job: Experiences of new professionals in student affairs. *NASPA Journal, 44*(2), 367–391.

Schein, E. H. (2004). Learning when and how to lie: A neglected aspect of organizational and occupational socialization. *Human Relations, 57,* 259–273.

Tierney, W. G. (1991). Organizational culture in higher education: Defining the essentials. In M. Peterson (Ed.), *ASHE reader in organizations and governance in higher education* (pp. 103–117). Lexington, MA: Ginn Press.

Whitt, E. J. (1997). "Don't drink the water?" A guide to encountering a new institutional culture. In E. J. Whitt (Ed.), *College student affairs administration* (pp. 516–523). Boston: Pearson Custom Publishing.

10

PROFESSIONAL ASSOCIATIONS AND SOCIALIZATION

Steven M. Janosik

P rofessionals have different motivations for belonging to associations. Carpenter (1991) and Nuss (1993) identified some of the common reasons individuals belong to associations. They desire to (a) enhance administrative skills, (b) gain new perspectives, (c) develop leadership skills, (d) develop collegial relationships, (e) grow professionally, and (f) influence the profession. Others suggest that involvement in professional associations can help advance careers (Chernow, Cooper, & Winston, 2003).

Professional associations and the activities connected with them can also provide valuable resources for new professionals and can be of great assistance in socializing them to the field of student affairs. Properly constructed and coordinated, these programs can help with the transition from the new professional's educational experience to the real world of work. Professional associations can provide needed skill development to enhance a new professional's repertoire of competencies. Moreover, they can help the new professional begin to develop a professional identity that may lead to increased validation and success. When well executed these mechanisms may result in increased retention of good and satisfied professionals at their home institutions or in the field.

The purpose of this chapter is to provide the new professional with a brief overview of the historical development of professional associations in the field of student affairs and to illustrate how they serve as an important tool in the socialization process. After a brief review of the development of professional associations, how these organizations help with the transition to the field of student affairs is discussed.

Continuing professional development is an important component of most professions, and so a review of how professional associations assist with training and skill acquisition of new professionals will make up the third major section of this chapter. Professional associations also help new members establish their own professional identity and help foster a sense of commitment to the profession and one's chosen career. These issues will be addressed in turn and will culminate in a list of recommendations on how new professionals can maximize their association experience.

Finally, the chapter concludes with several specific suggestions on how professional associations might improve their services to their members.

The Development of Professional Associations in Student Affairs

It does not take too long for organizations to be created any time a group of individuals gets together to share a common interest or purpose. Educators, in particular, seem driven to share their knowledge, advocate for issues, and establish common expectations. Indeed, less than 10 years after the first deans of students were appointed, they realized that to be more effective they needed to "gather together" and learn from one another (Gerda, 2003, p. 151). By 1916 the first professional association in student affairs was established. It was known as the National Association of Deans of Women (Nidiffer, 2000). As the organization evolved, it became known as the National Association of Women Deans, Administrators, and Counselors (NAWDAC) and later the National Association for Women in Education (NAWE). NAWE disbanded in 2002 after 86 years of service to the profession.

In the early 1900s, the popular thought was that men and women belonged in different realms (Hanson, 1995), so it did not take men long to develop their own parallel structure of professional associations. In 1919 Scott Goodnight hosted the first meeting for deans of men attended by his colleagues from Minnesota, Iowa, New York, Michigan, and Illinois. This conference established the National Association of Deans of Men (National Association of Deans and Advisers of Men, 1938), which eventually became the National Association of Student Personnel Administrators (NASPA).

Moore and Neuberger (1998) suggest that professional associations fulfill "the general role of advancing the interests of the profession and the professional by providing continuing education, establishing standards and expectations for practice, advocating for professional issues to a broader, and sometimes, external constituency, and transmitting knowledge about the field to their members and other interested parties" (p. 61). Nuss (1993) described the purpose of associations as "advancing the understanding, recognition, and knowledge in the field; developing and promulgating standards for professional practice; serving the public interest; and providing professionals with a peer group that promotes a sense of identity (p. 365). Elder (1984) suggested further that associations also encourage excellence and creative leadership.

Some associations do this by emphasizing one particular function in student affairs and establishing an organization for a specialized group of professionals. As examples, the Association of Student Judicial Affairs (ASJA) focuses on judicial affairs and the administration of student disciplinary systems. The Association of College and University Housing Officers–International (ACUHO–I) focuses on the needs of professionals in housing and residence life (Sauter, 1994). The Association of College Unions International (ACUI) addresses the needs of college union and student activities professional staff members (ACUI, 1995). Other organizations such as College Student Educators International (ACPA) and NASPA take a more generalist approach and serve as the two major umbrella organizations for student affairs professionals.

The oldest professional associations in student affairs have existed for almost 100 years and continue to develop and evolve. Today more than 35 national professional organizations serve the contemporary student affairs profession. (Sandeen & Barr, 2006). All of these organizations can help the new student affairs professional with the transition from graduate student to professional or the transition from another career field to the field of student affairs and higher education administration. Most professionals in student affairs belong to one or more associations. In their study on staffing practices, Winston and Creamer (1997) found that 80% of vice presidents for student affairs, 66% of major department heads, and 83% of professionals with the title of coordinator held association membership. Indeed, it is very common to hold membership in one of the major national associations and at least one association that focuses on the member's primary area of responsibility.

Helping With the Transition From Student to Professional

Professional associations and the activities connected to them help new professionals make the transition from their previous careers or their graduate school experiences. Some of this assistance may be less than obvious to the casual observer. Providing professional support, creating mentoring opportunities, and assisting new professionals with maintaining important professional networks are important services that should not be overlooked.

Support Versus Challenge

When new professionals take their first job they have several important decisions to make. Many opt to stick with the familiar and stay close to home. They may even choose to work at the same institution where they received their graduate or undergraduate degree. Staying in a recognizable environment offers new professionals a great deal of support and comfort—familiar environs, familiar faces, and familiar organizational cultures. Others may decide to challenge themselves by taking jobs in unfamiliar locations at institutions they know little about. Regardless of the decisions made, creating a network of peers and similarly situated colleagues through professional associations can help new members make the transition from student to professional. Using this network to learn more about the higher education enterprise and professional expectations, discussing common work experiences, and discovering trends in current practice is an important key to making an effective transition from student to new professional.

Using Mentors

Many professional associations sponsor mentoring programs for new professionals. In such programs, new professionals indicate their willingness to be matched with more experienced professionals who volunteer to spend time with those who are less experienced. Usually these mentoring programs take place at the annual conference of the association, but these relationships can extend well past a few days at the conference location. ACPA's most recent program is referred to as the Convention Colleague program. ASCA recently instituted its program called Conference Mentors as another example.

Many professional associations also offer special institutes where individuals are nominated and selected as participants. These institutes serve as another kind of mentoring program. In these programs, a small group of participants work with a select group of seasoned professionals, or faculty, in an intensive program especially designed to build skills, create a more significant professional network, and develop long-lasting relationships.

One example involving two generalist organizations is the New Professionals Institute (NPI) cosponsored by NASPA Region III and the Southern Association for College Student Affairs (SACSA). The sponsors describe NPI as a professional development opportunity for new student affairs professionals in the South, which includes "an intensive, interactive week of learning, sharing, networking and professional and personal development. This opportunity allows new professionals to draw on their first years of experience to improve their effectiveness and to learn from others. It is a time of professional and personal renewal and assists new professionals in the development of their careers" (SACSA, 2008). NPI requires a commitment by the new professional to work intensively over five days with other new professionals and a team of six to eight seasoned faculty members who are usually deans or vice presidents. To ensure that new professionals' participation in the institute is fully endorsed by the current senior student affairs officer at their institution, registrants must have a letter of support submitted by their senior student affairs officer.

ACHUO–I's James C. Grimm National Housing Training Institute serves as an example sponsored by a specialty organization (a focus on housing and residence life). The specific goals of this program are to provide a thorough professional development experience for younger professionals who want to further their careers in housing. Participants meet and interact with other colleagues, establish mentor relationships with experts in the field, design professional development plans, and gain skills and competencies needed to meet the current and future demands of the profession (James C. Grimm National Housing Training Institute, 2008).

Participating in these matching programs and institutes can be powerful learning opportunities, and they can serve as important socialization tools, but these experiences are only the first step in a true mentoring relationship. According to Johnson (2007) mentoring consists of three important components: psychosocial support, career development support, and role modeling. Psychosocial support includes being accessible, being selective, providing encouragement, nurturing the dream, and counseling. Career development support includes teaching and training, demystifying the system, encouraging risk taking, clarifying expectations, providing exposure, and initiating sponsorship. Finally, role modeling includes being a model, self-disclosing when appropriate, fostering networks, and allowing increased mutuality and collegiality (Johnson).

Clearly, mentoring takes commitment and time. It can, however, be one of the most effective ways to become socialized in the field of student affairs and an effective way to launch a career.

Beyond these structured opportunities, new professionals should know that they can initiate mentoring relationships on their own by seeking out their own mentors. To be successful, the relationship must be clearly defined and it must be mutual.

While immediate supervisors can be mentors, creating a mentoring relationship with supervisors can create some difficulties. Generally, mentoring is a professionally close relationship, where the person being mentored may benefit in ways that other staff members may not. This can create ethical problems for the supervisor. In addition, not every supervisor has the skill to be a mentor, and to be sure, not every supervisor wants this responsibility.

Supervisors who are unfulfilled in their positions and who may be just clocking time can be a negative influence on new professionals and colleagues (Coleman & Johnson, 1990). Other supervisors who have advanced beyond their abilities or have little interest in the profession rarely make good mentors. Mable (1984) refers to these individuals as "driftwood professionals" and suggests that new professionals are not likely to receive the direction and support they need from this type of supervisor. Of course, one way to widen the pool of potential mentors is to join a professional association and attend its conference activities.

The benefits of this special relationship are clear. Johnson's (2007) review of the research on mentoring leaves little doubt that new professionals who enter into relationships that can truly be defined as mentoring advance in their careers faster, gain more knowledge about their field, contribute in more significant ways, and have a stronger connection to the field than those who do not. More about the role of the supervisor in the socialization of new professionals and the mentoring process can be found in chapter 7.

Finding Comfort in the Company of Old Friends

Joining associations also offers new professionals an easy way to stay in touch with classmates and other peers. Most conference planners are well aware of the need and desire of their members to connect with colleagues in similar positions and similar types of institutions. Round tables and institutionally sponsored socials are a regular part of conference schedules. Clearly we find comfort in the company of old friends and that is a good thing. In fact, it is much more purposeful than one might think.

Networking is not just an up/down issue (Reesor, 2002). While there are benefits to meeting people at higher levels in organizations and the profession, there are many benefits in maintaining contacts with peers and classmates. These individuals work at other types of institutions and have different life experiences. New professionals can learn valuable lessons from old friends and those in this horizontal network. In fact, this peer mentoring, discussed at greater length in chapter 8, can produce some of the longest-lasting and most rewarding relationships a new professional can have. Professional associations are a natural place to engage in this type of learning and reconnecting.

The Need for Immediate and Additional Skill Development

New professionals in student affairs come from a wide variety of backgrounds and experiences. Although many may have already been socialized in the profession through their undergraduate and graduate experiences, others may not have been. Many will have experience in higher education and will enter their new jobs with appropriate professional preparation, but others may not (Janosik et al., 2003). Upcraft (1998) suggested that even when student affairs professionals graduate from excellent preparation programs, they still may not be ready for the environment they will work in. One reason for this skill gap has to do with our preparation programs themselves. Many of these programs have their historical roots in counseling and student development theory, not administration, organizational management, and higher education more generally (Sandeen & Barr, 2006). And regretfully, it is not always clear that our classroom and field experiences adequately prepare new professionals to be effective in their first postdegree position (Amey, 2002).

Several well-respected practitioner-scholars suggest that preparation programs do not currently include sufficient course work in diversity and multicultural issues (Upcraft, 1998), the legal system and current case law (McEwen & Talbot, 1998), supervision (Komives, 1998), budget administration (Winston & Creamer, 1997), and organizational culture and institutional politics (Upcraft) to prepare new professionals for their positions on today's college campus. Moreover, other currently needed skill sets, such as program evaluation, technology, and representing the university to external constituencies, are often overlooked in graduate preparation programs (Burkard, Cole, Ott, & Stoflet, 2005). Thus, it is likely that even those who graduate from some of our best preparation programs will need immediate and additional training.

But even if one were to be well-prepared to enter the field, the knowledge and skills needed to remain effective even in the same position will surely change as time passes. Technology, legislation and the law, the characteristics of our student bodies, management practices, and developmental theory all change more rapidly than we might wish to acknowledge.

To remain effective, individuals in all professions acknowledge the need to be involved in continuing education. In fact, Creamer, Janosik, Winston, and Kuk (2001) argue that regardless of institutional support, it is the individual's responsibility to maintain professional knowledge and skill required of fully functioning professionals in student affairs. Indeed, staying current in the field is the very essence of being professional. The need to be involved in continuing professional development is especially important for those who enter the field without the appropriate preparation and for those who work in institutions where appropriate in-service training is not available.

To date there is no requirement, however, for individuals to document their continuing education activities or to demonstrate their professional competence. ACPA and NASPA members have debated the value of developing continuing education programs where members would be encouraged to participate in educational activities throughout their careers. Both organizations also have considered the development of a standard exam that would test the knowledge of practitioners. Professionals who pass the exam would become certified or licensed as student affairs professionals. While such programs are commonplace in other professions, neither approach has been endorsed in the field of student affairs. Despite the lack of consensus on how we might help ensure professional quality, professional associations remain one of the best sources for additional skill development.

Finding and Using Resources

In an earlier time, new professionals had only a limited number of choices with respect to their own professional development. Reading books or journal articles, registering for formal course work, and attending in-service or conference programs were the primary delivery methods for staff development. Today, with the incorporation of technology, many more options are available. Webinars, audio conferences, electronic newsletters, interactive CDs, and streaming video have become commonplace delivery methods. Beyond this increase in delivery methods, the number of programs offered by the major student affairs associations has grown by leaps and bounds. State, regional, and national associations of all descriptions have developed comprehensive professional development programs. Private entities and special-interest groups have entered this market too. When properly constructed and delivered, these programs can reinforce the central values of the profession (Winston & Creamer, 1997) and play an important role in socializing the new professional.

Intentional Professional Development

With all of these opportunities available to new practitioners, deciding which professional development program to attend can be a daunting task. Carpenter (1998) has observed that many of these programs are offered with little continuity and less coherence from year to year. Others have concluded that depending on the issue, the quality, timeliness, and relevance of these programs may vary markedly (Moore & Neuberger, 1998).

Doing more for its members in the way of continuing professional education has been the subject of much study and debate. Creamer et al. (2001) have suggested that professional associations should create and offer (a) incentives to members for continuing education, (b) differentiated programs of high quality for members of varying statuses in educational attainment, and (c) rewards for educational growth of members. Although recent studies (Janosik & Hirt, 2005; Janosik, Carpenter, & Creamer, 2006) suggest that there is a great deal of support for such an approach, especially among new professionals, none of the national associations in the field have acted on this recommendation in a concrete and comprehensive manner.

To address some of these concerns, Janosik et al. (2006) have proposed that professional association leaders use a student affairs curriculum matrix to organize their conference programs. This matrix (Figure 10.1) was adapted from the work completed by Janosik (2002). NASPA and some of its regional associations have adopted this matrix and encourage their members to divide their conference time among the six topical areas found in the matrix.

FIGURE 10.1
The Student Affairs Professional Development Curriculum

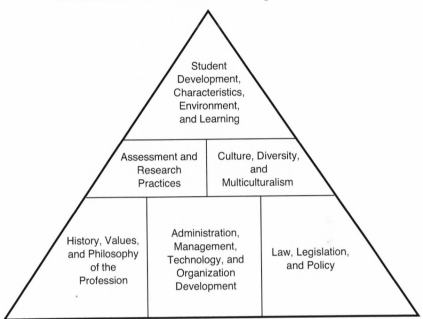

Adapted from Janosik (2002, p. 7). Used with permission.

The first of these areas involves the history, values, and philosophy of the profession. New professionals who have entered the field without the benefit of completing graduate preparation, in particular, will benefit greatly from a review of these topics.

Administration, management, technology, and organizational development make up the second topical area. Counseling-based preparation programs often leave these important skill areas unaddressed, and new professionals who graduated from such programs will find that additional training in these areas fill a crucial void.

The third topical area in this matrix includes law, governance, and policy. Regretfully, student affairs professionals are not immune from the threat of lawsuits. State and federal laws, and their interpretation, change over time and so it is important to continually update one's knowledge in these areas.

Assessment and research practices make up the fourth general area of staff development, and new professionals are well advised to develop skills in this area as quickly as possible. No student affairs professional can escape the call for accountability. More and more practitioners are being required to show how their work affects students and what students learn as a result of their participation in the myriad of programs offered on college campuses. Being able to demonstrate results through something more than anecdotal data and satisfaction surveys is becoming increasingly important.

Culture, diversity, and multiculturalism serve as the fifth general content area. Skill development in this area is designed to help new professionals understand and appreciate the backgrounds and cultures of an increasingly diverse student body.

Finally, the sixth area of skill development includes student development, characteristics, environment, and learning. These topics attend to understanding who students are, how students develop in early adulthood, and how the environments we create influence what they learn. This last set of skills is purposely placed at the top of the matrix, for it is these competencies that represent the essence of what the student affairs profession is about.

A working group of ACPA's Steering Committee on Competencies submitted a report that included a synthesis of student affairs literature related to the knowledge needed to be successful student affairs educators (Schoper, Stimpson, & Segar, 2006). In the report, the authors identified nine themes related to competencies, values, basic attributes, and skills. These are culture and organizations, multiculturalism, leadership, history and future trends, ethical and legal issues, budgeting, technology, learning and development, and assessment. From this report the Steering Committee identified eight areas of competence and recommended that these form the basic structure of a professional development program for the association (Love et al., 2007). The eight areas of competence are

1. Advising and Helping
2. Assessment, Evaluation, and Other Research Activities
3. Ethics
4. Legal Foundations
5. Leadership and Administration/Management
6. Pluralism and Inclusion

7. Student Learning and Development
8. Teaching (p. 5)

Subsequently, the conference program committee for the 2008 ACPA annual conference included a competency checklist in its conference program to help attendees reflect upon their current skill set and select programs that might add to their professional competencies.

While such a matrix and checklists provide a helpful way to organize conference programs, they do not, in and of themselves, ensure that new professionals choose those programs that would provide the optimal learning experience given their respective positions within their organizations. Winston and Creamer (1997) speak directly to this issue.

They suggest that professional development activities should be part of a staff development plan that is (a) constructed around the needs of the staff member and the supervisor, (b) focused on processes and products, and (c) anchored in the day-to-day work of the staff member. They contend that several problems that limit the effectiveness of current staff development activities can be overcome if

1. The staff development activities are connected to the performance appraisal process.
2. A systematic determination or assessment of staff needs is completed.
3. The staff development activities selected sufficiently meet the needs of the employer.
4. The staff development activities are able to remedy the staff member's deficiencies.

New professionals, regardless of their preparation and skills, will need to pay immediate attention to their professional development if they are to remain current and relevant in the field. Gaining new knowledge and competence will allow them to improve their practice and begin to establish their professional reputation.

Helping Establish a Professional Identity for the New Professional

Student affairs is a welcoming profession. Most professional associations make a concerted effort to attract graduate students and new professionals to their ranks and many of the major student affairs associations provide opportunities for new professionals to become meaningfully involved.

Orientation programs, socials, involvement fairs, and targeted programs are common conference activities. New professionals can become members of task forces, commissions, and committees. They can volunteer to be part of conference-planning groups and career placement activities. And they do. In fact, research shows that entry-level professionals attend workshops separate from conferences and serve in elected/appointed offices other than a committee chair more than chief student affairs officers, advanced middle, and middle-level professionals (Chernow, Cooper, & Winston, 2003). This is important for two reasons. First, membership and involvement increases the leadership skills, productivity, job satisfaction, and sense of professional identity of the individual. Second, the new professional's employer benefits, as the individual professional uses the knowledge and skills gained to improve student services at the home institution (Zimmerman, Radoye, & Itzkowitz, 1991). Most important, all these activities can be an important part of a new professional's socialization to the profession.

Helping Maintain the Passion for Student Affairs and Increasing Retention

Large numbers of student affairs professionals leave the field after five or six years. Some researchers suggest the number hovers around 33% (Wood, Winston, & Polkosnik, 1985). Others have placed the number as high as 40% (Holmes, Verrier, & Chisholm, 1983). To be sure, some of the reasons for this attrition have to do with poor professional fit, little room for appropriate advancement, and family circumstances. All these issues may fall well beyond the control of the employer.

Alternatively, however, there may be elements of the work environment that contribute to attrition among professionals. These elements might be addressed by the employer. Tull (2006) suggested that one common reason for attrition is job dissatisfaction. Further, it may be that the new professional's job dissatisfaction results from role ambiguity, role conflict, role orientation, perceived opportunities for goal attainment, professional development, and career advancement (Berwick, 1992; Conley, 2001). While poor supervision and a poor work environment may make for a very uncomfortable situation, meaningful involvement with professional associations where a person's worth can be reaffirmed and where new perspectives can be defined may ameliorate some of these conflicts. The power of networking and mentoring in particular may provide an important respite for new professionals.

Recommendations for New Professionals

Given this brief overview, new professionals should view professional associations as an important resource. To take the greatest advantage of these organizations, new professionals should consider the following:

1. Join one national or regional umbrella organization, such as ACPA, NASPA or SACSA, and keep this membership active.

2. Join at least one national or regional specialty organization that focuses on your current functional area (i.e., ACUHO–I or SEAHO for those employed in housing and residence life).

3. Consider joining one other association that focuses on a related area of professional interest (i.e., ASJA for those interested in student conduct administration).

4. Attend these conferences regularly even if institutional funds are not available. Scholarships to defray the cost of conference attendance are offered to select groups of members by some associations, and research grants may also be used to reduce this expense.

5. Volunteer to assist with convention activities. Reviewing program proposals, assisting with conference program evaluations, and helping with placement services are excellent ways to participate.

6. Attend the business meetings and award luncheons held by the associations you belong to. Participate and introduce yourself to the officers and facilitators of these events.

7. Maintain and develop your own professional network by introducing yourself to those professionals you would like to work with or learn from.

8. Seek out and develop mentoring relationships when these opportunities present themselves.

9. With the help of your employer, colleague, or mentor, create a systematic professional staff development plan based on one or more of the models presented in this chapter and be intentional about the

types of programs and training activities you attend. Keep a log of your activities and summarize what you learn in writing.

10. Read faithfully the journals that you receive as part of your association memberships. Discuss articles of particular interest with coworkers and colleagues at other institutions.

11. Subscribe to or obtain the *Chronicle of Higher Education* and read it on a regular basis.

12. Subscribe to free online media sponsored by professional associations that focus on higher education issues.

13. Begin building your professional library by using your membership benefits to purchase books and other publications at reduced cost.

14. Consider asking a colleague to join with you and submit a program proposal on a topic of mutual interest.

15. Become a member of an association committee or task force of professional interest.

Clearly, the best practitioners are active professionals. Indeed, some argue that the recommendations listed here are not optional; rather they are obligations all student affairs administrators should subscribe to. The real payoff to incorporating these activities in one's daily practice is increased job satisfaction in the short term and an enhanced career path in the long term.

Challenges for Professional Associations

Professional associations and their leaders play an important role in socializing new professionals. The positive effect of national, regional, state, and even institutional organizations cannot be overstated. All the activities mentioned in this chapter make significant contributions to the early orientation, assimilation, and success of those new to the profession.

Many of our associations are vital and in good financial shape, but some suggest that their programs and services could be stronger and better focused (Carpenter, 1998; Sandeen & Barr, 2006). To that end, the following are some suggestions.

Improve and Expand Mentoring Programs

As mentioned previously, several associations offer mentoring programs for their new professionals. Most conference matching programs where attendees with some experience are paired with new professionals operate on a volunteer basis with few selection criteria, little training for mentors or mentees, and even less follow-up. Coordinators of more formal institutes tend to invite faculty members who have demonstrated their own dedication to the field and have established themselves as scholars of practice. These efforts are laudable but could be much more powerful experiences if the definition that Johnson (2007) uses to define mentoring was better incorporated in these programs and the experiences themselves were offered to greater numbers of new professionals. Mentoring is a complex, labor-intensive, long-term process that requires a real commitment on the part of both parties. The benefits accrued by the mentor and the new professional, however, are just too powerful to ignore.

Continuing Professional Development

With respect to continuing professional development, more than 35 national professional associations now respond to the needs of the new professional in student affairs. Most of these associations are vibrant organizations supported by dedicated volunteers who want to create mechanisms to support and aid in the professional development of their peers.

Private for-profit organizations in specialized markets have also been created to provide training and support. The National Center for Higher Education Risk Management (NCHERM, http://www.ncherm.org/), Student Affairs.Com (http://www.studentaffairs.com/) and ResLife.Net (http://www.reslife.net/) are three most recent examples. Sandeen (1998) suggests that while this proliferation of organizations may be viewed as strength and may signal the maturing of the profession, it may also represent a real threat to the profession. Excessive fragmentation may dilute the real effectiveness of our associations.

New professionals have limited resources. Perhaps the two most important of these are time and money. Joining multiple organizations with similar purposes is an expensive proposition and may not be the most efficient way to use these resources.

Moreover, Sandeen (1998) suggests that multiple and overlapping associations may dilute the voice of student affairs to their own members and to important external constituents. NASPA's and ACPA's competing "models for continuing professional development" is just one of the latest examples that demonstrate this inefficiency. Association leaders, while well meaning, spend too much time protecting turf and trying to differentiate the same product.

All our professional associations hold annual conferences. In addition, these same organizations sponsor special institutes that focus on developing the skills of individuals within specific levels of the organization (i.e., new professional, midlevel managers, or senior). They also sponsor programs on special topics such as assessment, diversity, and campus crisis planning. Regretfully, these programs are not well coordinated and little effort is made to ensure quality. This redundancy may add to the revenue stream of these associations but may do little to benefit the individual.

Consolidating some associations, especially the larger generalist ones has been tried before, and while these efforts have been unsuccessful, new professionals should encourage the leadership in these organizations to try again. At the very least, members of these associations should insist on more joint efforts such as developing one set of expectations for continuing professional development.

Generativity

Finally, as someone who has served on a number of executive boards of our associations, I am continually struck by one agenda item that comes up all too frequently. The question is usually phrased, "How can we get our senior members to participate?" This is a serious question.

Carpenter and Miller (1981) define the final stage of their proposed model for professional development as Generative. This stage involves upper-level practice through retirement and includes mentoring, top-level leadership, consulting, and editorial positions (Carpenter, 1991). Younger and younger professionals hold these leadership positions in our associations and this may be some cause for concern. Keeping those with the most experience involved in our professional associations is crucial to the sustainability of our profession.

Student affairs associations are crucial to the development of the field. Many of the important issues facing the associations have been raised by well-meaning professionals who want to move the profession forward. So far, consensus has not been achieved. Only time will tell if we have the courage to act on those convictions.

Conclusion

Participating in professional associations in strategic ways can have several positive outcomes for new professionals. In fact, there may be no better way to create professional networks, improve one's knowledge and skills, enhance one's career, and make lasting contributions to the field. As previously discussed, however, the sheer number of opportunities for involvement can be overwhelming. Association dues can sometimes be unnecessarily high. Association leadership can be territorial and inconsistent, and association activities can be wastefully redundant. Positive results are not guaranteed.

Despite these shortcomings, new professionals, working closely with their supervisors and mentors, should plan their association participation carefully if its true potential is to be realized. Being involved is not the same as being intentionally involved. Choices should be made carefully and with purpose. Hopefully, the recommendations presented in this chapter will help new professionals with their journey.

References

Amey, M. J. (2002). Unwritten rules: Organizational and political realities of the job. In M. J. Amey & L. M. Reesor (Eds.), *Beginning your journey: A guide for new professionals in student affairs* (pp. 13–30). Washington, DC: National Association of Student Personnel Administrators.

Association of College Unions International. (1995). About the Association. In *Association of College Unions International membership directory and sourcebook* (pp. 2–3). Bloomington, IN: Author.

Berwick, K. R. (1992). Stress among student affairs administrators: The relationship of personal characteristics and organizational variables to work-related stress. *Journal of College Student Development, 33,* 11–19.

Burkard, A., Cole, D. C., Ott, M., & Stoflet, T. (2005). Entry-level competencies of new student affairs professionals: A Delphi study. *NASPA Journal, 42*(3), 283–309.

Carpenter, D. S. (1991). Student affairs profession: A developmental perspective. In T. K. Miller & R. B. Winston, Jr., (Eds.), *Administration and leadership in student affairs: Actualizing student development in higher education* (2nd ed., pp. 253–279). Muncie, IN: Accelerated Development.

Carpenter, D. S. (1998). Continuing professional education in student affairs. In N. J. Evans & C. E. Phelps Tobin (Eds.). *The state of the art of preparation and practice in student affairs* (pp. 61–79). Lanham, MD: University Press of America.

Carpenter, D. S., & Miller, T. K. (1981). An analysis of professional development in student affairs work. *NASPA Journal, 19*(1), 2–11.

Chernow, E. K., Cooper, D. L., & Winston, R. B., Jr. (2003). Professional association involvement of student affairs professionals. *NASPA Journal, 40*(2), 43–58.

Coleman, D. D., & Johnson, J. E. (1990). The new professional. In D. D. Coleman & J. E. Johnson (Eds.), *The new professional: A resource guide for new professionals and their supervisors* (pp. 1–16). Washington, DC: National Association of Student Personnel Administrators.

Conley, V. M. (2001). Separation: An internal aspect of the staffing process. *College Student Affairs Journal, 21*(1), 57–63.

Creamer, D. G., Janosik, S. M., Winston, R. B., & Kuk, L. (2001). *Quality assurance in student affairs: Role and commitments of NASPA.* Washington, DC: National Association of Student Personnel Administrators.

Elder, P. (1984). The importance of professional involvement. *Journal of the National Association of Women Deans, Administrators, and Counselors, 48*(1), 13–19.

Gerda, J. J. (2006). Gathering together: A view of the earliest student affairs professional organizations. *NASPA Journal, 43*(4), 147–163.

Hanson, G. S. (1995). The organizational evolution of NAWE. *Initiatives, 56*(4), 29–36.

Holmes, D., Verrier, D., & Chisholm, P. (1983). Persistence in student affairs work: Attitudes and job shifts among master's program graduates. *Journal of College Student Personnel, 24*, 438–443.

James C. Grimm National Housing Training Institute. (2008). Retrieved January 28, 2008, from http://www.acuho-i.org/brEventsbrPrograms/JamesCGrimmNHTI/tabid/202/Default.aspx Janosik, S. M. (2002). *A national student affairs registry: A proposal.* Washington, DC: National Association of Student Personnel Administrators.

Janosik, S. M. (2002). *The development and implementation of a national registry for student affairs administrators.* Washington, DC: NASPA.

Janosik, S. M., Carpenter, S., & Creamer, D. G. (2006). Intentional professional development: Feedback from student affairs professionals. *NASPA Journal, 44*(1), 127–146.

Janosik, S. M., Creamer, D. G., Hirt, J. B., Winston, R. B., Jr., Saunders, S. A., & Cooper, D. L. (2003). *Supervising new professionals in student affairs.* New York: Brunner-Routledge.

Janosik, S. M., & Hirt, J. B. (2005). *A qualitative analysis of the comments contained in the Membership Survey on Certification: A report to ACPA's Task Force on Certification.* Washington, DC: American College Personnel Association.

Johnson, W. B. (2007). *On being a mentor: A guide for higher education faculty.* Mahwah, NJ: Erlbaum.

Komives, S. R. (1998). Linking preparation with practice. In N. J. Evans & C. E. Phelps Tobin (Eds.), *The state of the art of preparation and practice in student affairs* (pp. 177–200). Lanham, MD: University Press of America.

Love, P., Bleiberg, S., Carpenter, S., Haggerty, B., Hoffman, D., Janosik, S., et al. (2007). *Professional competencies: A report of the Steering Committee on Professional Competencies*. Washington, DC: American College Personnel Association.

Mable, P. (1984, November). *Consultant-in-residence with new professionals*. Paper presented at a meeting of the Upper Midwest Region Association of College and University Housing Officers Conference, Aberdeen, SD.

McEwen, M. K., & Talbot, D. M. (1998). Designing the student affairs curriculum. In N. J. Evans & C. E. Phelps Tobin (Eds.). *The state of the art of preparation and practice in student affairs* (pp. 125–156). Lanham, MD: University Press of America.

Moore, L. V., & Neuberger, C. G. (1998). How professional associations are addressing issues in student affairs. In N. J. Evans & C. E. Phelps Tobin (Eds.). *The state of the art of preparation and practice in student affairs* (pp. 61–79). Lanham, MD: University Press of America.

National Association of Deans and Advisers of Men. (1938). *Proceedings of the 20th annual conference*. Madison, WI: Author.

Nidiffer, J. (2000). *Pioneering deans of women: More than wise and pious matrons*. New York: Teachers College Press.

Nuss, E. M. (1993). The role of the professional associations. In M. J. Barr (Ed.), *The handbook of student affairs administration* (pp. 364–378). San Francisco: Jossey-Bass.

Reesor, L. (2002). Making professional connections. In M. J. Amey & L. M. Reesor (Eds.), *Beginning your journey: A guide for new professionals in student affairs*. Washington, DC: National Association of Student Personnel Administrators.

Sandeen, A. (1998). Creeping specialization in student affairs. *About Campus, 3*(2), 2–3.

Sandeen, A., & Barr, M. J. (2006). *Critical issues for student affairs: Challenges and opportunities*. San Francisco: Jossey-Bass.

Sauter, J. (1994). *Association of College and University Housing Officers–International report*. Columbus, Ohio: Author.

Schoper, S. E., Stimpson, R., & Segar, T. C. (2006). *ACPA Certification Taskforce synthesis: A professional development curriculum*. Washington, DC: American College Personnel Association.

Southern Association for College Student Affairs. (2008). The New Professionals Institute. Retrieved February 20, 2008, from http://www.sacsa.org/displaycommon.cfm?an = 1&subarticlenbr = 8

Tull, A. (2006). Synergistic supervision, job satisfaction, and intention to turnover of new professionals in student affairs. *Journal of College Student Development, 47*(4), 465–480.

Upcraft, M. L. (1998). Do graduate preparation programs really prepare student affairs professionals? In N. J. Evans & C. E. Phelps Tobin (Eds.), *The state of the art of preparation and practice in student affairs* (pp. 225–237). Lanham, MD: University Press of America.

Winston, R. B., Jr., & Creamer, D. G. (1997). *Improving staffing practices in student affairs.* San Francisco: Jossey-Bass.

Wood, L., Winston, R. B., Jr., & Polkosnik, M. C. (1985). Career orientations and professional development of young student affairs professionals. *Journal of College Student Personnel, 26,* 532–539.

Zimmerman, L. J., Radoye, V., & Itzkowitz, S. G. (1991). *Developing leadership skills: A program model and its impact.* Detroit, MI: Wayne State University. (ERIC Document Reproduction Service No. ED 336671)

PART FOUR

IMPLICATIONS AND FUTURE DIRECTIONS FOR EFFECTIVE SOCIALIZATION

11

CONCLUSIONS AND RECOMMENDATIONS

Ashley Tull, Joan B. Hirt, and Sue A. Saunders

E ffective socialization of new student affairs professionals is essential, for the individual success of these practitioners and for the work of a college or university that promotes student learning. How a new professional is socialized in his or her first position has long-term effects. Socialization influences whether new professionals will manage the important personal and professional transitions they experience throughout their careers, whether they engage in continuous professional development, whether they achieve high levels of productivity, and even whether they persist in the student affairs profession (Saunders & Cooper, 2003). Additionally, if new student affairs professionals are socialized to work at peak proficiency, students who bring a variety of challenging needs to campus will in turn be better educated.

The intent of this book has been to depict the process of socialization and the contextual elements that influence that process. Further, the authors describe explicit strategies that can be used by new professionals, their teachers, their supervisors, and the profession's leaders to enhance socialization. This concluding chapter synthesizes some of the major themes in the book and addresses several current and future trends in higher education that are likely to affect the socialization process. We also offer recommendations on how to optimize the socialization of new professionals that chief student affairs officers, supervisors, new professionals, and graduate preparation program faculty might consider.

Processes of Socialization and Their Importance

To start, let's revisit the definition of socialization. As discussed in the first section of the book, the socialization process for new professionals includes formal and informal elements that influence success and quality of work life. This process is far more complex than a single orientation program organized by a unit or division. It is rather a comprehensive process where the new professional and organization learn about and from each other in ways that will influence working relationships and individual and organizations outcomes (see chapter 1).

Socialization to student affairs work begins early. Indeed, new professionals often first learn about the values of our profession before they are even aware there is a profession called student affairs. Undergraduate students are frequently attracted to student affairs work because of a mentoring relationship they form with a caring student affairs professional. Much of that early socialization occurs in the context of these important relationships. Understanding the nuances of the profession's history, mission, culture, and role in academe are often discussed in graduate school courses or in a variety of informal graduate student networks. Socialization to a particular position begins as soon as one first reads a position announcement, and it continues well beyond the early adjustment period. Socialization is complex and requires extensive time so that new professionals can move through distinct stages and eventually combine personal and work identities in a way that enhances commitment to the organization and to the profession (Thornton & Nardi, 1975).

Socialization, then, is a process with implications that reach beyond transitory commitment to a particular organization. This process can occur through several realms of professional practice (Hirt & Creamer, 1998). These realms (personal, institutional, extra-institutional, and professional) each present new professionals with challenges and insights into the world of work in student affairs and higher education, and into their own professional capacities. New professionals can never be fully cognizant of the challenges and successes they may encounter when entering student affairs work. However, through knowledge of socialization processes, such as the realms of practice and socialization stages, organizations and new professionals can design workable strategies to achieve important institutional outcomes.

Effective socialization is perhaps most important in helping new professionals develop a rewarding quality of work life, thus reducing attrition

among practitioners in student affairs. Those new professionals who successfully navigate entry into student affairs work and commit to the profession
will be less likely to leave their position, institution, or the profession alto-
gether. To help new professionals develop a high quality of work life, several
dimensions of work life must be addressed, primarily through supervisory
relationships (see chapter 2). These dimensions are varied and include supporting career development and advancement, providing meaningful recognition for competence, facilitating collegial relations between departments,
and helping the new professional build useful external relationships across
the campus and community. Further, the quality of work life can be
improved by ensuring reasonable compensation and working conditions,
and by eliminating perceptions of discrimination or unfairness.

Effective socialization for new student affairs professionals involves a
series of complex and varied processes that integrate personal needs, organizational priorities, and diverse individual leadership styles. To support new
professionals as they are socialized requires commitment of time and fiscal
resources over an extended period. Since socialization is not a passive process,
new professionals themselves must also devote energy to their own socialization. Further, it is clear from the chapters in part one of this volume that
effective socialization must be intentionally planned with a focused yet wide-
ranging agenda.

Creating an Agenda for Intentional Socialization: Considerations

Senior student affairs officers, by their leadership and access to fiscal and staff
resources, can infuse a commitment to intentional socialization of new professionals in their divisions. It is essential for division leaders to ensure that
supervisors of new professionals possess and use resources to purposefully
support effective socialization from the moment the new professional first
encounters the organization. Senior student affairs officers would be well
advised to frequently monitor the quality of work-life issues among new professionals. Articulating and demonstrating a commitment to improve work-
life-related problems can do much to enhance morale among new professionals. Further, role modeling a healthy work-life balance and continued
passion for professional growth are powerful strategies to promote effective
socialization.

Supervisors of new professionals often have the most direct influence on a new professional's socialization process. Socialization processes must be carefully designed before the position announcement is even published. Supervisors would be well advised when crafting job announcements to carefully think through what coherent, consistent, and accurate messages will be sent about such elements as working conditions, professional development opportunities, departmental relationships, and organizational expectations. It is also important to recognize that while anticipatory socialization is a key component, the effective socialization process is an extended one in which the individual's professional identity eventually meshes with the organization's priorities. Therefore it is essential that supervisors learn about their supervisee's professional goals and values and, further, that supervisors try to integrate individual goals with those of the unit.

New professionals are not passive recipients of socialization. They can and should be active players in creating an intentional socialization process for themselves. On an individual basis they can strive for optimal work-life balance by finding time to meet personal priorities outside work. Continuing to nurture relationships outside those with colleagues is another important strategy for effective socialization, because it allows one to regain perspective in times of stress. Further, new professionals should be setting their own professional learning and development goals. They should be able to address specific questions about what skills they want to develop, what concepts they want to explore, and what professional activities they want to pursue. Additionally, new professionals should be able to advocate for their own professional development needs and to openly request assistance to rectify problems related to role conflict, role ambiguity, role orientation, role stress, and burnout.

Graduate preparation program faculty members are key agents of anticipatory socialization for new professionals. They have many varied opportunities to help students create their own agenda for effective socialization. Faculty can facilitate focused discussions about the adjustment process between graduate school and professional life. Further, students can be encouraged to identify role conflicts and stressful situations, and to develop effective strategies to create work-life balance while they are still students so that they might practice those strategies in their assistantships or internships. Finally, it is important that graduate preparation faculty maintain contact with practitioners who hire their students. In that way, the faculty can identify any common trends or difficulties in becoming socialized to new professional positions and address those with new students. It is essential that graduate preparation program faculty remain current with the necessary skills and competencies required for effective practice in the contemporary college environment.

Influential Contexts in the Socialization Process

Institutional type and changing student characteristics are influential contexts in the socialization process. To fully understand the culture of one's new institution, it is essential that the new professional be cognizant of institutional type and student characteristics. With so many different types of postsecondary institutions in the American system of higher education, one cannot assume that the missions, goals, student characteristics, and work environments are similar. New professionals should clearly examine during the preparation process or anticipatory phase the type of institution(s) and student(s) they desire to work with. Because of the variety of cultural elements within institutions, new professionals cannot broadly assume that all institutions within a type are similar. Yet, understanding how institutional type differentially affects one's work life and opportunities to serve students is an important starting place (see chapter 3). Institutional contexts often influence the type(s) of administrators and students attracted to an institution. This in turn can influence the important elements of the institutional and student culture, the programs and services offered, how problems are addressed, as well as intrinsic or extrinsic rewards for new professionals.

Understanding the type of students served is another important element of the culture of a new institution. Regardless of institutional type, college students often create their own distinctive traditions, rituals, values, and ways of being that definitely affect the work of student affairs professionals. The characteristics and motivations of any institution's students are also affected by a variety of societal trends (see chapter 4). New generations of students bring new issues, new challenges, and new opportunities even before they arrive on campus. Being aware of the interrelationship between particular student customs on a given campus and the broader societal trends affecting students everywhere is important for understanding the culture of a new campus.

Knowing and navigating a new culture is an important skill for a new professional. The contexts described in part two of this book are springboards for explicit examination of institutional culture that can be furthered by the efforts of institutional leaders, supervisors, graduate preparation faculty, and new professionals themselves. The recommendations that follow guide these efforts to make the organizational and student cultures explicit for new professionals.

Making the Organizational and Student Cultures Explicit: Considerations

Chief student affairs officers should regularly communicate institutional and division mission, goals, and objectives to new professionals, and they should do this early in the socialization process when the view of the organization is more malleable. Understanding the particulars of the student culture is an important step to building awareness of the organizational culture. Since rapid changes in our society have an impact on students, it is essential that careful assessment of students' needs, values, and background characteristics be completed regularly. Senior student affairs officers are often in a position to devote time and resources to such assessment efforts.

Supervisors of new professionals should regularly help their novices interpret the mission, values, and goals of the department as well as those of the division and of the institution. These conversations about the overriding espoused purposes should not simply be a didactic reiteration of the words of the mission but should involve making explicit the connections between action and mission. Campus politics, for example, are often baffling to new professionals as they try to make sense of what they see and hear. Supervisors need to be careful about how they communicate the political elements of culture and avoid biasing new professionals before they start to develop their own independent opinions. However, supervisors should be prepared to help new professionals understand how the culture is revealed through the political dilemmas and conflicts.

Further, it is important that new professionals understand fully the characteristics of students served by their institutions. If new professionals can learn this information early, in a straightforward and comprehensive fashion, they will be more likely to feel comfortable as they begin their direct work with students.

New professionals should give careful consideration to the types of institutions that would be the best fit with their skills, values, and preferences before they even begin the search process. It is important to try to discern elements of the institution's organizational and student culture before accepting a position, as socialization is facilitated when the new professional and institution share common values and preferences about the nature of student affairs work. Learning about an institution's culture is becoming easier because there is so much information on the Internet. New professionals would be well served to spend some time looking at published material from the institution as well as engaging in conversations with others who have worked there or with students who have attended the institution. Obviously, it is important to critically analyze information since some of it may be unreliable or incomplete. However, a new professional can make tentative hypotheses about a particular college or university when considering a job at that institution that can then be addressed during interviews.

Graduate preparation program faculty should use the opportunities they have with students in classes, in internship supervision, and in general conversations to discuss the implications of institutional type and student characteristics as elements of campus culture. Further, faculty are in a position to facilitate discussions about the importance of determining fit with organizational and student culture. These discussions can lead to questions that students can ask themselves and their potential new supervisors before accepting a position.

Strategies to Enhance Socialization of New Professionals

A variety of strategies and agents of socialization are examined in part 3 of this book. Specifically, socialization strategies focusing on graduate preparation, orientation, supervision and mentoring, peer relationships, institutional initiatives, and professional associations are discussed. Socialization strategies occur in each of these arenas and together form the total socialization experience for new professionals. Although each arena is important at different times in the socialization process, we argue that all are important if new professionals are to be fully socialized to student affairs work.

The messages sent during the socialization period are also vitally important to the success of this comprehensive process. It is clear that new professionals desire and require increasingly explicit expectations to navigate an ever more ambiguous higher education milieu. To meet the needs of students and other stakeholders, new professionals must be expected to demonstrate high levels of proficiency in terms of their task completion, ethical behavior, and interpersonal competency in intervening with students and other constituents. Yet these high expectations must be balanced with support. New professionals need assistance to translate the signals given in their new environment, to integrate their professional goals with the demands of the position, to receive guidance in resolving difficult problems, and to understand how others have grown through challenges. The importance of a supportive supervisor, a former faculty member, or a professional network of colleagues cannot be overstated.

Most professionals enter student affairs work after the completion of a graduate preparation program with a focus on student affairs and/or higher education administration. Through the graduate preparation process, new professionals are first exposed to the skills and competencies necessary to be effective in their work. Additionally, the graduate preparation process provides formal and informal socialization opportunities (see chapter 5). From a formal socialization perspective, new professionals encounter the established curriculum of their graduate program along with opportunities for practice, generally graduate assistantships and internships. Informally, new professionals are socialized through opportunities to interact with a diverse group of peers and with preparation program faculty. Each of these socialization opportunities allows new professionals the chance to establish their roles within the field of student affairs administration by putting their newly acquired skills and competencies into practice. New professionals also form key peer relationships that often serve as their first supportive professional network of colleagues as they enter student affairs work.

New professionals participate in more formal socialization processes through orientation programs that come with the acceptance of a job in student affairs. These regularly occur at the departmental, divisional or organizational, and institutional levels. In some cases, new professionals may be required to participate in orientation programs at each one of these levels. Orientation programs have been found to increase organizational commitment and job satisfaction among new professionals (see chapter 6). Student affairs organizations, therefore, have a vested interest in providing formal orientation programs. These programs not only assist new professionals with their entry into student affairs work but also assist those currently on the job by ensuring that their new professional colleagues are equipped to effectively meet challenging position expectations. Even though orientation programs can be seen as expensive and time consuming, student affairs divisions should not overlook their importance in preparing new professionals to be successful. The time and attention given to new professionals through this process will surely pay dividends in the long run to the student affairs organization employing them. Orientation is not simply a short-term event occurring at the start of a new professional position. Just as new student orientation has evolved into a semester or year-long intervention, so too should institutions promote continuous learning for new professionals that encourages reflection and incorporation of newly acquired knowledge and skills.

Supervisors are best positioned to support new professionals as they make the transition to student affairs work. Supervision and mentoring relationships provide formal and informal mechanisms that can effectively aid new professionals in the socialization process. Although there are several types of supervision models, one of the most influential is synergistic supervision (see chapter 7). Synergistic supervisors help new professionals meet their own personal and professional goals while contributing to the organization's mission and strategic initiatives. Through the synergistic approach to supervision all parties in the supervisory relationship make important gains, including the employing organization. Mentoring, unlike supervision, remains a more elusive concept (as presented in chapter 7). Although some formal mentorship programs have clear goals, contracts, or other intentional structures, most mentoring relationships remain informal in nature. We support the varied forms outlined in this book as important to the socialization process. Scores of current student affairs administrators and graduate preparation program faculty have had and currently have mentors who counsel them in their personal and professional lives. Many would argue that they owe their careers and professional success to those who have mentored them over the years. Supervisors and mentors make up a local and expanded network of professional colleagues that is important for personal and professional support in student affairs work.

Staff-peer relationships, like those with supervisors and mentors, are critical to the successful socialization of new professionals. As noted above, many new professionals develop their first important peer relationships while in graduate preparation programs. Supportive peers can have a more significant and lasting impact on new professionals than any other relationship formed while entering student affairs work (see chapter 8). New professionals are generally more satisfied if they are surrounded regularly by supportive colleagues as well as by a caring supervisor. These relationships with peers and supervisors in turn affect success on the job and ultimately retention in the position and in the profession.

Institutional socialization initiatives are important on several levels—personal, unit/divisional, and institutional (see chapter 9). New professionals hold some responsibility in the socialization process but need assistance in making sense of the culture and formal and informal structures of a particular institution. Many, if not all, of the socialization strategies discussed in this book can occur at the institutional level. The institutional socialization process should commence once a hiring decision has been made. This can occur through the interactions and materials that are shared prior to a new professional's arrival on campus. Once on campus, new professionals need assistance in understanding simple tasks like where to park, and more difficult tasks such as how to navigate subcultures that may not be so apparent. Relationships with supervisors, colleagues, and institutional leaders are critical to the institutional socialization of new professionals. Each should take an active interest in new professionals to ensure their proper socialization to the division, to the institution, and to student affairs work.

Professional associations in student affairs are facilitators of the socialization process for new professionals as well as places where socialization occurs, as in the case at association conferences. Nearly all the socialization strategies described in this book can be accomplished through professional associations. Many new professionals will attend their first professional conferences while in graduate school and will continue to attend and become more active in them as they enter the field. Through professional association activities new professionals will continue to acquire skills and competencies important to their work in the field. Associations provide a means for new professionals to remain in touch with peers they met through graduate preparation or other channels. They also offer multiple and varied opportunities for formal and informal mentoring (see chapter 10). Associations provide a connective tissue to keep student affairs professionals in touch with one another personally and professionally. This is no more important than in the initial socialization process for those entering student affairs work. Associations also provide a structure and opportunities for those who may be entering student affairs work through less-traditional methods. In these cases, new professionals have a forum for acquiring skills and competencies and connecting with those already working in student affairs administration.

It is vital that varied agents or processes associated with socialization strategies communicate similar messages about high expectations balanced with meaningful support. The recommendations that follow are designed to help those concerned about socialization to strive for this balance.

Balancing High Expectations With Adequate Support: Considerations

Chief student affairs officers can provide support for organizational professional development initiatives and resources so that new student affairs professionals can participate in activities off campus. Further, chief student affairs officers create a climate within their organization that values supportive rather than overly competitive interactions with new professionals. Finally, chief student affairs officers can consistently recommend new professionals for intense training institutes and recognition opportunities sponsored by professional associations.

Supervisors would be well advised to practice synergistic supervision with new professionals and with other professionals they supervise. The character of the supervisor–new professional relationship deserves considerable attention. Supervisors should develop explicit professional development plans in partnership with their new professionals, and both supervisee and supervisor should assess progress in achieving these plans. Professional development and socialization are definitely facilitated by providing regular and frequent formal and informal appraisal to new professionals. It is critical to provide feedback as soon as the supervisor is aware of problematic, or conversely, exceptionally good performance. New professionals not only need high expectations, but they need to know on a regular basis whether they are meeting those expectations. Supervisors are uniquely positioned to provide that reality check.

Advocating for a well-planned and expertly delivered orientation program should be an important initiative for supervisors. It is vital that orientation efforts continue throughout the new professionals' first year. With creativity, supervisors can create a seamless learning experience that starts with the new professional's first encounter with the institution through the formal orientation process and continues through the department's or division's professional development initiatives. Role modeling is a highly effective strategy that supervisors can use to encourage continued professional development through involvement with professional associations and through active participation in on-campus training opportunities. Since peer relationships are so important for the socialization of new professionals, supervisors should be fostering a climate where meaningful peer networks can develop within a department and across departments within the entire student affairs organization.

New professionals themselves can take the initiative to identify their own professional development goals and discuss those goals and challenges with supervisors and peers. Since peer relationships are so important for professional development, it is important that new professionals actively develop meaningful peer relationships throughout the graduate preparation process and as soon as they enter a new institution. The best peer networks are those where individuals can openly discuss issues and receive constructive feedback. Because effective supervision is a two-way street, it is important that new professionals plan intentionally for formal and informal meetings with their supervisor. Supervision meetings are opportunities to discuss short- and long-term professional development goals as well as to solicit feedback about performance. It is also recommended that new professionals identify and establish a relationship with a mentor either on their own campus or from their graduate preparation program, or through professional association activities. Participating in professional development activities on local, regional, and national levels is an important way to not only establish a network but to develop vital skills and competencies. Improving skills can also occur through on-campus activities by volunteering for new and challenging assignments and by being intentional in selecting these opportunities. Further, new professionals should view orientation programs as not simply a hurdle to be jumped but as yet another opportunity to learn about the culture of their institution. Finally, establishing and maintaining the habit of reading the *Chronicle of Higher Education,* student affairs journals, and other higher education–related materials are important ways to enhance socialization.

Graduate preparation program faculty can tweak numerous teaching and curricular opportunities to help students think through socialization opportunities before they begin the position search process. The informal aspects of a preparation program, such as brown bag lunches or presentation opportunities, are important socialization opportunities where meaningful peer networks can be fostered. The interview process is often a catalyst for beginning the socialization process. When encountering the stress and decision making associated with interviews, graduate faculty can be crucial supportive assets. Often graduate preparation faculty assume a long-term mentoring role with their graduates by giving feedback, offering insights, and thinking through dilemmas of practice. Although this mentoring role is often not part of a faculty job description, it is a worthwhile use of time because it can be an essential part of the socialization process.

Implications of Higher Education Trends on Socialization

The purpose of this book is to depict the socialization process as well as to offer practical and usable strategies for graduate preparation faculty, for institutional leaders, for supervisors of new professionals, and of course for new professionals themselves. Our hope, though, is to do more than simply depict the current state of affairs. We also want to stimulate a dialogue, a conversation, about what we can do to improve the socialization of new professionals, and how trends in higher education might affect this important process.

One important trend is the demand for accountability. We are beginning to see more severe budget cuts at private and public institutions. Concern about potential enrollment stagnation is also becoming more prevalent. The corollary to apprehension about finances is the more fervent push to demonstrate that resources, particularly personnel, are being used efficiently. Thus, the relatively high number of new professionals in student affairs who decide to leave the profession after only a short time should be of grave concern to graduate faculty and institutional leaders. This attrition of new student affairs professionals is clearly an inefficiency—a waste of hours of training, a waste of time and money in recruitment, and a waste of talented new professionals who are well educated and somewhat experienced in achieving important institutional outcomes. How then can this waste be reduced?

One way to decrease attrition is to pay careful attention to the socialization process from one's first awareness of the field. We need to ask the hard questions. For example, are practitioners who mentor those interested in the profession accurately communicating the nature of student affairs work, including the administrative responsibilities as well as the educational activities such work entails? Is there actually a disconnect between the concepts taught in graduate preparation programs and the tasks that new professionals face on the job? How can we determine through formal research or informal local assessments the specific challenges and effective strategies that affect those involved with the socialization process?

Another important trend is the ubiquitous nature of technology. We know that nearly 100% of full-time college students consult their e-mail daily, that 80% use a social network daily, and that more than 80% send instant messages daily (Salaway, Caruso, & Nelson, 2007). Our full-time students and most of our part-time students are wired to communicate instantly and in turn expect immediate responses from administrators. Not only do students expect immediacy, but many parents communicate with their students daily, and they too expect instant responses. The wired generation, 24-hour cable news, blogs, and social networks make it increasingly difficult for a new professional to take the time to carefully construct a well-reasoned response. Therefore, we need to think about new ways to ensure that our new professionals are expert in the mechanics of technology. More important, we must help them discover how to find the time and the mental space to make good decisions. How then can graduate faculty adjust the curriculum in light of the social pressure for instant communication? How can supervisors and institutional leaders clearly identify expectations about who communicates with whom? Further how can we define what constitutes a timely response to the variety of communiqués we receive? One element of increasing reliance on technology—social networks—can be particularly troubling for new professionals. Since such social networks as Facebook or MySpace are considered student-only communication venues, their use often blurs the lines of authority and propriety. How then do we teach new professionals to use these tools in a way that will encourage accessibility and yet maintain professionalism?

The instantaneous nature of communication today parallels extraordinarily high expectations about the quality of service owed to students and their families. With tuitions rising, families are expecting more service for their hard-earned dollars. New professionals are often required to provide that higher level of service, sometimes even with decreased levels of staffing.

For example, new professionals often are expected to staff late-night programs that run until 2:00 a.m. They are often required to conduct frequent, late-night rounds in the residence hall and to make more personal contacts with residents, some of whom exhibit more troublesome behavior. On some campuses new professionals are required to be on call for major events that could erupt into violence. Concerns about safety after the tragedies at Virginia Tech, Northern Illinois University, and other campuses around the nation are exacerbating the expectations of families that student conduct matters be handled swiftly and that troublesome students be dealt with in a way that is efficient and that ensures campus safety. These heightened expectations require significantly more work in a more stressful environment for new professionals. How then will graduate faculty, institutional leaders, supervisors, and new professionals themselves develop strategies that reinforce stress reduction, balanced lifestyles, and continued capacity building among staff? Institutional leaders in particular need to be ever vigilant about ensuring that staffing levels are appropriate to address the kinds of problems and issues that students are bringing to campus.

Conclusion

Throughout this book we address important issues surrounding the socialization process for new professionals. Our purpose for doing this is to promote success on an individual and organizational level. By understanding the purposes and importance of the socialization process we are best able to assist new professionals with entry and quality of work-life issues. Many different, but related, contexts influence the socialization process in student affairs. Each of those, addressed in the book, is important to review when preparing for and going through the socialization process as a new professional. Chapter authors have provided effective strategies that are informative and useful to new professionals and those who employ them. We encourage readers to implement these strategies and to take our recommendations into account when socializing new professionals in student affairs. Above all, we hope we have substantiated the importance of socialization to the success of new professionals, and the importance of new professionals' success to supervisors and institutional and professional leaders. Our intent is to initiate a dialogue about this often overlooked or understated process. We urge our colleagues at all levels to sustain the conversation.

References

Hirt, J. B., & Creamer, D. G. (1998). Issues facing student affairs professionals: The four realms of professional life. In N. J. Evans & C. E. Phelps Tobin, *State of the art of preparation and practice in student affairs: Another look* (pp. 47–60). Lanham, MD: University Press of America, American College Personnel Association.

Salaway, G., Caruso, J. B., Nelson, M. R. (2007). *The ECAR study of undergraduate students and information technology, 2007.* Boulder, CO: EDUCAUSE.

Saunders, S. A., & Cooper, D. L. (2003). Orientation: Building the foundations for success. In S. M. Janosik, D. G. Creamer, J. B. Hirt, R. B. Winston, Jr., S. A. Saunders, & D. L. Cooper (Eds.), *Supervising new professionals in student affairs* (pp. 17–42). New York: Brunner-Routledge.

Thornton, R. & Nardi, P. M. (1975). The dynamics of role acquisition. *American Journal of Sociology, 80,* 870–885.

ABOUT THE CONTRIBUTORS

Linda Carpenter is associate professor of clinical nursing and chair of the Family and Public Health Nursing and Nursing Systems Division at the University of Texas at Austin School of Nursing. Carpenter earned a BSN from the University of New Mexico, an MNSc from the University of Arkansas for Medical Sciences, and a PhD in higher education administration with a minor in nursing from the University of Arizona. She has held teaching positions at the University of Arkansas for Medical Sciences, the University of Arizona, and the University of Texas at Austin, and earned a national certification as a nurse educator through the National League for Nursing. She has held many administrative positions including coordinator of academic affairs at the College of Nursing at the University of Arizona, director of the Blinn College associate degree in nursing program, and assistant dean for student and clinical affairs and assistant dean for community relations at the School of Nursing at the University of Texas at Austin. She has developed work-study programs for nursing students and established a study-abroad program for nursing students in Mexico. She was selected to serve a three-year term on the Task Group on Innovations in Curriculum Design for the National League for Nursing.

Stan Carpenter is professor and chair of the Educational Administration and Psychological Services Department at Texas State University–San Marcos. He earned a BS degree in mathematics from Tarleton State University, an MS in student personnel and guidance from Texas A&M–Commerce, and a PhD in counseling and student personnel services from the University of Georgia. He joined the faculty at Texas State in 2003 after over 20 years at Texas A&M University. He has held many administrative positions including dean of students at the University of Arkansas at Monticello and executive director of the Association for the Study of Higher Education (ASHE) from 1987 to 1997. He has served as chair of the Senior Scholars of the American College Personnel Association (ACPA) and completed terms as national board member at large of the National Association for Student Personnel

Administrators (NASPA) and chair of the ACPA Media Board. He has also served as a directorate board member for Commission XII (professional preparation) of the ACPA. He is a past member of the *Journal of College Student Development* editorial board, *NASPA Journal* editorial board, and the review board for the *College Student Affairs Journal.* He has received major awards in research/scholarship, teaching, and service.

Denise Collins is assistant professor of educational leadership, administration, and foundations and an affiliated member of the women's studies faculty at Indiana State University. She serves as the coordinator of the student affairs and higher education program. Collins earned her bachelor of general studies from the University of Maryland–College Park, where she also earned a master's in college student development. She earned her PhD in higher education and student affairs at Virginia Polytechnic Institute and State University (Virginia Tech). She worked for 13 years in residence life at Grinnell College, the University of Iowa, and the State University of New York College at Cortland. She also served as the assistant director of the Women's Center and as special assistant to the provost at Virginia Tech. Collins is an associate editor for the *College Student Affairs Journal* and a member of the American College Personnel Association (ACPA) books and media editorial board. She has been recognized by the ACPA with the research and scholarship award from the Standing Committee for Women and the Annuit Coeptis Senior Professional Award.

Diane L. Cooper serves as professor in the Student Affairs Administration Program at the University of Georgia. Cooper earned her bachelor's degree in business administration from Miami University, master's degree in counseling from the University of Missouri–St. Louis, and her PhD in counselor education–student development from the University of Iowa. Cooper has held teaching positions at the University of Georgia, Appalachian State University, the University of North Carolina–Greensboro, and the University of Iowa. She has held professional positions of assistant to the vice-chancellor for student affairs and director of Disabled and International Student Services at the University of North Carolina–Greensboro. Cooper has authored or coauthored several books including *Identity Development of Diverse Populations* (2003; ASHE-ERIC); *Supervising New Professionals in Student Affairs* (2003; Brunner-Routledge), *Learning Through Supervised Practice in Student*

Affairs (2002; (Brunner-Routledge), and *Beyond Law and Policy: Reaffirming the Role of Student Affairs* (1998; Jossey-Bass). She has authored or coauthored 11 book and monograph chapters and published numerous refereed journal articles in student affairs and higher education journals. Cooper received the Outstanding Contributions to Student Affairs Through Teaching Award in 2004 from the National Association of Student Personnel Administrators, Region III.

Michael J. Cuyjet is associate professor in the College of Education and Human Development at the University of Louisville in Louisville, Kentucky, where he has been teaching in the College Student Personnel program since 1993. Prior to that, he served more than 20 years as a student affairs practitioner and an affiliate assistant professor at Northern Illinois University and at the University of Maryland–College Park. He received a bachelor's degree in speech communications from Bradley University and a master's degree in counseling and a doctorate in counselor education from Northern Illinois University. He is the editor and one of the authors of the 2006 book, *African American Men in College* (Jossey-Bass), and a coauthor of the 2002 book, *How Minority Students Experience College* (Stylus). Dr. Cuyjet has edited two other books, published more than 20 other journal articles or book chapters, and has made more than 80 presentations at national and regional conferences. He currently serves on the editorial board of the *National Association of Student Affairs Professionals (NASAP) Journal*, on the editorial board of the *Journal of College and Character*, and as an associate editor of the Books and Media Board of the American College Personnel Association (ACPA). He has received ACPA's Annuit Coeptis award as an exemplary student affairs professional twice, once as an emerging professional in 1981 and as a senior professional in 1998, and has received the Bob E. Leach Award for Outstanding Service to Students from Region III of NASPA. In 2006 he was named a Diamond Honoree by the ACPA Educational Leadership Foundation. In spring 2007, the College Personnel Association of Kentucky (CPAK) named its annual award for outstanding graduate student of the year in his honor.

Jerrid P. Freeman is the director of the Arkansas Union and an adjunct assistant professor in the higher education leadership program at the University of Arkansas. He has previously held positions in student affairs at Elon University, the University of North Carolina at Chapel Hill, Bowling Green

State University, and the University of Nebraska at Kearney. Freeman received his bachelor's of science degree in_secondary mathematics, physics, and coaching from the University of Nebraska at Kearney and his master's of arts in college student personnel from Bowling Green State University. He completed his doctorate of education in higher education administration from North Carolina State University. He is a certified emotional intelligence evaluator and has served on the board for the North Carolina Housing Officers Association. He has also been the chair of the National Association of Student Personnel Administrators (NASPA) national volunteer committee for three years. Freeman has been awarded the NASPA Region III New Professional Award and the Region IV-W Rising Star Award. Some of his research interests and areas of publication and presenting are integrated strategic planning (ISP), spirituality, student retention, leadership, and the changing economy's effect on higher education and the underserved populations in the United States.

Joan B. Hirt is associate professor of higher education in the Department of Educational Leadership and Policy Studies at Virginia Polytechnic Institute and State University (Virginia Tech). Hirt earned her BA in Russian studies from Bucknell University, her MAEd in student personnel from the University of Maryland–College Park, and her PhD in higher education administration from the University of Arizona. She spent 15 years as a student affairs professional, working in residence life, housing and dining services, and in a dean of students office before becoming a faculty member in 1994. In the course of her career, Hirt served as president of the Western Association of College and University Housing Officers. She is the recipient of numerous awards, including the Annuit Copetis Emerging Professional and Senior Professional awards conferred by the American College Personnel Association; the Outstanding Contribution to Student Affairs Through Teaching Award presented by the National Association for Student Personnel Administrators (NASPA), Region III; the Thomas M. Magoon Distinguished Alumni Award conferred by the Counseling and Personnel Services Department at the University of Maryland; and the Robert H. Shaffer award from NASPA. Hirt has authored or coauthored over 30 refereed articles, books, and monograph chapters. She cowrote two volumes on professional issues in student affairs, *Supervising New Professionals in Student Affairs* (2003) and *Learning Through Supervised Practice in Student Affairs* (2002). Her recent book,

Where You Work Matters: Student Affairs Administration at Different Types of Institutions (University Press of American, 2005), examines professionalization issues more closely.

Steven M. Janosik is senior policy analyst and associate professor of higher education in the Department of Educational Leadership and Policy Studies at Virginia Polytechnic Institute and State University (Virginia Tech). In addition, Janosik serves as the director of the Educational Policy Institute of Virginia Tech. He received his BS degree in business administration from Virginia Tech, MA degree in counseling and student personnel services from the University of Georgia, and his EdD degree in educational administration from Virginia Tech. Prior to assuming his faculty position, he served as deputy secretary of education for the commonwealth of Virginia where he worked closely with the State Council of Higher Education for Virginia, the Virginia Community College System, the Council for Information Management, and the state Department of Education. Janosik has more than 20 years of experience in college administration. He has authored or coauthored 2 books, 13 book or monograph chapters, and 44 refereed journal articles on campus crime, college administration, ethics and professionalism, higher education law and policy, liability and risk management, residence life, and student development. Janosik received the Outstanding Research Award from Commission III of the American College Personnel Association and the D. Parker Young Award for outstanding scholarship and research in the areas of higher education law and judicial affairs.

Jan Minoru Javinar is director of Co-Curricular Activities, Programs, and Services, and an adjunct instructor for the College of Educational Administration, University of Hawaii at Manoa. He is a graduate of the University of Hawaii at Manoa College of Education, where he earned a bachelor's degree in secondary social studies education, a master's degree in educational administration, and a doctorate of education in higher education administration. He is a student affairs educator with over 26 years of work experience as an academic advisor in federally funded projects, financial aid administrator, student employment counselor, student activities advisor, orientation coordinator, and leadership development educator. Javinar provides teaching, advising, and program support for student governance organizations, clubs and organizations, and students. He currently serves as director of a comprehensive student activities/student union department that includes student government, student publications, student broadcast media, college union governance, college union programming, intramural sports, leisure recreation, fraternities and sororities, new student programs, and leadership education. Javinar is active with the Association of College Unions International (ACUI), member of American College Personnel Association (ACPA), and member of National Association of Student Personnel Administrators (NASPA) where he is completing his term on the NASPA Journal Board.

Linda Kuk is associate professor of education and program chair for the graduate program in College and University Leadership at Colorado State University. Prior to her faculty role, she served as vice president for student affairs for over 22 years at Colorado State University; the Rochester Institute of Technology, in Rochester, New York; and State University of New York at Cortland. Kuk brings diverse experiences to her post, from her consulting work in China and France, to sitting on boards of directors for a family counseling center and a women's sports advocate group, the YMCA, Funding Partners of Fort Collins, and EDUCO of northern Colorado. She has served on the National Association of Student Personnel Administrators (NASPA) Board of Directors as Region II vice president, the NASPA Foundation Board, NASPA Journal Board, and the American College Personnel Association (ACPA) Board of Directors. She also serves on the editorial board of the *Spectrum* journal. In October 2003 she was named Alumni of the Year for the College of Education at Iowa State University, and in March 2004 she was named a Pillar of the Profession by the NASPA Foundation. Kuk earned a PhD in professional studies at Iowa State University, a master's in education, and a bachelor's with distinction in social work from Colorado State University. She has written and presented on varied subjects in the areas of higher education administration, organizational behavior, gender studies, and career development, and serves as a student affairs organizational consultant.

Vicki J. Rosser is associate professor of higher education and codirector for the University Council for Educational Administration's Center for Academic Leadership in the Department of Educational Leadership at the University of Nevada–Las Vegas. She received her PhD in higher education (with a cognate in sociology) from the University of Hawai'i at Manoa. Her research interests include faculty members and (midlevel) administrative work-life issues. She has conducted systemwide and national studies on work life, satisfaction, morale, and the intended mobility of faculty members and midlevel administrators in higher education. An executive board member for the Association for the Study of Higher Education, Rosser also reviews manuscripts for more than 10 refereed journals and serves as a consulting editor for *Research in Higher Education*. Rosser's research has been published in a variety of journals throughout higher education (e.g., *Journal of Higher Education, Research in Higher Education, Review of Higher Education*, and the *Journal of College Student Development*). She has co-edited a New Directions for Higher Education Series monograph titled *Understanding the Work and Career Paths of Midlevel Administrators* (2000, Jossey-Bass).

Sue A. Saunders serves as associate extension professor and coordinator of the Higher Education and Student Affairs Administration Program at the University of Connecticut. Her career includes service as a faculty member in the College Student Affairs Administration Program at the University of Georgia. In addition to teaching and research positions, Saunders has served as dean of student affairs at Lycoming College, PA; dean of students at Longwood University, VA; and in other administrative positions in Virginia, Georgia, and West Virginia. Saunders earned her bachelor's degree in journalism and a master's degree in counseling, both from Ohio University. Her PhD in counseling and student personnel services is from the University of Georgia. She is the author of 40 publications, including *Supervising New Professionals in Student Affairs* (2003: Brunner-Routledge) and *Learning Through Supervised Practice in Student Affairs (2002:* Brunner-Routledge*)*, both written with Diane Cooper, Don Creamer, Joan Hirt, Steve Janosik, and Roger Winston. Her research interests include staff supervision, patterns of professional development, and translation of student development theory to practice. She has served on the American College Personnel Association (ACPA) Executive Council and as chair of ACPA's Core Council for the Generation and Dissemination of Knowledge, and currently serves on the editorial board of the *Journal of College Student Development*. She is a recipient of the ACPA Annuit Coeptis Award, and was named an ACPA Leadership Foundation Diamond Honoree and an ACPA Senior Scholar.

Terrell Lamont Strayhorn is associate professor of higher education and sociology in the Department of Educational Leadership and Policy Studies, special assistant to the provost, and director of the Center for Higher Education

Research and Policy (CHERP) at the University of Tennessee–Knoxville. In addition, he serves as visiting scholar in the Carter G. Woodson Institute for Afro-American and African Studies at the University of Virginia. A leading expert on college student retention and success, Strayhorn has authored or edited five books/monographs, over 50 peer-reviewed journal articles, book chapters, reviews, and reports. His work appears in the *Journal of Higher Education, Review of Higher Education, Journal of College Student Development*, and *NASPA Journal*, to name a few. He has secured several highly competitive external grants, including the prestigious National Science Foundation Career Research Award, and he has presented over 100 invited and/or refereed papers at international and national conferences, meetings, and symposia. In recognition of his early career success, Strayhorn received the Outstanding Junior Scholar Award sponsored by the Council on Ethnic Participation within the Association for the Study of Higher Education, the Benjamin L. Perry Professional Service Award from the National Association of Student Affairs Professionals, the 2007 American College Personnel Association (ACPA) Emerging Scholar Award, and the 2008 ACPA Annuit Coeptis Emerging Professional Award. A member of six editorial boards, Strayhorn also has been appointed to the national advisory committees for the Thurgood Marshall College Fund, Frederick D. Patterson Research Institute, and American Association of University Professor's Committee on HBCUs and Scholars of Color. Strayhorn earned his undergraduate and master's degrees from the University of Virginia and a doctorate in higher education from Virginia Polytechnic Institute and State University (Virginia Tech), along with certificates of advanced graduate studies in graduate teaching and race and social policy.

Colette M. Taylor is an assistant professor in higher education in the Department of Educational Psychology and Leadership at Texas Tech University. Taylor earned her BS in psychology, MEd in counselor education, and her EdD in educational leadership from the University of Florida. She spent 14 years as a student affairs professional, working in residence life, student activities, and in a dean of students office before becoming a faculty member in 2008. Prior to her faculty appointment, Taylor served two years at Middle Tennessee State University as associate dean of students. She has previously held positions at University of Florida, Nova Southeastern University, and Wake Forest University. Taylor is 2007–2008 president of the

Southern Association for College Student Affairs after serving on the Executive Committee for several years. Taylor has also served as a faculty member and coordinator of the National Association of Student Affairs Professionals (NASPA) Region III Mid-Manager's Institute and as the Southern Association for College Student Affairs with the NASPA Region III Conference local arrangements chair. Taylor was also on the conference team for the American College Personal Association's Conference in 2001 and 2004. Taylor has published and made presentations to professional organizations, most recently with "Leading From the Middle," a chapter in *The Mid-level Manager in Student Affairs: Strategies for Success,* edited by R. Ackerman, (2007) and *African-Americans and Community Engagement in Higher Education,* edited with Stephanie Evans, Michelle Dunlap, and DeMond Miller (New York: SUNY PRESS, in press).

Ashley Tull is the associate dean of students for campus life and adjunct assistant professor of higher education leadership at the University of Arkansas–Fayetteville. He has previously held positions in student affairs at Florida State University, Georgia Highlands College, and Middle Georgia College. Tull earned a bachelor of science with honors in social and rehabilitation services and a master's of education in college student personnel services from the University of Southern Mississippi. He received a graduate certificate in human resource development and a doctorate of education in higher education administration from Florida State University, where he was a Hardee Scholar. He has served as the National Association of Student Affairs Professionals (NASPA) Region III chair and national chair of NASPA's New Professionals and Graduate Students Knowledge Community. Tull serves on the editorial boards of the *Journal of Happiness Studies, Oracle: The Research Journal of the Association of Fraternity Advisors, Journal of College and Character, College Student Affairs Journal,* and the *NASPA Journal.* His research has been published in *Net Results,* the *NASPA Journal,* the *Journal of College and Character,* and the *Journal of College Student Development.* His research interests center on management concepts and supervision in student affairs and higher education.

accountability, 94–95, 105, 180
adult learners, 71–72
Allen, N. J., 187
Amelink, C. T., 178
American College & University Presidents Climate Commitment, 76
American College Personnel Association (ACPA), 6, 76, 160–161
Amey, M. J., 115, 182, 183–184, 185
anxiety, competency, 177–178
associate's colleges, 57–59
Association of College and University Housing Officers-International (ACUHO-I), 6, 196
Association of College Unions International (ACUI), 196
Association of Student Judicial Affairs (ASJA), 196
attrition
   factors affecting, 28–31, 36–38
   professional fit and, 206–207
   staff relationships and, 155, 159–166, 168

baccalaureate colleges, 48–52
Barr, D. I, 39;, 117
Baumgartner, L. M., 120–121
Beeny, C., 37
Benge, E., 30
Berdrow, I, 90
Bluedorn, A. C., 29
Boehman, J., 187–188
Burkard, A., 97, 102, 177

Caffarella, R. S., 120–121
career support, 31–33
Carnegie classification system, 47–48
Carnegie Foundation for the Advancement of Teaching, 47
Carpenter, 97, 179, 194, 202, 210

Carroll, D. D., 70
certification, 201
Chronicle of Higher Education, 228
classification systems, institutional, 47–48
Cole, C. D., 97, 177
College Student Educators International (ACPA), 196, 197
colleges
   baccalaureate, 48–52
   community, 57–59
   tribally controlled, 59–60
communities, of practice, 123–124
competence
   anxiety, 177–178
   areas of, 204–205
competencies
   basic, emphasizing in orientation, 140–141
   developing through continuing education, 200–206
   developing within graduate preparation programs, 97–102
   keeping up with changing, 103–105
   key, 99
continuing education. see also professional development
   need for, 201–206
   trends in, 229–231
Cooper, D., 114
Council for the Advancement of Standards in Higher Education (CAS), 6
Craig, J. R., 30
Creamer, D. G., 4–6, 113, 115, 196, 201, 202, 205
culture, organizational
   improving, 38–39
   understanding, 13–14, 18–22, 181–189, 222–223
   work unit socialization, 178

curriculum
    evaluation, student affairs, 95–97
    professional development, 202–206, 203t
    and socialization, 91–92, 103
Cuyjet, M., 100

Dalton, J. C., 34–35
Dean, L., 115
DeBard, R., 69
discrimination, perceptions of, 37–38
diversity, discussing in orientation programs,
    117–118
doctoral-granting universities, 54–56

education
    continuing professional, 201–206
    trends in, 229–231
Edwards, R. L. R., 30
El-Khawas, E., 117
employee development, principles of,
    119–124
enrollment patterns, 72–74, 73t
Evers, F. T., 90

faculty
    cultures, understanding, 20–21
    interactions with, 92–93
    recommendations for, 220–221
    role in socialization, 103
feedback, 33–34, 141
fit, organizational, 176–177
Freeman, M. A., 117

Garland, P. H., 97
generational differences in students, 77–78
Goodnight, Scott, 195
Grace, T. W., 97
graduate preparation, 90–91, 102–103
Grimm, James C. National Housing Train-
    ing Institute, 198
Gruenberg, M. M., 30
Guthrie, V. L., 37

Harned, P. J., 130
Herdlein, R. J., 102, 178, 179
Hickey, J., 30
Higher Education Research Institute, 79

Hirt, J. B., 178, 186–187
Hirt, R. B., 4–6, 14
Hispanic-serving Institutions (HSIs), 60–61
historically Black colleges and universities
    (HBCUs), 56–57
Hodges, J. P., 15, 16, 23, 112, 177
Horn, L. J., 70

information sharing, 184–185
institution type
    associate's colleges, 57–59
    baccalaureate colleges, 48–52
    classification system, 47–48
    doctoral-granting universities, 54–56
    Hispanic-serving Institutions (HSIs),
        60–61
    historically Black colleges and universities
        (HBCUs), 56–57
    influence on socialization, 63
    master's institutions, 52–54
    and socialization, 221–222
    tribally controlled colleges, 59–60
institutional culture
    improving, 38–39
    mission and, 45–46, 183–184
    six elements of, 182–189
    socialization within, 13–14, 182–189, 226
    understanding, 18–22
internships, 93–94

Janger, I., 111
Janosik, S. M., 201, 202
Javinar, J. M., 31
job satisfaction
    factors affecting, 28–31
    mentoring relationships and, 142–143
    orientation programs and, 110
    and staff-peer relationships, 159–165
Johnson, W. B., 198, 199, 209
Johnsrud, L. K., 30, 155

Klein, H. J., 110
Komives, S. R., 99
Kuk, L., 99, 201

Lawler, E. E., 30
leadership, 185–186

learning. *see also* education
　goals, 122–123
　organizational, 118–119
Lee, T. W., 29
Levin, J. S., 71

Mable, P., 199
Madron, T. W., 30
master's institutions, 52–54
Mendel, R. M., 30
mentoring
　at graduate level, 8–9
　obstacles to effective, 143–146
　outcomes of effective, 140–143
　peer, 135–136
　professional associations and, 197–199
　programs and staff orientation, 162,
　　208–209
　relationship types, 135–139
　resources for, *132t, 133t*
　roles and responsibilities, 130–134
Merriam, S. B., 120–121
Merton, R. K., 155
Meyer, J. P., 187
millennial students, characteristics of, 69,
　77–78
Miller, T. K., 210
modeling professionalism, 191
Moore, L. V., 196
morale
　definition of, 30–31
　improving, 38–39
　and orientation programs, 109–110
Mowday, R. T., 29
multicultural competence, 38–39
Murphy, M. C., 130

Nardi, R. M., 4–5, 6, 15, 22, 24
National Association for Women in Educa-
　tion (NAWE), 195
National Association of Deans of Men, 195
National Association of Deans of Women,
　195
National Association of Student Personnel
　Administrators (NASPA), 6, 160–161,
　195
National Association of Women Deans,

Administrators, and Counselors
　(NAWDAC), 195
National Career Development Association
　(NCDA), 6
National Center for Higher Education Risk
　Management, 209
National Orientation Directors Association
　(NODA), 6
National Survey of Student Engagement, 79
Neuberger, C. G., 196
New Professional Needs Study, 17
New Professionals Institute (NPI), 198
nontraditional students, 69–74
Nuss, E. M., 117, 194

organizational culture
　improving, 38–39
　understanding, 13–14, 18–22, 181–189,
　　222–223
organizational fit, 176–177
orientation programs
　benefits of, 109–110, 224–225, 227–228
　effective, 111–118
　including technology policies in, 118
　and job satisfaction, 162–164
　and learning goals, 122–123
　message and tone within, 189–190
　as part of formal socialization, 13–15
　preparation for, 114–118
　self-guided, 124–125
　and supervisory relationships, 139–140
Ott, M., 97, 177

Pascarella, E. T., 153
peer relationships
　and socialization, 135–136, 164–166, 168,
　　225–226
　study of, 156–161
personal socialization, 22–23, 175–178
pre-employment preparations, 179
Principles of Good Practice for Student Affairs,
　186–187
professional associations
　activities and opportunities, 205–206
　benefits of, 194–197, 199–200
　continuing professional development and,
　　209–210

level of involvement in, 22
mentoring programs, 197–199
recommendations for utilizing, 207–208
and socialization, 166, 226–227
professional development
basic skills and competencies, 140–141
need for expanded, 200–206
and socialization, 190–191, 194–195
tasks to improve, 34–35
through professional associations, 209–210
professional practice
challenges to, 179
contexts of, 5–6
experiential opportunities for, 93–94
professional roles
and personal identity, 22
personalizing, 15
preparation for, 7–12, 91–97
professionalism, modeling, 191
professionals, new
and competency anxiety, 177–178
core competencies for, 97–102, 140–141
development of, 34–35
orientation study and, *116t*
recommendations for, 220
protégés, problems for, 146

recognition, 33–34
recruitment, staff, 137–138
reflection, 120–121
relationships
building professional, 34–36
importance to socialization, 16
peer, 135–136, 164–166, 168, 225–226
study of staff-peer, 156–161
supervisory, 14, 130–146
Renn, K. A., 15, 16, 23, 112, 177
retention and job satisfaction, 28–31
Rhoads, R. A., 153
role conflict, 143–144
Rosser, V. J., 31, 155
Rush, J. C., 90

Sandeen, A., 209
Saunders, S., 114
Schaef, A. W., 116
Schein, Edgar, 174, 178, 185

Schneiter, S., 178
sectarian baccalaureate colleges, 50–52
secular baccalaureate colleges, 49–50
skills and competencies, developing, 97–102,
103–105, 140–141, 200–206
socialization. *see also* orientation programs;
peer relationships; professional
development
anticipatory stage, 7–12
definition, 3, 218–219
formal stage, 13–15
higher education trends and, 229–231
informal stage, 15–22
and information sharing, 184–185
and institution type, 221–222
institutional, 182–189
personal, 22–23, 175–178
stages of, 3–23
strategies for, 223–227
study of, 153–165
unit/division, 178–182
Southern Association for College Student
Affairs, 161
staff development. *see* professional
development
staff-peer relationships. *see* peer relationships
stages of socialization
anticipatory, 7–12
formal, 13–15
informal, 15–22
personal, 22–23
Stein, E. L., 90
Sternberg, R. J., 123
Stimpson, M., 179
Stoflet, T., 97, 177
stress, role, 143–144
Strong, L. J., 39;
student affairs
curriculum evaluation, 95–97
curriculum matrix, *203t*
future skills requirements, 103–105
Student Affairs History Project, 6
student culture, understanding, 78–81,
222–223
students
enrollment patterns, 72–74, *73t*
expectations of, 76–77

generational differences in, 77–78
graduate preparation and socialization, 102–103
millennial, characteristics of, 69
nontraditional, 69–74
traditionally aged, 68–69
trends impacting, 74–77
supervision
obstacles, 143–146
outcomes of effective, 140–143
resources for, *132t, 133t*
synergistic approaches to, 134–139
supervisors
importance to socialization, 225
recommendations for, 220
relationships, 134–139
roles and responsibilities, 18–22, 34–35, 129–134

technological changes, 74–75
technology, discussing in orientation programs, 118
Terrell, P. S., 37
Thornton, R., 4–5, 6, 15, 22, 24
Tierney, W. G., 90, 153, 154, 182

tribally controlled colleges, 59–60
tuition, impact of rising costs of, 75–76
Tull, A., 206
Twale, D. J., 90

universities
characteristics of, 52–56
doctoral-granting, 54–56
historically Black, 56–57
Upcraft, M. L., 99, 200

Van Maanen, J., 165–166

Waple, J. N., 100–102
Weaver, N. A., 110
Weidman, J. C., 5, 90
Wenger, E., 123
Winkler, K., 111
Winston, R. B, 113, 115, 196, 201, 205
work unit socialization, 178–182
working conditions, 36

York-Barr, J., 121

Zachary, L. J., 145